Imbibed In Faith

Imbibed In Faith

Susant Pal

ISBN: Hardcover 978-1-4828-1257-2
Softcover 978-1-4828-1258-9
Ebook 978-1-4828-1259-6

Cover Photo by Susant Pal

To order additional copies of this book, contact
Partridge India
000 800 10062 62
www.partridgepublishing.com/india
orders.india@partridgepublishing.com

Contents

Dedicated

To the

Loving Memory of

My Father

Indu Bhusan Pal

Jan 30, 1926 - Dec 6, 2010.

Preface

My inspiration to write this chronicle stemmed from the curiosity that I witnessed amongst my friends and fellow travelers from around the globe arriving India to discover a hidden myth. Religious belief is one of the many facets of this country. It is so deep rooted in the culture and customs of the society that it forms an inseparable way of life. Most Indians travel only to fulfill religious pursuits. Those who travel for pleasure or business too can seldom escape a visit to a temple. In other words there is no place on this land where there isn't a place of worship. A sizable chunk of an Indian (non-atheist) household budget accounts for puja (diety worship) and festivals carried out in different scales but round the year. Festival spendings are also very huge. Its impact on the local economy is also quite significant. Some community festivals collectively spend nearly a billion rupees in a matter of days. I feel astonished to hear that annual donations received by some of the temples reach more than Rupees 10 billion. Indian import from China of goods connected with to puja and festivals is estimated to be close to a billion dollars. Such is the magnitude of religious faith in this country that makes it distinctly overwhelming and indeed enigmatic. I thus thought of portraying these fascinating places of worship before my readers. Along with are narrated some prevalent tales and historical episodes. What is provided in this book is neither exhaustive, as it can never be nor is it exploratory but it is informative enough to provoke thoughts to go deeper in the matter if one so desired.

Hinduism unlike other religions of the world has no date of origin or originator. Every other religion has a founder based on whose teachings the religion has flourished and followed a uniformity of sorts. Hinduism on the other hand has become the religion of the people of India where even the origin of its holy texts is not specifically known. Also described as 'Sanatan Dharma' meaning eternal path Perennial Philosophy that has no beginning or ending. Without following ideological divisions the faith is built on experience rather than belief. It is perhaps for this reason that practice of rituals and customs differ from place to place although the principles of belief remain largely the same across the county. Hindu deities are in multitude and are worshipped according to their sanctified recognition. For example Goddess Lakshmi is worshipped for wealth and prosperity, Mother Saraswati for knowledge, Lord Ganesh for wisdom and so on. The list is endless and covers all situations in human life where adversities or deficiencies call for salvation. There is a deity, a destination, and a ritual each for every possible disorder be it wading away evil, respite from diseases, protection from wild animals, fear of deluge, escape from draught, fear of fire, pacifying mother earth, washing away sins, running of machinery and equipments', business success, global positioning, crop yield, food supply, cookery, success in exams, fickle mindedness, litigation and court cases, love making, procreation, warfare, composure, taming an adversary, long journey, self-possession, respite from wife beating, domestic violence, neighbours' envy, etc., etc., till death and after. Prayers and performances are carried out intensely round the year on sanctified days provided in the ephemeris. While 'pundits' and 'purohits' perform religious rites, the present day astrologers are seen making hay in sunshine. Astrologers (mostly sham) perched at every prospective commercial corner like a predator to entrap a trouble-torn victim. These god men offers them remedy in the form of occult guidance based in mysticism. Enticed by their hype people too are drawn in to their folds. Faith runs so deep that some use God images to dissuade road side nuisance doers, and it works. Even television channels rake up good TRP to up their media ratings. I wonder why this inspite the wretched lives of people still remain submerged in misery. Why then their well being still remains a distant dream. Indeed many a legendary saint from this very country have urged to keep God in one's own heart and mind and follow what He says is right. Never should one fail to carry 'kartavya' (assigned duties) with sincerity and without snooping for the fruits it will bear. Never cheat and never hurt any living being. These practices perhaps ignored, but can bring out the righteousness in oneself and usher in a life of well being and enlightenment. One needs to work towards it with patience. If Godliness is absent within no amount of pomp in deity worship and faith in the occult can be of help.

Acknowledgement

I express my gratitude to all the learned writers who have authored those valuable books and manuscripts that I have read while compiling this documentary. All authors may not find mention here but without their contribution an ignorant enthusiast like me couldn't have compiled this publication. I am unable to acknowledge each one of you individually but collectively I give credit to all of them for their contribution in making this book manifest while I remain a humble carrier of what has already been said to a new set of people. With this in view I intended not to gain out of this book rather have priced it so low as only to recoup a portion of the expenses incurred on it.

I remain grateful as always to my respected teachers and elders for having imparted in me the light of knowledge to move forward life. My travel across the varied terrains of this vast country has been painstaking but worthwhile. At no stage of my travel was I unaccompanied. I wish to thank them all who gave me company out of sheer affection.

My deepest indebtedness will always remain with my parents for whom I am here and my dear wife Madhu who always made my life comfortable in spite of all odds.

In my effort to thank the Almighty for his gracious blessings and plentiful pleasures in life I wish to bow before Lord Ganesha, the supreme epitome of wisdom and the embodiment of all knowledge without whose blessings my innumerable publications would never have materialized.

Tribute

Ever since civilisation dawned the lives of mankind his compelling urge to travel started on. Earleiest ones may have travelled hunting in search for food, later it was for acquiring wealth and knowledge followed by the desire to conquer distant lands. Some travelled in the persuit of peace and better livelihood while there were others who migrated for refuge. Human minds too never remained static. It explored to invent newer and newer means to travel. Be it the dugout canoes of the stone age-era or Kautilya's maritime schemes of 300 BCE, invention of hot-air-baloon in 1782 by the Montgolfier brothers or George Cayley's discovery of gliders followed by German engineer, Otto Lilienthal's invention of long distance gliding or Leonardo da Vinci's winged aircraft during 1480's that culminated into Orville and Wilbur Wright's invention in 1905 of an airplane—all were intended to accomplish one goal, that of travel, to explore faster and quicker. I pay my tribute all for their courage and devotion that cannot be acknowledged in words.

My admiration will also remain with those who ventured to travel into the unknown and became the pathfinders for mankind. Hannu the earliest known Egyptian explorer of 2750 BCE who travelled along the Red Sea and enriched his tribe with many a treasure or XuanZang of 610 BCE a resolute Chinese monk also known to be the first amongst travel writers travelled alone through the treacherous deserts and mountains of

China and Central Asia into India to learn the roots of Buddhism, are the unignorable ones. Special mention is made of Adi Shankaracharya Indian philosopher saint (788 CE to 820 CE) who in his 32 years of existence travelled extensively throughout India by foot wearing a saffron robe and wooden sandals. His preachings succeeded in awakening a common spiritual heritage that still keeps this diverse country bonded in allegiance. Thus there have been many great and famous travelers whom we know of besides those about whom we are oblivious. But all have left behind the treasure of experience and knowledge that mankind will always learn from.

If I were to mention three individuals of recent times, in my mind comes the following but for no great reason of their superiority over others. I give below quotes in their own words:

"*Go not to the temple to put flowers upon the feet of God, First fill your own house with the Fragrance of Love . . . Go not to the temple to light candles before the altar of God, First remove the darkness of sin from your heart . . . Go not to the temple to bow down your head in prayer, First learn to bow in humility before your fellow-men . . . Go not to the temple to pray on bended knees, First bend down to lift someone who is trodden-down . . . Go not to the temple to ask for forgiveness for your sins, First forgive from your heart those who have sinned against you*". **Rabindranath Tagore**—Nobel prize-winning Indian, Bengali poet, author, songwriter, philosopher, artist, and educator whose ardent desire to travel contributed in introducing the Indian race to the western world.

"*Travel opens your eyes to history of all types, whether recent or distant, obscure or commonplace and disputed or agreed. The danger of not travelling is that we have to take someone else's word for what a country is like, and that's not always responsible. We shouldn't retreat behind barriers and say it's costing the world a lot of pollution to travel. I don't think the ability to use Google or virtual devices is enough. Again, I think you've got to get feet on the ground, I think you've got to go sniff, smell the earth, see it, look at it. That's the sort of geography that I think is still important*". **Michael Palin**—Actor, writer, comedian and a world traveller in a conversation with Globe's editorial board Toronto during his visit to accept a Gold Medal for contributions to geographical literacy from the Royal Geographic Society of Canada.

Another European and the first amongst them to have journeyed across Central Asia into Mongolia, China and India for over 24-year (from 1271 at age 17) was a man of multifaceted charm. Over perilous mountains, fiery desert sand, wilderness and scarcity of resources he travelled with undaunted spirit. His mannerism and modesty gained him the affection of the people and confidence of the rulers whose land he explored. He may not have introduced pasta to Itally but certainly he acquainted Europe about what impressed him in China. To mention a few is the concept of paper-money, description of the use of coal, eyeglasses and most importantly the Mongol 'post and courier' system. Perhaps to silence his sceptics he is said to have remarked on his deathbed, "*I did not tell half of what I saw.*"—**Marco Polo,** the merchant of Venetian origin an adventurer and traveller who preferred to be called a "wayfarer."

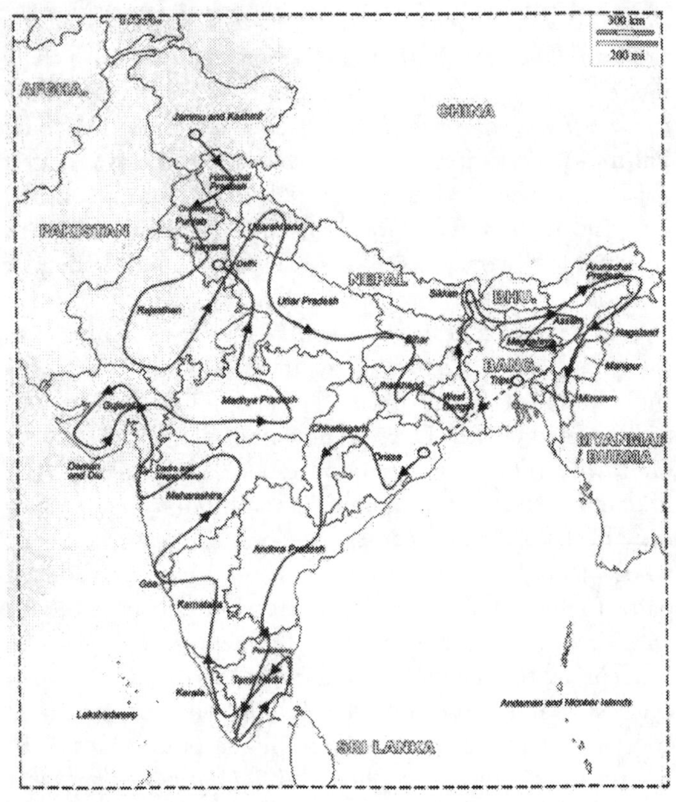

Red line shows route map of journey as it proceeds in the book.

India's federation comprises of a number of states that were initially carved out from British provinces and princely states and subsequently reorganized on linguistic lines. With the passage of time and following the ongoing linguistic agitations and administrative convenience further division were made forming smaller states. The principles adopted is one of unitary government with strong centre and distribution of powers between central and state governments along with placing residuary powers with central government. India presently comprises of twenty-eight states and seven union territories.

1

Introduction

India is a country with multiple religions and varied faiths. Amongst the Hindus themselves, which comprise majority of the population in India, one can find diversity in devotion amongst sects and towards different Gods, Goddesses and idols. As a consequence innumerable temples of worship have cropped-up throughout the country and over the centuries. During the course of my travel to different parts of the country I have had the privilege of getting company of many friends and hosts who took me around. In India generally people tend to take their outstation guests to a popular temple of his town. It is also true that if there in no place of tourist interest in any city there would surely be a temple or a shrine where the locals generally throng on holidays. I have thus been escorted to several such shrines. I visited not always out of great devotion (except a few) but to respect the faith that my hosts have towards their respective divine being. I confess that I have little knowledge about religion and religious beliefs and would refrain from contesting any form of faith and thereby not hurt the sentiments of anyone. But I do believe that the magnitude of sanctity of most places of worships is not as much as they are made out to be. To my humble understanding all religious sites in India are not the same and do not stand in equal sanctified footing. Some Hindu places of worship are referred to in religious manuscript or epics (Dharmic Granth—as called in Hinduism) where worshipers have been visiting and offering their prayers and where hymns and spiritual chanting have been conducted even thousands of years ago. I have broadly segregated all temples into three categories, first the genuinely designated ones that constitute locations that have historical significance or has reference in some holy epic or belongs to a time in antiquity like some of the 'Pithasthan' (*usually denotes where the sacred parts of Mahashakti's body are believed to have got scattered. Places where they fell were treated consecrated holy places called 'Pithasthan'. This has been dealt with in some details later*). Similar are auspicious Jyotirlingas (*places where Shiva is believed to have appeared as a fiery column of light*) or the Char Dham defined by Adi Shankaracharya. The second category to my mind would be shrines that were set-up in the later stages say about 200 to 500 years old or may be more but have little or no direct mythological connections. History would reveal that some maharaja or a person of eminence or a warrior or a stanch disciple might have built one such. Many of these sites have their own historical tales, which narrate to us how the temples came into being. Some would say that God appeared in the dream of the king or a rich landlord who then followed the sermon and constructed the temple, or a warrior king built it as an expression of gratitude towards the deity he worshipped and in memory of a victory at war or it could even be a place where a devotee attained some feat or enlightenment that later became a place of pilgrimage. Some stories are true some could be imaginary but there are little evidences and time to test the truth. Then there is a third category where temples have been set up in recent times or prayers are performed to congregate worshippers. These could be found in conspicuous places or especially where a Banyan tree has taken a formidable shape (in Hindu Mythology the banyan tree is also called 'kalpavriksha' meaning 'wish fulfilling tree'. It represents eternal life because of its seemingly ever-expanding branches and people have great respect for it. There are many stories about it in ancient literature. Many feel it to be a sin to uproot or cut these trees even if it wrecks havoc on the roof of a house). These temples are fake and do not have any mythological significance. These are meant to draw attention of the passers-by who would be drawn to offer donations. These establishments are mostly set up out of commercial interest. India being a country of blind faith it is easy to allure people in the name of satisfying the God. Some can be found even on the roadside occupying a portion of the walkway. I do not consider these correct. This is more of disrespect towards the faith as well as the deity for having them installed in obnoxious places and where people even commit nuisance nearby. Generally these would be small structures or a make shift arrangement which later get better with time as they get enriched. Many are patronized by tradesman in the vicinity or a political persona to obtain mileage of some material kind under the garb of devotion. On a higher altar I would put those temples that are larger and set up by communities that are organized and solvent and are run by trustees. These establishments are built with great devotion and ornamentation. Here religious performances are also performed following ritualistic norms. They generally do not obstruct public passages or create inconvenience rather are charitable in their work. These establishments are maintained and managed well (though several instances of scams, scandals and stain have been reported) but are generally peaceful places for families to congregate and hang around. Some have also become places of tourist interest.

In this book I wished to relate to some of religious places that I have visited. Not all of them but atleast those that are too important to forget. But then I realised that it would be unreasonable not to appraise my readers about other important and popular places of worship in the region that I may not have visited. These however may belong to any of the categories that I have segregated above. These may even include such sanctified places that may not be related to religion of faith. I have traveled to most places of this large country. But surely I have not visited every place as the country is so large and the terrain so diverse that my entire life would be insufficient to cover it all. Just to give an idea about the size of India from Kashmir to Kanyakumari and from Kutch to Kohima this country occupies a total area of about 3,287,590 sq km or 1,269,345 sq miles, of this 78,932 sq km (30,476 sq mi) are under the de facto control of Pakistan and 42,735 sq km (16,500 sq mi) are held by China. It extends 3,214 km (1,997 miles) N-S and 2,933 km (1,822 miles) E-W. India is bordered on the north by China, Nepal, and Bhutan; on the east by Myanmar, Bangladesh, and the Bay of Bengal; on the south by the Indian Ocean; on the west by the Arabian Sea; and on the north-west by Pakistan. The total boundary length is 21,103 km (13,113 mi), of which 7,000 km (4,340 mi) is coastline.

2

Religion in India

Before going into my recount let me give you a brief idea about religion in India as taken from the Encyclopedia of Nations: India "India is the cradle of two of the world's great religions, Hinduism and Buddhism. The principal texts of Hinduism—the Rig Veda (Verses of Spiritual Knowledge), the Upanishads (Ways of Worship), and the Bhagavad-Gita (Song of the Lord)—were written between 1200 and 100 BC. The teachings of Buddha, who lived during the 6th-5th centuries BC, were first transmitted orally and then systematized for transmission throughout Asia. Jainism, a religion that developed contemporaneously with Buddhism, has largely been confined to India. Islamic influence arrived India in the early part of the 7th century. Historians have found evidence of Muslim travelers and Arab traders arriving India during those times. It is believed that in 628 AD during the lifetime of Muhammad (c. 571-632) itself the 'Cheraman Masjid', first Indian mosque was built in Kodungallur, Thrissur district of, Kerala. The Sikh religion began in the 15th century as an attempt to reconcile Muslim and Hindu doctrine, but the Sikhs soon became a warrior sect bitterly opposed to Islam".[1]

---

1 http://www.nationsencyclopedia.com/Asia-and-Oceania/India.html—for convenience of readers

India today is a secular democratic republic and every citizen has his freedom to practice the religion of his choice. The population of India as per the census of 2011 is 1,220,200,000 (1.22 billion) which is about 17.31% of the world's population meaning that one out of every six people on this planet live in India. Followers of Hindu religion here have an absolute majority in all areas except Nagaland, Jammu and Kashmir, and the tribal areas of Assam. Sikhs (about 2% of the population—2001 census) are concentrated in the state of Punjab. Other religious groups include Muslims (nearly 14% in 2002 mostly Sunni) and Christians (2.3%). The remaining religion followers consist of Buddhists, Jains, and other groups. Muslims comprise more than 10% of the population in Maharashtra, Bihar, Karnataka, and West Bengal, and more than 30% of the total population in Assam and Kerala. Christians are a sizable minority in Nagaland and in Kerala as are Jains in Rajasthan and Gujarat, and the Parsis (Zoroastrians) in Maharashtra". Although there have been instances of communal violence in the country but by and large there is no imperative animosity amongst communities. The law in the country is also very vigilant and strict on neutralizing hate feelings if and when they surface. Different communities thus live in harmony in respective localities across this peace loving country. (*Figures above are indicative, may not be entirely accurate*)

Hinduism has tens of thousands of deities.

'Brahma'—the Absolute, is seen as the creator of the universe. The creator has three incarnations: Brahma, the creator, Vishnu, the preserver and Shiva, the destroyer. 'Sakthi' (or power / energy) is represented by Goddess power in the forms of 'Saraswathi' (embodiment of knowledge), Lakshmi (the personification of wealth and prosperity) and Parvathi (the consort of Lord Shiva is the epithet of strength and supreme conquest). The caste system is a distinct feature of Hinduism, wherein every person either is born into one of four groups—Brahmans (priests and scholars), Kshatriyas (warriors and rulers), Vaisyas (shopkeepers, artisans, and farmers), and Sudras (farm laborers and menial workers)—or is casteless and thus untouchable (now known as Harijan, from the term used by Mahatma Gandhi meaning persons of God). Within the four major castes there are over 2,500 sub-castes based upon occupation, geographic location, and other factors. The Indian constitution however prohibits caste distinctions and discrimination and untouchability stands abolished in all forms.

Other religions that originated in India are Buddhism, Jainism and Sikhism. Buddhism and Jainism originated 500 years before the start of the Christain Era and Sikhism was established in the 15th century A.D. Other religions that were also attempted to be established in India like Din—E—Elahi, Lingayat faith the Brahmosamaj could not sustain to establish an identity of their own.

There are quite a few religions of non-Indian origin as well that occupy prominace in India. Well-known amongst them are Islam, Christianity, Judaism, Zoroastrianism and Bahaism.

Islam one of the most practiced religions of the world emerged in India prior to the Muslim invasion of India. Trade relations of the Arabs prevailed much before the rulers set foot in this country. It is beieved that Islam in India began with the settlement of Arab Muslims in India some time in the 7th century A.D.,[2] and the setting up of the first mosque in that was built here in Kerala. This happened during the lifetime of The

---

2 Ancient and Medieval History of India by H.G. Rawlinson. Delhi, Bharatiya Kala Prakashan, 2001, xvii, 356 p., plates, figs., maps, $61. ISBN 81-86050-79-5.

Muhammad the messenger and prophet of God. "The Arab world had trade contacts with Kerala coast from very early times. As the tradition goes, a Chera king, Cheramanperumal of Kodungallure, left for Makkah, embraced Islam, and accepted the name Thajudeen. He married the sister of then King of Jeddah. On his return trip, accompanied by many Islamic religious leaders, led by Malik-ibn-Dinar (RA), he fell sick and passed away. But he had given introductory letters for the team to proceed to 'Musiris' (Kodungallur), the Chera capital. The visitors came to Musiris and handed over the letter to the reigning king, who treated the guests with all respect and extended facilities to establish their faith in the land. The king also organised help for the artisans to build the first Mosque at Kodungallur, by converting Arathali temple into a Juma-Masjid. It was built in 629 A.D., and the area around it had been earmarked for the team's settlement. The original Mosque has undergone extensive repairs, but traces of the original construction are seen in the plinth, the columns and the roof which are in the old traditional styles of Hindu temples".[3] Later the religion was professed and propagated by the Sufi Saints linke Hazrat Nizam-ud-din, Amir Khusro, Hazrat Khawaja Muin-ud-din Chisti, Waris Pak Shah Jalal, Auliya, Sarkar Sabir Pak and the like during the 10th century A.D. Indians then who were converted to Islam belonged mostly to the lower echelon of the Indian society. There were however rulers too who got converted to Islam. Indian Muslims like those in other parts of the world are divided into two main sects, Sunni and Shia. Amongst this faith are different communities like

---

3 Cheraman Juma Masjid A Secular Heritage By P.A. Muhammed. *Islamic Voice,* Jamadi-Awwal / Jamadi Thani, June 2004. Volume 17-06 No: 210

Bohra, Khoja, Nawait, and Pathan etc. Hindu culture had a direct influence in the development of caste system amongst Muslims. Ashrafs who consider themselves as superior being the direct descendants of the Arab are subdivided into four castes, Sayyads, Shiekhs, Mughals and Pathans. The non-Ashrafs are alleged to be converts from Hinduism. This segment is subdivided into castes that are based on the occupation they practice or their ancestors practiced.[4] "The non-ashrāf Muslim castes are of three levels of status: at the top, converts from high Hindu castes, mainly Rājputs, insofar as they have not been absorbed into the Shaykh castes; next, the artisan caste groups, such as the Julāhās, originally weavers; and lowest, the converted untouchables, who have continued their old occupations. These converts of Hinduism observe endogamy in a manner close to that of their Hindu counterparts."[5] During the early 12th century many Rajput clans were converted to Islam for political reasons as they could thus occupy poweres of authority in the Government. But by and large they remained loyal to their faith. "The fact of subsequent conversion to other faiths, did not deprive them of this heritage; just as the Greeks, after their conversion to Christianity, did not lose pride in the mighty achievements of their ancestors, or the Italians in the great days of the Roman Republic and early empire . . . Christians, Jews, Parsees, Moslems. Indian converts to these religions never ceased to be Indian on

---

4 Social Stratification Among Muslims in India" by Zarina Bhatty in *Caste: Its Twentieth Century Avatar*, edited by M. N. Srinivas, Viking, New Delhi, 1996.

5 Islamic caste. (2008) in *Encyclopædia Britannica*. Retrieved on August 18 from from: http://www.britannica.com/EBchecked/topic/295708/Islamic-caste. Encyloperia Britannica.

account of a change of their faith . . . ."[6]. Mughal dynasty encouraged such Islamisation of the warior Rajput clans. This process continued even during the British Raj in the 19th century. It may be of interest for many to know that the ancsestors of the father of Pakistan Quaid e Azam Muhammad Ali Jinnah and his sister Fatima Jinnah belonged to Rajput Bhatia clan and hailed from the Paneli village in Gujarat. Similarly, Zulfikar Ali Bhutto and Muhammad Khan Junejo both of whom served as Prime Ministers of Pakistan and Sardar Sikandar Hayat Khan leader of Pakistan occupied Kashmir bear their lineage to the Rajput community.

Christianity arrived in India long before America was discovered, and much before it arrived in Europe. It is believed that the first amongst the Indians converted to Christianity was by one of the Apostles named St. Judas Thomas who arrived first in Kerala in 52 AD. Later several missionaries appeared as they arrived with the European merchants 15th century onwards. First amongst them were the Portuguese under the leadership of Vasco DaGama in 1498. But the British allowed missionaries to operate only from 1813. The main division of Christians in India is like in the Christian world, Protestants and Catholic. There are also different denomination among them, Syrian Church, Armenian Church, Anglican Church and others. Mostly the Portuguese converted of the Indian to Christianity. "The Syrian Christians along the Malabar Coast, descended from 1st-century converts of high birth, retain mid-rank status in Hindu society. Portuguese missionaries of the 16th century converted lower-caste fisherfolk. Missionaries in the 19th century

[6] The Discovery of India By Jawaharlal Nehru. Published by Oxford University Press, 1985 ISBN 0195623592, 9780195623598. 582 pages.

insisted on social reform and tended to draw from the lowest classes. Caste distinctions are breaking down at about the same rate among contemporary Indian Christians and other Indians".[7]

Anglo-Indian community in India are a significant segment of the Indian population though they may be insignificant in number compared to the population if the country. They are decendants of the British who came to India on assignment from Britain under the British rule in the late 18th century. The East India Company during those days did not allow its staff and employees to travel to India with wives. During their long stay on duty they began having relationships with Luso-Indian and Indian women. Luso-Indians are those who were born under similar mixed marriages between the Portuguese and Indians a practice encouraged by Alfonso d'Albuquerque the Portuguese Governor of India in the 1510's. Thus children born out of these cross-cultural marriages came to be known as Anglo Indian. The term Anglo-Indian means an Indian citizen whose paternal line can be traced to Europe. This continued till the late 19th century when British women began migrating to India in good numbers. Anglo-Indians have always been Christains who were during the British rule supported financially by the East India Company and were recognized as members of British Society. Studies have shown that during the mid 20th century most of the Indian Christains were Anglo-Indians. Now the number is very few and is not the only Christains. Many have migrated to other commonwealth countrues and many others have got mingled into other communities through marriage. But their condition is precarious in the sense that they are not quite accepted by the British whom they 'look-up' to and

---

7 'Christian Caste'. Britannica-Concise Encyclopedia 2007.

somewhat marginalized by the community it 'looks-down' upon.[8]

Jews in India are segregated into different communities. The largest amongst them are called the Bene Israel arrived and settled in a village called Navgaon. Those who arrived in India during the King Solomon's time (around 800 BC) call themselves Cochini Jews. Baghdadi Jews or Iraqi Jews arrived from Baghdad, Yemen, Iran and Syria. Most in this community were rich businessmen who first settled in Gujrat. Manipuri Jews are yet another community found in the Indian states to Manipur and Mizoram. Some believe they were persecuted in their own land when they migrated to China, later moved to Burma and settled in India. Later many were converted to Christianity. In recent times there was a movement to get reconverted to Judaism and emigrate to Isreal. For a short span prior to India's Indepedence there came Jews from European countries. They were mostly professionals like doctors who eventually migrated to England and America. Although there is no codified caste system amongst the Jews but the Hindu caste system did have an impact on the Jews as well. Thus division came about amongst the settlers in different places in India. Like the Baghdadis considered themselves superior to others. The Kochis considered them superior to the Bene's who were treated at par with the Sudras under Hindu casts as they worked in pressing oil like the 'Teli' community in India.

Two other religions that arrived in India were Zoroastrianism and Bahaism. Both of these faiths arrived from Iran and got migrated to India because of

---

8 Anglo-indians: Vanishing Remnants of a Bygone Era By Blair R. Williams. Published by Calcutta Tiljallah Relief Inc, 2002. ISBN 0975463918, 236 pages

religious mistreatment in their country. Zoroastrians are immigrants from Persia who eventually settled in urban India are popularly known as the Parsi Community. Their numbers are on the decline but their enterprising skills have tured them into economically rich and honorablefor their prudent approach. Bahá'ís of India as they believe are the largest Bahá'í Community of the world, numbering some 2.2 Million. Associated with the central figures of the Bahá'í Faith from its very inception in 1844, the Bahá'ís in India today live in over 10,000 localities spread all over the country.[9]

K'ung Fu Tzu (commonly pronounced Confucius in English) who started Confucianism like Taoism and Buddhism started by Lao Tzu and Buddha respectively is a religion followed by most amongst the Chinese settled in India, mostly in my home town Kolkata. Ancestor worship and worship of the immortals like Lao Tzu, Buddha, and Confucius are a part of the religious faith that the reigion ascribes to.

---

9 Retrieved from www.bahai.in. Official Website of the Bahá'ís of India

3

Journey

While scripting my recollections I decided to move geographically rather instead of going chronologically. I wished to present this like a journey from place to place. This would also enable a reader to refer back to any portion with ease. I thus decided to go state-wise.

India comprises of a union of several states. Nestled at the top is the state of **JAMMU & KASHMIR**. According to Nilamata Purana 'the oldest literary document of Kashmir'[10] the present Kashmir Valley was once a gigantic lagoon and was called 'Satidesa' and was surrounded by high mountains. In that lake lived 'Jalodhbava' an enormously powerful demon who was invincible under water. In order to obliterate this demon Sage Kashyap wedged a crevice in the mountains that drained off all the water and then emerged the valley that is now known as Kashmir, after Kashyap. To give an idea about the topography of the palce I quote here an excerpt from Kashmir: Land of Mountain Ranges written by Mohammed Saleem. It goes thus "The State of Jammu and Kashmir has predominantly three geographical

10 The Nīlamata Purā Vol. II *by Ved Kumari* Journal of the American Oriental Society, *Vol. 97, No. 4 (Oct.-Dec., 1977), pp. 554-556*

regions—i. The Lesser Himalayas, also called "Jehlum Valley" (Kashmir), ii. The Inner Himalayas or the "Indus Valley" (Ladakh & frontier areas) which is also called as "Trans-Himalayas" and, iii. The Outer Himalayas, also called as "Southern Mountain range" (Jammu). The Valley of Kashmir is a longitudinal depression in the north-western Himalayan range carved tectonically, and situated at an altitude of 1590m. Its latitude stands between 23-4' and 37-6' North & longitude between 72-31' and 77-30' East. The length of this oval shaped valley has a parallel axis to the general direction of the mountains bordering it which include: the middle mountains, the Pir Panjal, the Himalayas, the Zanaskar, the Ladakh, the Korakaram, and the Shivaliks. Uniquely the valley of Kashmir is covered with majestic mountain ranges which possess a source of most of Earth's fresh water, repositories of biological diversity, popular destinations for tourism and recreation, areas of important cultural diversity, knowledge & heritage. Mountain regions also provide food, energy, timber, flood and storm protection and prevention of erosions. Mountains and hillside areas hold a rich variety of ecological systems". Today one of the most admired and a venerated place of Hindu pilgrimage is here—the shrine of 'Amarnath'. ('Amar' meaning immortal and 'nath' signifies the guardian lord, the almighty that is 'Shiva'). Gradual drips of icy cold-water waxes inside a cave to take a rounded, elliptical form similar to the sacred 'Lingam' (lingam is a form or symbol of Lord Shiva). In Hindu tradition this is a sacred symbol of sublimity, serenity and strength. This natural formation of the 'Lingum' in the cave of Amarnath happens during May to August every year. I suppose this is more a miracle of nature than a religious place in true sense as it is made out to be. But the strange thing is that this icy formation grows and shrinks with the phases of the moon. Discovered by a non-Hindu shepherds boy named Buta Malik while he tread that way one day some two hundred years ago. The Amarnath cave, where the lingam is formed, is situated in a narrow gorge at the far end of the Lidder valley at an altitude of 3,888 meters and about 140 Km from the capital city of Srinagar. But again there is a story behind this pilgrimage site. Bhole Shankar (or Lord Shiva, 'Bhole' generally indicates happy-go-lucky, absent-minded) entered this Holy Amarnath Cave along with Parvati Maa to tell her about the secrets of immortality. To ensure that no living being is able to hear the Immortal Tale, he created Kalagni and ordered him to spread fire to eliminate every living thing in and around the Holy Cave. After this he started narrating the secret of immortality to Parvati. But as a matter of chance a pair of pigeon overhead the story and became immortal. Many pilgrims report seeing the pair of pigeons at the Holy Shrine even today and are amazed as to how these birds survive in such a cold and high altitude area. It is a long walk across the mountains over steep inclines and cascading streams covering a distance of 45 km from Pahalgam, which is located about a hundred kilomerets from capital Srinagar. This journey generally takes four days to cover. The icy cold conditions restrict the movement to only a few weeks of summer each year when tens of thousands of devotees walk their way up chanting incantations and singing bhajan as priests perform aarti and puja invoking the blessing of Shiva.

The other most popular place of worship is near Jammu a place called Katra where at an altitude of 5300 feet on the holy Trikuta Hills of the Shivalik Mountain Range is the abode of Maata Vaishno Devi. The Holy cave is 13 Kms from the Base Camp Katra. I visited this temple twice so far. Devotees to this shrine come from all walks of life, be poor or rich all of whom while taking the 13 Km pathway over the inclines of the mountain walk like equals. Some devotees are very rich and famous.

Even celebrities and prominent political leaders make their way-up walking. Although a helicopter service is available but it is said that the offering is complete only if the devotee takes the difficult path up. The first time I went with my wife Madhu. She had an ardent desire to visit the shrine. Our visit always got deferred, as neither of us was confident that we could walk so much up the mountain. But as they say in India, when God desires, He paves the way for you. Indeed this plan was finalized in a short span of time and our journey from Delhi too went smoothly and with much ease. After reaching Jammu we took a bus to Katra. The place then being infested with extremist elements and militants aggressively active all over we had to pass through several stringent security checks. At Katra (on the foot of the hill) we had a wash in the state tourist house and began our journey. It took us about 6 hours to reach the top. We started at about 5 in the evening and reached at 11 in the night. The walkway is well paved all through and very well lit. So walking during the night is not difficult. Though we reached at 11 we had to wait for our turn for the Darshan (getting a glimps of the deity). By the time we were out of the temple it was almost getting dawn. We rested for a while in a hotel room nearby. When we woke up at about 8 am we were neither in the mood nor had the strength to walk back. We thus decided to take the helicopter to descend. They charged us Rs. 900/—each and in less than four minutes we were back in Katra. Two thousand hard-earned rupees were wiped out in under four minutes. But that served a very good purpose. Our train to Delhi was at night and we had the entire day at our disposal. We decided to explore the temple city of Jammu situated on the banks of river Tawi. Indeed apart from the scenic beauty of Jammu, the dry fruit market and the Amar Mahal Palace the only other places of attraction in Jammu are the innumerable temples. Amongst the temples in

Jammu, the Raghunath Mandir, Bawey Wali Mata is inside the Bahu Fort, Panchbakhtar temple and the Ranbireshwar temple dedicated to Lord Shiva. Each has its own legend, its devotees and specific days of worship. In Ranbireshwar Temple, there are twelve Shiva 'lingams' of crystal measuring 12" to 18" and galleries with thousands of 'saligrams' (oval shaped auspicious stones which depicts Lord Narayan) fixed on stone slabs. Other important temples in Jammu are the Lakshmi Narayan temple, Duda Dhari temple and the Panj Mandir in Gandhi Nagar. Peer Mitha is another famous Muslim shrine in Jammu where the Peer would accept nothing more than a pinch of sugar in offering from his devotees (thus the name 'meetha' meaning sweet). Other places of worship include the St. Paul's Church and the Garrison Church. The Sunder Singh Gurudwara, Tali Sahib Gurudwara, Kalgidhar Gurudwara are amongst many Sikh temples that adorn the winter capital of the state of Kashmir. The second time I visited the Maata Vaishno Devi shrine was a couple of years later when I was on an official visit to Katra. After finishing with the assignment I, accompanied by two of my officers decided to pay a visit to the holy shrine. As we had to catch a flight the next morning we had no option but to take the helicopter ride both ways. We not only saved a lot of time but with practically no crowd up there we also had a very good darshan that was better and more prolonged than my earlier visit.

Srinagar the summer capital of the state of Jammu and Kashmir is situated about 900 Kilometers from Delhi and at an altitude of nearly 6000 feet above sea level. Many describe Srinagar as 'heaven on earth'. I too endorse the view. I cannot deny that the immaculate beauty of the valley around and its changing colors stunned me on every visit. This place itself is sacred by the virtue of its sheer purity that makes it no less than a place of pilgrimage. The Hazratbal shrine built by the Mughal Emperor

Shahjahan's Subedar, Sadiq Khan, in 1623 that was later converted into a prayer House by the Emperor during his visit in 1634. It is said that The Holy Relic in the form of the hair strands of Prophet Muhammad is said to be preservd here. Another important place of worship is located in the center of the city the holy Jama Masjid that was built by Sultan Sikandar sometime in 1400 AD. The great saint and philsopher from the south of India 'Shankaracharya' is said to have visited Srinagar in the in 9th Century A.D and propagated the `Siva Sutrar', as revealed by Lord Shiva himself and prayed at the Shiva Temple located at the foot of Mahadeva mountain nearby. He did this as a part of his mission to contain the influence of Buddhism that was taking strong roots here and in other parts of the country. In memory of his visit the temple began to be called the Shankaracharya Temple. Some are of the view that this temple was originally constructed some 2500 BC. The main deity in this temple is of Lord Shiva.

On the western side of the state between the mighty Karakoram and the Himalayan range of mountains is another region with a completely different landscape. The region of Ladakh, a desert plateaus ten thousand feet above the sea level. Some ascribe the stone carvings found here to 'neo-stone age era that date back to 10,000 BC. But the more recent and authentic traces are found in the Kushana Dynasty of the first century. Buddhism arrived here during the 2nd century AD and still is the predominant religion here. Thus there are several Buddhist monastries here. These monasteries are called 'Gompas' generally situated atop a hill. The largest one is the 'Hemis Gompa'. Amongst the other important Gompas are the 11 century AD called the 'Likhir Gompa', the 'Cave Gompa' and the 'Sanker Gompa'. Added in the modern time by a Japanese Buddhist organization 'The Japanese for World Peace' is the peaceful shrine called 'Shanti Stupa'.

Inaugurated by His Holiness Dalai Lama this Stupa was constructed in 1985 to commemorate the 2,500 years of Budhism on earth.

Below the state of Jammu and Kashmir is the tiny picturesque state of **HIMACHAL PRADESH** that encompasses tourist destination like Chamba, Kullu, Manali, Dharamshala, Kufri, and Dalhousie. A mention ought to be made of the suburban towns of McLeodganj and Forsythganj whose colonial ambiance reminds us of the British era. McLeodganj named after David McLeod, once the Lieutenant Governor of Punjab is situated in the Kangra district. A hill resort at an altitude of nearly 1800 metes McLeodganj is presently the official residing place of His Highness the Dalai Lama. Arrived in 1959 after the Chinese military occupation of Tibet, the Tibetans sought refuge and are now settled in this land and from where they run the Tibetan government-in-exile. Due to its large population of Tibetan refugees McLeodganj is also called the "Little Lhasa". His Holiness is the present crusader of peace who has spoken strongly for better understanding and respect among the different faiths of the world. Imparting the message of universal responsibility, love, compassion and kindness he speaks of "The need for simple human to human relationship is becoming increasingly urgent. . . . Today the world is smaller and more interdependent. One nation's problems can no longer be solved by itself completely. Thus, without a sense of universal responsibility, our very survival becomes threatened. Basically, universal responsibility is feeling for other people's suffering just as we feel our own. It is the realization that even our enemy is entirely motivated by the guest for happiness. We must recognize that all beings want the same thing that we want. This is the way to achieve a true understanding, unfettered by artificial consideration"[11]. A large monastery with a majestic image of Lord Buddha inside is an important place of worship for Buddhist followers. St. John's church and the final resting place of Lord Elgin, a British Viceroy of India during the 19th century are situated close by. The hustle-bustle of the Tibetan inhabitants, their life and life-style, shops with display of curios, and handicrafts have made the place to be popularly known as land of Lhasa.

State of Himachal came into eistance in 1948. Later some more areas of neighbouring Punjab were annexed in 1972 to give it the geographical shape that it is now. One such district now adjoining Punjab is Bilaspur in the southwest part of the state. About about 65 Km from Bilaspur town and about 151-Km from the state capital Shimla is loicated one of the fifty-one 'Shakti Pitha Sthaans'. Pitha Sthaans, as have been described earlier have all grown into sacred places of worship. Here temple of 'Shri Naina Devi' stands in commemoration of that holy occurrence, where people gather to offer their prayers particularly during the month of 'Shravana'. (Month of 'Shravana' generally falls during post-summer, coinciding with the English calender months of July & August). It is believed that of the several parts of 'Sati's' body that were strewn across the country, the eyes of the Goddess fell at this place, hence the name 'Naina' (also 'nayana', 'nayan' means eyes). The temple located at an altitude of 1200 meters is said to have been built in reverence by Raja Bir Chand in the 8th century AD. Raja Bir Chand belonged to the Chanderwanshi Rajputs who ruled over Madhya Pradesh. This adventurous kings persuit of expanding his kingdom brought him here and established a state making

---

11 *Universal Responsibility and the Good Heart*—by H.H. the Dalai Lama, Library of Tibetan Works and Archives, Dharamsala, 1977

Naina-Devi his capital.[12] This dynasty went on to rule till the India became a republic.

Amongst the several religious places in Himachal the oldest and presumably the most famous place is 'Vyas Gufa' ('gufa means cave) A few thousand years ago, Sage 'Vyas' came to the bank of the Satluj River where he lived and meditated in this Gufa. Vyas Rishi (sage) is considered as the original source of all learnings. Amonst the several philosophical works of his, is the depiction of the great epic of 'Mahabhatara'. The 'Vedas' that form the ethos of all Hindu practices and viewpoint that was downloaded from the head of Lord Brahma and handed over to Vyasa through the hands of 'Narad Muni' (muni is sage). Vyasa having studied it all edited them and organised them for propagation and learning. I share with the readers a little more about this great recitor of auspicious divinities. This will also be a tribute to this great composer.

Vyas's real name was 'Krishna Dvaipayana Badarayan Vyas'. Krishna because he was black, Dvaipayana (dweep means Island) he was born on an island (dveep) in Yamuna River and Badarayan he was a loner in the Badri forest (now in Uttaranchal) region of the Himalayas. A grandson of the great sage Vashishtha and son of sage Parashar, Vyas is considered as immortal. His mother Satyavati was from an unknown community as she was born out of a fish. Once when a boatman netted a large fish and cut it open this girl child was found inside. The boatman took her home and brought her up. Though a foster patrent he treated her like his own daughter and named her 'Satyavati'. But as she was retrieved from a

[12] The Princely and Noble Families of the Former Indian Empire: Himachal Pradesh Vol-1. By Mark Brentnall. Compiled by Mark Brentnall. Published by Indus Publishing, 2006. ISBN 8173871639, 9788173871634. 374 pages

fish she had a fishy stench on her body so she was also called 'matsyagandha' ('matsya' meaning fish and 'gandha' is smell or odour) When she grew up she began to help her father in ferrying people across the river. Once sage Parashar while travelling in her fery realised the auspiciousness of the moment to procreate a child. His eyes fell on this impulsive, ebullient beauty that was in her full bloom of puberty. She was the only other person on the boat, standing on the far end slowly rowing the oar. It was getting close to dusk as she stood silhouette against the silvery sky. The contour of her body so defined against the dimming light that she appeared nude. Unfettetred and uncontrolled amidst the serenity she was irresistible. Parasar advanced towards her and unveiled his desire. Satyavati agreed to submit to the passionate advances of the sage but on three conditions. She knew he was able and accomplished enough to fulfill her desire so she thought this to be an opportunity to make use of. The three things she asked for were that her body must get rid of the fishy stench, that no one should be able to see her love making and that her virginity must be restored after a child was born. Parasar agreed to all and through his devine power created a screen of fog around the boat that engulfed them in secrecy and through his divine powers also removed the unpleasant odour from her body. Out of this association 'Vyasa' was born. Sage Parashar restored Satyavati's virginity and left the place with his son. This young boy later grew up to become one of greatest preceptors of all times. He classified the Vedas (under four heads—Rig, Yajur, Saama and Atharva), composed their background narrations, scripted the eighteen Puranas, and for the common masses set down the moral and spiritual percepts from the stories of our great heroes and saints. Interestingly, Vyas is said to have approached the 'Lord of learning' the 'auspicious God of knowledge' and the 'obviator of all obstacles' Sri Ganesh to write the epic Mahabharata. Lord Ganesh agreed to this with a forewarning to Vyas that he must dictate the entire manuscript in one go. Vyasa too put a condition that Ganesh would not interrupt his flow if he failed to understand any portion that he would dictate. With this reciprocal agreement the task of putting down the epic in writing began and in due course the '6,00,000 verse' composition of the great epic became manifest. Kisari Mohan Ganguli in his book 'The Mahabharata of Krishna Dwaipayana Vyasa' states "The wisdom of this work, like unto an instrument of applying collyrium, hath opened the eyes of the inquisitive world blinded by the darkness of ignorance. As the sun dispelleth the darknes, so doth the Bharata by his discourse on religion, profit, pleasure and final release, dispel the ignorance of men. As the full moon by its mild light expandeth the buds of the water lily, so this purana, by exposing the Sruti hath expanded the human intellect. By the lamp of history, which destroyeth the darkness of ignorance, the whole mansion of nature is properly and completely illuminated". [13]

Hindus hold sage Vyasa in the highest esteem and is thus venerated as a true 'Guru'. It is for this that Hindus' have dedicated the full moon day in the month of 'Ashadh' (month preceeding 'Sravan' that falls in July-August according to the English calendar) to this Guru. The day is observed as a festival of 'Vyas Purnima' more popularly known as 'Guru Purnima' ('purnima' means fullmoon) and is celebrated throughout India.

The capital town Simla is a historical place in many respects. Discovered and established by the British as the summer capital during British rule this beautifully

---

[13] The Mahabharata of Krishna Dwaipayana Vyasa By Kisari Mohan Ganguli Published by Kessinger Publishing, 2004. ISBN 1419171259, 9781419171253 532 pages

decked capital has several religious places like Temples dedicated to Lord Ram, Lord Krshna, Goddess Kali and Sri. Hanuman. But standing majestically on the mall and the most prominent of all is the Christ Church built some time in the mid 1850s. A couple of kilometers to the west is the sprawling Viceregal Lodge. This majestic edifice was built in 1888 for Viceroy Lord Dufferin. It may be of surprise to many that this palace had a tennis court inside. Till the time of India's independence thirteen different Viceroys stayed at the Lodge, starting with Lord Dufferin and ending with Mountbatten. It was during the time of Lord Mountbatten when this was the venue of the Simla Conference in 1945. In 1947, the decision to partition India by carving out the states of Pakistan on either side of India was also taken here. After Independence this mansion was handed over to the government of India. This is now a study center and ofcourse a place of visit for the numerous tourists who come here to get a feel of the historic past that are now embedded in the pages of history.

I visited Simla in 2004 when I went to organise a conference that was attended by a Cabinet Minister, senior officials from the government and UNDP, local elected representatives and a large number of our beneficiaries. The local authorities arranged a visit for the minister (Mr Kansi Ram Rana) to the famous Hanuman temple popularly known as the Jakhu Temple in Shimla. This temple is situated on the top of Jakhu Hill, at an altitude of about 2500 meters. Jakhu is derived from Hindi word Yakhsa (Yakshas are the mythological character in Hindu mythology, who are a link between human and gods). As I was accompanying the minister with his aide-de-camp and a local political leader I got the privilege of climbing the hilltop in a car with the minister. We reached early in the morning lucky to catch up with the morning prayers and engaged our mind in the chanting of the auspicious mantras (hymns). After the puja the minister and I offered nuts to the monkeys that are in plenty there (like many other Hindu places of pilgrimage). It is considered sacred to feed the monkeys there. I hope I picked up a few 'blessing points' on that. One of the legend here is that Lord Hanuman (the monkey God who was not only a leader of the monkey army but an disciple of Lord Rama) when flying through the sky on his way to the Himalayas in search of the 'sanjeevani' plant (a herb) that was needed to cure Lord Laxmana (brother of the Hindu mythological hero Lord Rama) who lay mortally wounded in the battle field in Lanka (now Sri Lanka), made a stop over here on top of this hill. He left behind his footprint (some say one of his sandals). It is around this footprint that a temple has been built and worshippers who come to Simla pay a visit to this place and offer their prayers.

The Minister and I stayed at the Wildflower Hall Mashobra. This manor is now a hotel operated by the Oberois' for the exclusive and selective. This property is somewhat as elitist as the Viceregal Lodge, an imposing but rambling 19th century house where Lord Kitchener is said to have lived. Later Robert Hotz a Swiss hotelier bought the property and developed it further. The premise is ostentatious covered with deep green deodars and overlooks the snow-capped mountains and the Shimla Reserve Forest in the foreground.

The neighboring state is the prosperous and industrious state of **PUNJAB**. The 400 years old city of Amritsar and one of the most sacred places in India is situated here on the north—western border of the country. The fourth guru of the Sikhs, Guru Ramdas had founded the city. This place has been the seat of the Sikh religion and culture from its very inception. Here in Amritsar is the holiest shrine of Sikhism the Harimandir Sahib (meaning Temple of God). This temple is popularly known as the Golden Temple that houses the Darbar

Sahib (Divine Court). Amritsar literally means 'Pool of Nectar'. The holy pond around the temple signifies this. The Moghul Emperor Akbar had gifted the land for the pool. I visited this temple first in 1982 when I was just studying in the University doing my Masters Degree. I had accompanied my parents on that tour. Those were dreadful days in Panjab. The Khalistan Movement for right to self-determination for the state of Punjab was in full valor and the common people intimidated by the acts of repression and terrorism spread across the state and neighboring Delhi. As we were non-Sikhs it was indeed scary to move around. But we never faced any serious problem except for being in a state of wariness all the time. Inside the temple the local people including the Sikhs were very cordial in their interaction. Out of anxiety and caution I had kept my camera hidden under my shirt. I remember having circumspectly asked one bye stander if I could take a photograph of this sacred monument. It was a splendid structure indeed. The shining splendor of the Golden Temple is witness to the high skill of the traditional craftsmen. The name 'Swarn Madir' (in Hindi) meaning Golden Temple is aptly so. The entire dome of the structure and the wall around is literally wrapped in gold. The bye stander was amazed at my question and said 'why not? You are free to take pictures . . .' and so on. This I remember was a great relief. I was young and knowing that photography in many places in India is prohibited and there could be sactions too I was a bit scary to carry my camera lest a militant member took offence. The unease of holding the camera under cover finally subsided and I took a few pictures with ease. Those days the cameras were big and cumbersome and keeping it camouflaged was quite a difficult task. But thereafter I could make good use of it.

Adjacent to the Golden Temple is the 'Jalianwala Bagh' an ancient garden arena for people to congregate.

Though not a religious place but its importance and sanctity has grown out of the sacrifice of over 2000 brave men and women who faced the bullets of the British soldiers under the command of Gen Michael O' Dyer who indiscriminately opened fire on April 13, 1919 while they were participating in a peaceful public meeting. Bullet marked walls have been preserved and still visible along with the memorial well in which many of them jumped to escape. After this massacre Mahatma Gandhi declared, "The impossible men of India shall rise and liberate their mother land". Rabindra Nath Tagore the noble laureate while returning his knighthood in retaliation wrote "This disproportionate severity of punishment inflicted upon the unfortunate people and method of carrying it out is without parallel in the history of civilized government".

Close to Amritsar is Ram Tirth, Amritsar dates back to the period of Ramayana. There is a hut where it is said that Luv & Kush (the twins of Rama) were born. Along side the hut of Rishi Balmiki, the well and steps where Sita (Rama's wife) used to take her bath as is believed, could also be seen. A four-day fair, since times immemorial is held here starting on the full moon night in November. These apart there are several other Hindu temples in Amritsar dedicated mostly to Goddess Durga and Lord, Shiva.

In the afternoon on the following day I set off from Amritsar to the border with our hostile neighbour Pakistan to a place called Wagha located 35 KM to the west of the city. The ceremonial flag retrieval can be witnessed here every day at sunset when the Border Security Force (BSF) on the Indian side and The Sutlej Rangers on the Pakistan side put up spectacular display of drill. The rhythm of the trumpet on the two sides reminds us that the nations were one at one time. This border on the Grand Trunk road between the two great cities of Amritsar and Lahore is the gateway from to Pakistan and beyond to Central Asia.

Annexed to the other side of the Punjab border is the state of **HARYANA** a territory that was once in Punjab. Separated in 1966 both these states of Haryana and Punjab have capitals in a common city in the Union Territory of Chandigarh. (Union territories are centrally administered territories and do not fall under the category of 'States' of India). I have been in Haryana on several occasions and have traveled by road through several districts and visited its remote villages. The people are very hospitable and ardently follow the culture of honoring their visitors. Very religious and God fearing in nature the Haryanvi's are also very industrious and fun loving much like the Punjabis. I remember having travelled to Panchkula 1997 by a local bus. It is about 8 km from the Chandigarh bus stand. Here lies the holy Temple of Sri Mata Mansa Devi a Consort of Lord Shiva in the form Shakti or Power. (The Goddess has many names like Chandi, Bhawani, Durga, Kalika, Ambika, Sharda, Kali and Mansa among others. There are two temples here. The Maharaja of Patiala built the more elegant one with a lovely garden in the foreground. But the temple near the parking lot is believed to be the original Mata Mansa Devi temple and reportedly built in 1815. While on my return there was a sudden strike and public transport were off the road. I had no way to reach back. As I was wondering what to do in the middle of a highway one Sardarji (*denotes Sikhs with turban for their leadership character*) came up to me and volunteered to give me a lift back to Chandigarh in his car. I was pleasantly surprised at this unsolicited offer and I had no option either. Perhaps the Mata was kind to me. But frank, as they are he said he would charge some fifteen rupees or so and that a few others will also be seated in the same car like me. I had no objection as I took a seat next to the Sardar who was driving, hardly mattered who else were in the rare of it. He dropped me at the doorsteps of my guesthouse. I am thankful to him still. But perhaps I too fulfilled a purpose of his that day.

Chandigarh also has a The Laxmi Narayan Mandir (temple). It is a modern Hindu temple dedicated to Laxmi (goddess of wealth) and Narayana (the preserver). This is also commonly called Birla Temple as known in several places across the country where the Birlas, a dominant business houses in the country, have built such temples. the late Raja Baldeo Das Birla or B.D. Birla as popularly known is said to have built this one.

Closer to Delhi are two very important locations that are of historical and religious importance. One is Panipat and the other is Kurukshetra. (Land that once was the territory of the Kuru Dynasty. Kshetra means territory) Both these places are historical and bear significance for the fact that they changed the course of history. The history of India is marked by arrival of various invaders from far away land. Their presence and actions have been important guiding force for the religious beliefs to emerge and faiths to manifest. It is for this reason that I chose to recount some historical sequence of events that will later help in relating to the anecdotes, as they will appear in bits and pieces at various places of visits in this book. I have even digressed at places to make the content meaningful and noteworthy. It is important thus to gather some information on Panipat and Kurukshetra as well. Both these places have been 'theaters of historical warfare' where the battles created and changed the course of history. Panipat was the venue where two significant battles were fought. The first Battle of Panipat as it is refered to was fought in April 1526 between the Moghul king Babur and the ruling Sultanate of Delhi Ibrahim Lodhi. Althoug the battle lasted only a few hours it terribly fierce. In those few hours about 25,000 troops on both sides were left dead or wounded. The war ended when Ibrahim Lodhis head was severed and taken to Babur. This resulted in the end of the Afgan Sultanate's Rule and marked the beginning of the Moghul Rule. Thirty years later in November 1556, Hemu the commander in chief of the Afgan King Muhammad Adil Shah, taking advantage of the untimely sudden death of Humayun decided to attack the Mughals and get rid of them from India. Humayun's son Akbar was only thirteen had ascended the throne then. During the course of the battle an arrow pierced through the eyes of Hemu and he fell down unconscious. He was immediately taken custody by the army and taken to Akbar. It is said that here his head was cut-off and sent to Kabul as a momento of the victory. This victory re-established the Mogul empire in India that was reduced to some territoties in Afganisthan and Punjab. A third battle of Panipat fought in January 1761 between the Afgans and the Marathas led to the defeat and downfall of the Marathas. Collapse of the Marathas and the death of Mughal emperor Aurangazeb paved the way for British Rule in India. But the battle at Kurukshetra fought thousands of years ago was a holi war that has a connect with the Hindu mythology and has special association with the 'Vedas'. This famous battle as depicted in the 'Mahabharata' was fought between the two families the 'Kurus' and the 'Pandavas' who were both decendents of the 'Bharata Dynasty'. It was in this battle here that the spontaneous deliberance of the tachings and sermons of Lord Krishna was addressed to the reluctant-at-war 'Arjun'. This reflection of Lord Krishna was later enshrined as the sacred inscription called the 'Bhagwat Gita'. Bhagwat Gita is one of the holiest of all texts of the Hindu Religion. The book is identified as the essence of the 'Upanish' and hence also called also called 'Gitopanishad' as well as 'Yogopanishad'. Mahatma Gandhi, throughout his life and his own commentary on the Gita, interpreted the battle as a metaphor in which "the battlefield is the soul and Arjuna, man's higher impulses struggling against evil".[14]

Mahabharata is the culmination of a dynastic struggle for the throne of Hastinapura. Hastinapur was the capital of a legendary king 'Bharat' who was the first and the only emperor to rule all of India. It is from the name of this emperor that the empire came to be known as 'Bhatatvarsha' Bharatvarsha encompassed total Indian subcontinent that includes most of Asia. Though the territory has shrunk with the emergnce of other countries in Asia, The Republic of India of the present time continues to be called Bharatvarsha even today. After the era of the Vedic Gods (estimated to be upward of 5000 years BC), the reign of the lunar dynasty decended starting with King Bharat. The Pandavas and the Kauravas the prominent adversaries in the Mahabhatara epic were the decendents of King Bharat and appeared about a thousand years later.

A gist of the Mahabharata is essential here to understand the significance of its role in the Hindu mythology. Invocation of all faith and belief in Hinduism are either imbibed in or emanate from the two epics namely the Mahabharata and the Ramayana. I am sounding like an authority in this but it is not so. It takes immence amount of learning before one can begin to learn the contents of these and other intricate holi writings. I am nowhere near but as a layperson I wish to put down to share some basic facts that I have gathered during the course of my life's journey. This will also introduce us to some of the important characters involved in shaping Hinduism.

---

14 Gandhi, Mohandas K., *The Bhagavad Gita According to Gandhi* Berkeley Hills Books, Berkeley 2000

It is said that it all started with the 'Mahadivya' the inexhaustible seed of all creation. But for our purpose we would start from the story of 'Vishwamitra'. Vishwamitra, an illustrious saint was in deep meditation when God Indra—the first amongst the extraterrestrial beings in heaven, deployed one of the finest celestial beauties of paradise 'Maneka' to disrupt his concentration fearing that his austere penance would become a challenge to his high position in heaven. Maneka was terrified at this assignment because she knew that Viswamitra was extremely ascetic and very short tempered. She requested Lord Indra to protect her in case she was in trouble. She also suggested advising 'Marut' the Lord of wind to spread the fragrance of suduction and rob her clothes when she would sport before the celebrated sage. So it happened. Invisible Marut disrobed her before the very eyes of the saint. Seeing this faultless beauty unclothed before him trying to blushingly get hold of her flying robe the sage was captivated. He could not take his eyes off the unblemished body that was blooming with femininity. Irresistable as she was the fire of energy within the saint got ignighted and he succumbed to the lust. He advanced towards her and firmly embraced the nude beauty close to his body. Maneka obligingly melted in his arms expressing her acceptance to his desire to have her companionship. They lived for some time when she became expectant. Viswamitra in the meanwhile was in extreme dismay for giving in to desire and loosing all the virtue gained over the years. He wished to resume his consecrated performance and seclude himself entirely from this falsehood. Maneka too was duty bound to return to paradise. Finding no option she left the newborn on the banks of river Malini atop the Himalaya Mountain and disappeared. The baby was looked after and protected by the 'shakuns' (vulture bird in Sanskrit). The baby girl thus came to be called 'Shakuntala'. Whilst on a gaming expedition King Dushyanta happened to arrive at the cottage of Kanva. The saint was away then. On seeing this beautiful girl the king fell in love and they got secretly married there in the forest. Having spent some time there the king left for his kingdom. The son who was born to Shakuntala grew up in the forest amongst the wild. Tuitored by his mother he learnt the sacred texts and also learnt to dominate the wild animals and nature. He was thus named Sarvadamana ('sarva' means 'every' and 'damana' meaning dominant). Later after the mother and child joined the King their son was renamed Bharata. He later ascended the throne and conquered the entire continent from Indian Ocean to the Himalayas. This became the land of Bharata and the empire named after him as Bharatavarsha. He was a virtuous king who is said to have equaled the valour of Indra himself.

With the passage of time and over the generations Bharata's decendent 'Shantanu' came to rule over Hastinapur. Shantanu married Goddess 'Ganga' and a son 'Devabrata' was born who later came to be known as 'Bhisma' who becomes the heir apparent. But as this marriage was short lived he decided to marry 'Satyavati' whom he accidentally met during a safari in the jungle. Satyavati the foster daughter of a fisherman who had once secretly given birth to 'Vyasa' was indecisive. Her father told to her not to marry unless Shantanu promised that the son who will be born out of their relationship was made the king after his death. King Shantanu was so obsessed that wished to agree to the offer but repented that Devabrata would be deprived. He loved Devabrata very much but the love of his son for him was even more. To fulfill the desire of his father and relieve him from the syndrome of worries Devabrata vowed that he would never ever stake claim to the throne and also vowed of lifelong celibacy to guarantee a future assurance to Satyavati and her father. Through this marriage Shantanu had two sons 'Chitrangada' and 'Vichitravirya'. After the death of Shantanu, Chitrangada and later Vichitravirya became the king of Hastinapur. In performance of his duty Devabrata decided to arrange marriage of his stepbrother King Vichitravirya. Hearing of a swayambar (marriage) ceremony in the court of the King of Kashi (now Varanasi) for the marriage of his three daughters namely Amba, Ambika and Ambalika Shantanu went to Kashi and in defiance of ritual whisked the three daughters away and brought them before Satyavati for marriage with her son. As Amba had other plans Ambika and Ambalika were married to Vichitravirya. Unfortunately Vichitravirya soon died without any heir. Satyavati immediately summoned her first son Vyasa to sleep with them and make them pregnant. Having followed rigorous restrictive practices and severe religious ritualistic harshness Vyasa had become unsightly horrid and ghastly over the years. Repelled by his appearance Ambika kept her eyes shut during the course of the involvement, while Ambalika turned pale with scare at first sight. For this reaction of their mothers at the time of procreation the two children born to the two, one was blind named 'Dhritarashtra' and the other 'Pandu' was born pale and weak respectively. But a maidservant whom Ambalika had initially sent to sleep with Vyasa enjoyed the feast and thus gave birth to a healthy flawless son who was named 'Vidura'. Shantanu thus became a grandfather and came to be known as 'Bhishma Pitamah'.

From the marriage of Dhritarashtra with 'Gandhari' were born a hundred sons who are refered to as the 'Kauravs' while Pandu's fathered five children born out of his two marriages with 'Kunti' and 'Madri'. These brothers are referred to as the Pandavas. Incidentally, Kunti had earlier mothered a son 'Karn' who was brought up by foster parents. He played an important role in the war of Kurukshetra. Due to Dhritarashtra's blindness Pandu took the throne but he later retired to the forest as he was cursed by a rishi called 'Kindama' that forbade him from engaging in any sexual act. Thus Dhritarashtra had to manage the kingdom despite his blindness.

Dhritarashtra's younger brother Pandu's eldest son 'Yudhisthir' was the eldest amongst all the one hundred and five brothers. Thus 'Duryodhana' the eldest amongst the Kauravas was younger than Yudhisthira the eldest Pandava. Both Duryodhana and Yudhisthira claim to the first in line to inherit the throne. But the Kaurava being the senior branch of the family there was a rivalry between the two families who should claim to be the first in line to inherit the throne, Duryodhana or Yudhisthira. This rivalry and enmity with the Pandava brothers was planted by 'Shakuni' brother of Gandhari who germinated and treacherously nurtured this hostility from their youth and into manhood. Shakuni was resolute and oath-bound to destroy the dinasty of the Kauravas, as he was severly insulted when his beloved sister Gandhari was getting married to a blind man. Thus very cunningly he chose to take the side of the Kauravas and yet remained their enemy. He strategised actions adverse to Kauravas with whom he lived but without ever letting them know of his ulterior designs. He succeeded in agravating the resentment between the two families that finally culminated in to the famous war at Kurukshetra. This war is also called the 'Dharma Yuddha' which in Sanskrit means 'war of righteousness'. The war finally resulted in total destruction and marked the end of 'Dwapar Yug' ('Yug' meaning era or age). Then on began the 'Kal-Yug' In Hindu philosophy the cycle of creation is divided into four 'Yugs'. They are the Satya Yuga, the Treta Yuga, the Dwapar Yuga and finally the Kal Yuga.

During the Kurukshetra war Bhishma Pitamah's (Devabrata and great-grandfather of the Pandavas and Kauravas) body was pierced by a hundred arrows and he

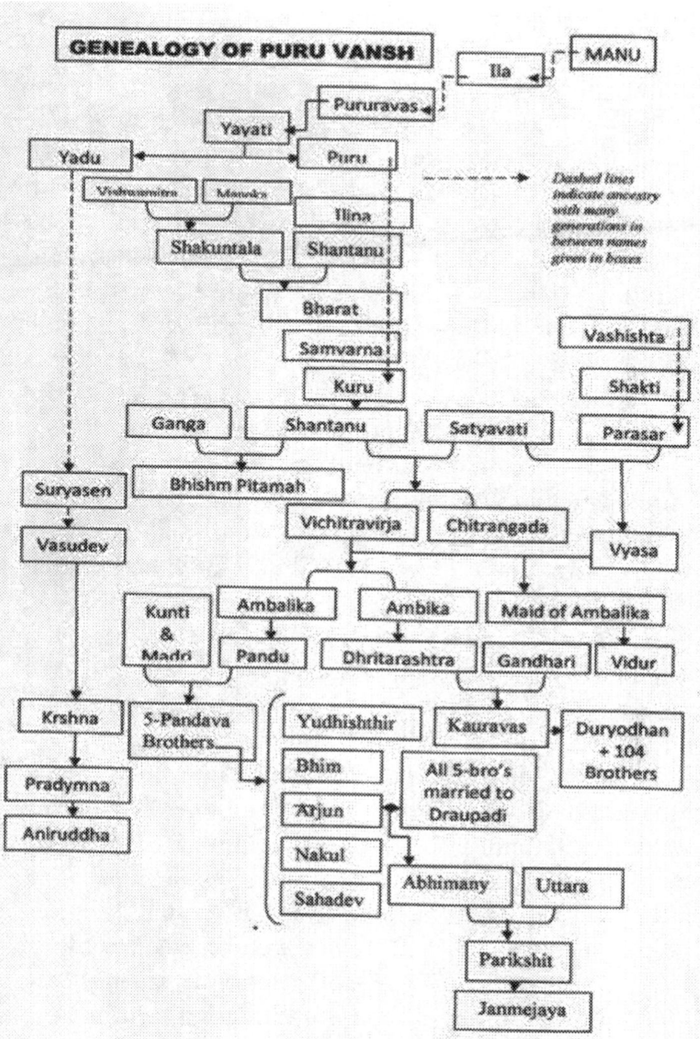
GENEALOGY OF PURU VANSH
MANU
Ila
Pururavas
Yayati
Yadu
Puru
Dashed lines indicate ancestry with many generations in between names given in boxes
Ilina
Shakuntala
Shantanu
Bharat
Samvarna
Kuru
Vashishta
Shakti
Ganga
Shantanu
Satyavati
Parasar
Suryasen
Bhishm Pitamah
Vichitravirja
Chitrangada
Vasudev
Vyasa
Kunti
&
Madri
Ambalika
Ambika
Maid of Ambalika
Pandu
Dhritarashtra
Gandhari
Vidur
Krshna
5-Pandava Brothers
Yudhishthir
Kauravas
Duryodhan + 104 Brothers
Pradymna
Bhim
All 5-bro's married to Draupadi
Aniruddha
Arjun
Nakul
Abhimany
Uttara
Sahadev
Parikshit
Janmejaya

lay there on a bed of arrow unable to move. At the time when he was nearing his death he asked for water. Wasting no time Arjuna shot an arrow into the ground and water squirted out into his mouth. Bhishma Kund (kund means a waterbody) and Narkatari Temple as seen today are believed to be the place where that event took place. Other sanctified places here are Brahma Sarovar (pond) dedicated to Lord Vishnu and Brahma (who created our planet), Nabhi Kamal a sacred tank dedicated to the trinity God Lord Bramha and 'Sthaneshwar' temple dedicated to Lord Shiva. The famous Ma Bhadra Kali temple located in the vicinity is considered a 'Pitha Sthana' and is called a 'Sidh Peeth' where Sati's lower limb fell. Near to Sthaneswar is a 'Gurudwara' ('Guru' means the beholder of knowledge and 'dwara' means the doorway) dedicated to eighth Sikh Guru Harkishan. Another one dedicated to the sixth Sikh guru Hargobind, stands near the Sinnihit tank. But the largest of all is Gurudwara Rajghat built in the memory of the Guru Gobin Singh. The Chini Masjid and Patthar Masjid are important Muslim places of worship here. Situated at Gurgaon closer to Delhi is a Sheetla Devi Temple dedicated to Mata Sheetla Devi that is considered a sacred 'Shakti Peeth' and hence a place of pilgrimage for all Hindus.

Coming down south from Punjab is the State of **RAJASTHAN**. This state not only has a legendary history of valor and heroism but also encompasses a wide display of creativity in art, architecture and scientific feats. This state also has the maximum diversity of terrain, from mountains to forests and from the enormous expanse of dry desert land to the myriad stretches of water-bodies. The land tells stories of the colorful festivities and also of the innumerable battles and bloodshed that come to pass on this land. This state has given birth to communities of tradesmen, merchants and businesspersons. People of Rajasthan or more notably the Marwari's are spread all across the country and the world. They have conducted business wherever they lived and brought prosperity for themselves as well as for the people with whom they lived. Today they are the richest communities in India and their contribution to the growth of the Indian economy is enormous. A recent survey of the world's richest persons show that four Indians figure amongst the top eight and three out of the richest five are Marwaris. With such an intense history of undaunted bravery and enormity of courage it is imperative that there will be a soaring concentration of deity worships and religious beliefs in this blessed land.

Jaipur the capital city and also called the pink city is the most popular of all places as the world also knows. Birla Temple is a major attraction of Jaipur. Made in pure white marble it looks stunning when lit up at night and during the day it dominates the skyline of Jaipur. The temple was built quite lately 1988 by house of Birlas. Also known as Laxmi Narayan Temple and is dedicated to Lord Vishnu (Narayan), the preserver and his consort Lakshmi, the Goddess of wealth. Govind Dev Ji Temple is another major tourist attraction of Jaipur. The Temple is dedicated to Govind (Other name of Lord Krishna). The temple is situated in the City Palace complex wherein the idols of Radha and Krshna are installed and worshipped by followers of Lord Chaitanya who walked this earth some 500 years ago. It may be known to many that Lord Krshna a significant character in the epic of Mahabharata was the eighth and the most popular and also the full and complete incarnation of Lord Vishnu. Radha symbolizes the individual soul that is awakened to the love of God and is absorbed in such love. The sound of Krishna's flute represents the call of the divine for the individual souls. Moti Dungri Temple is yet another illustration of the diversity of Hindu places of worship. The temple of Moti Doongri (meaning Hill of Pearls) is dedicated to the elephant head God known as 'Ganesha', son of Lord Shiva. Ganesha epitomizes auspiciousness. With his name and rememberance begins every auspicious event in any Hindu community. Situated atop a small hill it overlooks the city of Jaipur. A palace and a temple occupy the hill. It is said that Maharaja Madho Singh's son resided in that palace and it still belongs to the royal family. As I understand it was also the home of Rajmata Gayatri Devi (a queen of recent times) and her son, Jagat Singh. However, the palace is not open for public.

On way to Udaipur, another royal city in the state of Rajasthan falls a small town called Ajmer some 135 Km from Jaipur where the Dargah Shariff of Hazrat Khwaja Muinuddin Chisty is located. Although this is an important place for Muslim pilgrimage, but the holy Dargah (shrine) is revered by individuals of all faith. I have visited this shrine at least twice so far. Although I am a Hindu by birth I have found immense fulfillment and solace being here and listening to the qawwali (devotional songs sung in the praise of Allah). Emperor Humayun is said to have built this shrine in memory of Hazrat Khwaja Moin-ud-din Chisti a revered prophet who undertook to propagate Islam in India. The Khwaja by his noble teachings touched the hearts of everyone who came his way. He was a Sufi saint who came to Ajmer from Persia and died here in 1236. (Term Sufism denotes nothing but a direct interpretation of the cardinal principles of Islam and certain spiritual practices to be observed in this process. Its originator Abu Ishaq Shami was the first Sufi who preached this cult which was in conformity with all the basic principles of Islam). 'The life of a Sufi is the "life of the spirit" regulated strictly in accordance with Islamic theology and traditions. To attain this first lesson is unshakable belief in the existence of God and unconditional surrender to His will. This entails a strenuous life attended by rigid austerity and self-denial.

He has to undergo a course of training in regular prayers and meditation to attain the Divine Knowledge and realisation of Truth. One Sufi passes this particular knowledge on 'in secret' to another having the requisite qualifications (i.e. one who does not think evil does not see evil, does not hear evil and does not speak evil). Without this Divine Knowledge, one cannot fathom the hidden mysteries of the Nature and those of the soul. To sum up the whole object of Sufism is to attain the highest spiritual perfection'.[15] This final resting place of the saint is also considered as a shrine of wish fulfillment. Tourists, travelers and devotees visit this place to pray and tie a thread on the banister with their wishes wound in it. It is said that King Akhbar's wishes to have a son was fulfilled by his blessings.

Near Ajmer is a very holy place of Pilgrimage for the Hindus called Pushkar. It is a small town and its inhabitance is concentrated around the holy Pushkar Lake. Amonst the several important temples in the town like the 12th century Apteshwar Temple dedicated to Lord Shiva, Varah Temple has an idol of lord Vishnu (according to the Hindu legend Lord Vishnu took the form of a Varah (Wild boar) and descended on the earth to kill an atrocious demon Hirnayaksh), Rangnath Temple dedicated to Lord Vishnu and Savitri Temple (located at an altitude) dedicated to goddess Savitri, the first wife of Lord Brahma. The most significant is one dedicated to Lord Brahma. This 14th century monument is a very conspicuous structure in Pushkar and also the most revered one, as this is perhaps the only one temple in India dedicated to Lord Brahma, considered as the creator of the universe. One can see an idol of Brahma here with four hands and four faces facing the four directions. Beside

---

15 'Philosophy of Sufism' <http://www.dargahajmer.com/i_sufi.htm>

the Savitri temple on the hilltop is the Gayatri Temple. Gayatri was another wife of Brahma and was a proxy to his first wife Savitri during auspicious ceremonies if she were absent. To make a mention of yet another legend Gayatri was an untouchable and to purify her she was put into the mouth of a cow and taken out from the other end. The town of Pushkar stands out for one more reason and that is it holds an annual animal and livestock fair some time in November that is also the largest camel fair in the world (and indeed, world's largest cattle fair in general). It may be of information that the largest animal fair in Asia (or perhaps the second largest in the world next to Pushkar) is held at Sonepur in Bihar, India also called the Son Mela.

An overnight journey from Jaipur one can reach Udaipur also called the city of lakes. It is these large expanses of water that make this city unique and indeed very beautiful But I was struck with awe when during my third visit to the city in 2001 I noticed that the lakes had dried up and at many a places the mud has surfaced. This was in important source of water for this water-starved surrounding. I was told that some plan was underway but I thought restoring the lake and its water content was equally important to maintain the natural topography of the region. Apart from the Jagdish Temple in Udaipur dedicated to Lord Vishnu one can find Ekling Temple, Rishabdeo Temple, Ranakpur Temples, Nathdwara Temple, Jagat Temple and Kankroli Temple that are well known and located in and around Udaipur. All these temples are dedicated to several forms of God. Jagdish temple located within the City Palace complex of Udaipur the temple is dedicated to Lord Vishnu (Jagadish is another name of Lord Vishnu who is considered as the preserver of the Universe). Maharana Jagat Singh, who ruled Udaipur during 1628-53, built this temple. This is perhaps the largest temple in the city of Udaipur.

The Temple is majestic in sight with sculptures of dancers, elephants, horsemen and musicians adorning its surroundings. There are four shrines built around the main deity of Lord Jagdish. Seated in these four shrines are Lord Ganesha, Sun God, Goddess Shakti (meaning power) and Lord Shiva respectively. A brass image of Garuda (a figure of half-man and half-eagle) stands guarding the doorway of four-armed idol of Lord Vishnu. The Ekalinga temple is situated outside Udaipur about about 22 Km away and within is installed idol of Eklingji (Lord Shiva) made out of black marble. Built in 734 A.D. by Bappa Rawal, Eklingji has been the ruling deity of Mewar rulers. Its height ranges around 50 feet and its four faces depict four forms of Lord Shiva. The east-facing part is recognized as Surya (solar), the west-facing part is Lord Brahma, the north-facing part is Lord Vishnu and the south-facing part is Rudra i.e. Lord Shiva himself.

About a 115 Km northeast of Udaipur is the tiny district of Chittorgarh. This was the capital of Mewar from the 7th to the 16th century and the reminiscing fort of Chittor is the most endearing and appealing monument of the place making it more alluring for visitors than the holy temples that the people worshipped. My first visit to Chittorgarh was when I was 18. Fresh from the textbooks of history this visit was like history coming alive. The reminiscence is so vivid and virtual that I felt as if I was witnessing the replay of all the magnificent events that took place here. Indeed I cannot resist putting down a prologue to on of the splendid happenings in history that describes the heroic deeds of sacrifice and bravery displayed by the men and women who once lived here. The territory of Chittor came to Bappa Rawal, the legendary founder of the Sisodia dynasty as dowry of the last Solanki princess. The Bappa Rawal and his dynasty ruled Chittor then on for almost eight centuries. But all these years their existence was more turbulent than peaceful. The seemingly impregnable kingdom was provoked and attacked several times and always had to remain vigilant and in a state of readiness. The fort is located on a hilltop. The terrain is harsh and there is one road that leads to the fort atop. This passage used to be guarded by seven huge doorways, which still exists. As one drives upwards these gates would appear at definite intervals. Each of these are different in shape and size and were built as a mechanism to defend. The fort was also scientifically built so as to make it as self-sufficient as practicable. It had nearly a hundred water-bodies, which served different purposes for the army and the population that lived in the kingdom. It had space for enough livestock and provisions. There was enlightenment amongst people and had a rich culture to revere. But in spite of this the kingdom could never rest in peace. In 1303 Allauddin Khilji, Sultan of Delhi who once plundered Gujrat decided to capture Chittor as the Chttor would never submit to the rule of the Sultans. Knowing that it was not easy to invade Chittor a different plan emerged in his mind. He planted moles in the royal family who would bring information for him. While he would gather information about the Rajput king Rana Rattan Singh and his kingdom, his intelligentsia would never fail to make at least one mention about the enchanting beauty that was Padmini the queen of Chttor. Enthralled by tales of queen Padmini's beauty the Sultan Allauddin Khilji could not resist but having a glimpse of her himself. Knowing that he would not be permitted so easily he decided to besiege the territory and send a message to Rana Rattan Singh, Padmini's husband, that he would spare the city if he could meet the queen. After much squabble conciliation was finally reached. The sultan could only look upon a reflection of Padmini but he would have to come alone and disarmed. Kilji agreed and he was given the opportunity to see a reflection of the beautiful Padmini standing by a lotus pool. The Sultan was gratified but could not resist his yearn to possess the beauty. So he made an evil plan. As the host courteously escorted Allauddin down to the outer gate, the sultan's men ambushed and took the Rana hostage and sent a message to the kingdom that the Rana could be let free if Padmini came to take her back. Understanding the iniquitous design Padmini agreed but devised a counter strategyherself after discussing with Gorah, her maternal uncle. Padmini conveyed to the Sultan that she would be accompanied by a contingent of 700 of her maids who would come in palanquins (palki in Hindi). As the Sultans and his men waited at the foot hill, dozens of curtained palanquins set off down the hill, each carried by six humble bearers. Once inside the Sultan's camp, four well-armed Rajput warriors leaped out of each palanquin and they along with the palanquin-bearer drew out their sword. In the ensuing battle, Rana Rattan Singh was rescued. Gorah put up a brave front and he with his solders killed several of the Sultans army. When he reached Kilji's camp the coward Sutan flung one of his concubine to the fore knowing that a Rajput would never hurt a woman without arms, This momentary delay was enough for the soldiers of Khilji to pounce upon Gorah and finish him there. Gorah was killed and so were 7,000 of the brave Rajput warriors. The sultan now attacked Chittor with renewed vigor. Having lost 7,000 of its best warriors, Chittor could not hold out. But surrender was unthinkable. The queen and her entire entourage of women, the wives of generals and soldiers, sent their children into hiding with loyal retainers. They then dressed their wedding attire entered the main palace and singing the ancient hymns immolated themselves in an act called the 'Jauhar'. (an enormous fire, with ghee and sandalwood, lit to the chanting of mantras when all the women, 16000 of them, dressed in their wedding finery, jumped into the fire to perish).

The Rajputs were staunch Hindus and they built several temples here in Chuttorgarh. One such famous temple is the Meera temple dedicated to Meera Bai, the princess who committed her whole life to Goddess Krishna. Her ardent devotion was such that Krshna got invoked to save her when she was about to gulp down poison. It is said that Krishna emerged and consumed it instead to save her life and as a consequence Krshna's body turned blue. Such is the blessings of Krshna that even the barbaric attack on this land on so many occasions when temples and the palaces were destroyed and plundered this temple remained untouched and protected. Located in the premises of Shyam Kumbh there is a carved statue of five human forms with one head. This is said to signify the convergence of all sects, beliefs and faith in the indefinable Supreme.

Built by Bappa Rawal around 700 AD, the Kalika Mata Temple is the place for worship of Kalika, another incarnation of Goddess Durga who also is the patron goddess of Chittorgarh. Durga is an embodiment of 'Shakti' or power. It is said that this temple was originally built in the 8th century as a Sun Temple and later converted in its present form in the 14th century AD. The Goddess here is worshipped in her worrier incarnation and depicts the victory of good over the evil. Figures of the Sun God adorn the gates, shrine and walls of the temple precincts. It is located near Padmini's Palace. The temple was in ruins when I visited last but the architectural splendor that remains still is worth an appreciation.

One night train journey from Udaipur will reach you to Jodhpur. This is one of the last major cities on the western fringe of Rajasthan and the country and from where the desert of Thar begins. During the mid 16th century the city of Jodhpur was the capital of Marwar (the land of death) State. Founded in 1459 Rao Jodha, the chief of the Rathore clan, is considered as the originator of Jodhpur, the city that is named after him—previously known as Marwar. Like many other places across Rajasthan this kingdom too had fought many a war and several tales of bravery could be heard once here. Ruled by the Rathore clan this was the largest princely state of pre-independent India (after Jammu and Kashmir and Hyderabad). Rathors are believed to have their origins from Rama (hero of the epic Ramayana) and thence to Surya (the sun). Rathors thus consider themselves as belonging to the Suryavansha (solar race). Suryavansha is branch of the Kshatriyas, the warrior caste amongst Hindus. Later, in 470 A.D. Nayal Pal conquered the kingdom of Kanauj, near modern Kanpur in Uttar Pradesh. Kanauj remained the bastion for more than seven centuries, till they fell in 1193 to the Afghan invasion led by Muhammad Ghori.

Udai Mandir is the most exquisitely built temple in Jodhpur. Its architectural brilliance makes it worth visiting. The temple rests on a gigantic platform supported by 102 pillars. Several paintings adorn the inside walls. The paintings depict mudras (postures) of 'Yogasanas' (exercise of yoga). Nearby is the Rasik Bihari temple (also known as Niniji Temple) devoted to Rasik Bihari, Lord Krishna and Goddess Radha. Statues of other deities could be seen at the gates and around. Another temple dedicated to Krshna is the Kunj Bihari Temple in Jodhpur. Here a statue of Meera Bai, the great devotee of Lord Krishna of Krshna could also be seen. All these temples have been built by the royal family as gratitude towards the God or may be with an intention to appease and thereby ward off difficulties. Being rich and royal in their approach the rulers of Jodhpur had built more of forts and palaces than real temples of worship if compared by size and magnificence. One such example of palace here is Balsammand lake Palace built by Maharajah Sur

Sinhji in the 1600s. A lake in the foreground called the Balsammand lake is said to be one of Rajasthan's oldest artificial water reservoir created in 1159 AD.

Moving northward from Jodhpur is the start of the Desert. The two districts of Rajasthan that are predominantly desert covered are Bikaner and Jaisalmer. I traveled to Bikaner from Jaipur. Travelling on a meter-gauge train I reached Bikaner town early in the morning. Very thinly populated and deserted as it appears, the place is inhabited by very lively people whose lives I found were very tough. I gathered that one Rao Bikaji had founded Bikaner here in the year 1488 A.D. Here stands the Laxminath Temple where deities Vishnu and Laxmi are installed. From Bukaner I went to a remote village called Lunkansar. While traveling to this place I was told to abandon the car I was using in Bikaner town and board a desert jeep arranged by my hosts. Later during my journey through thr deep desert I realised that indeed without such a rugged vehicle it would be impossible to move around. Even this jeep once got stuck, with the wheel spinning at one place and gradually sinking into the sand. It was a fearful sight amidst the dunes where not a soul could be seen. The only glimpse of life I saw while waiting there was a sight of two small kids who appeared at a distance, waited and looked at us and in a short while disappeared. The driver of the jeep, my host and myself first tried to test our strength by trying to haul out the helpless machine but we failed utterly. Then the two of them ran down the dunes to collect the dry shrubs and put them under the wheels to create the friction that could pull the wheel out from the sand. After several attempts the vehicle finally came on its own. Though a bit delayed but I reached Bikaner quite after sunset, which is the ideal time to go around the place.

Temples in Bikaner are many but only a few of them are historical or noteworthy The beautifully sculpted

Bhandeshwar Temple decorated with gold-leaf work and rich mirror work and the Sandeshwar Temple covered with marble sculptures are two exceptional Jain temples built by two merchant brothers in the 16th century. A rarely seen monument dedicated to Kapil Muni (a saint who was an incarnate of Lord Vishnu and believed to have lived some 500 years BC. Kapil Muni preached amongst many other things, the philosophy of Sankhya, which is highly esteemed. It is a course of self-realization by those desiring freedom from the entanglement of unnecessary material desires). Also one could see here the Sri Kolayatji Temple. Shiv Bari Temple (bari means water)built in the late 19th century by Dungar Singhji houses a four-faced black marble Shiva statue and a bronze Nandi (the sacred bull and carrier of Shiva) facing the Shiva-Lingam. There are two large reservoirs of water known as bawaris.

The following day I set off for Jaisalmer. Although I had more comfortable and convenient options but I opted to travel by a common overnight bus, which normally the local people travel in. Those who know about Indian buses can perhaps imagine the plight that I went through. But I have no regrets. It is my country after all and all those who traveled with me are my own people deprived and devoid for no fault of theirs. The government will do little or perhaps nothing to ameliorate their condition but I hope the Gods who are worshipped in so large numbers could show them the way to well being. Our bus entered the Jaisalmer bus station when it was still dark. It was around 4:30 am and the conductor woke us all up. Half asleep I took a rickshaw (a two-seater, three wheeled manually paddled vehicle) and set off for the Tourist Lodge. Founded in 1156 AD, Jaisalmer is named after its founder Bhatti Rajput Rao Jaisal. This desert city of the medieval times is clad with the golden sand stone that is the only available and conducive material used for housing in that harsh and rugged climate. The fort of Jaisalmer is picturesque. Perched on a hill-top and housing its people, inside the citadel are three beautifully sculptured 12th-15th century Jain temples that are dedicated to the Jain Tirthankaras—Rishabdev, Sambhavnath and Parswanath. This fort was also invaded and plundered by the Sultan King Alla-ud-din Khilji before he invaded Chittorgarh.

Close to Rajasthan's border with the State of Gujarat is a magnificent mountain resort known as Mount Abu. A part of the Aravali range of mountains this hill retreat has a rich variety of flora and flowering shrubs. Its cool climate makes it unique in the province that is other wise known for its dreadful heat and dust. Of the many temples in Mount Abu the most well known and admired is the Dilwara Temple that was built in the 11th to 13th century AD. From outside the temple looks like any simple structure from inside it is awfully mesmerizing. No words can describe the immaculate artwork chsseled on stone along the walls and ceilings of the entire premises. The premise is actually a conglomerate of five Jain Tirthankara (Saints) temples namely the Mahaveer Swami Temple, Parshav Nath Temple, Rishabdaoji Temple Adi Nath Temple, and the Nemi Nath Temple. Adi Nath Temple was built by the rulers of Gujarat in 1031 AD and is dedicated to Shri Adinath Ji—The first Jain Trithankar. Rishabdaoji Temple was also built by Gujrathi rulers but much later in time. Tejpal and Vastupal two brothers and devotees are known to have built the Nemi Nath Ji Temple in 1230 A.D. They dedicated this temple to the 22nd Tirthankara of Jainism—Shri Nemi Nathji. The tallest amongst all is the Parshva Nath temple built by Mandika clan between 1458-59 A.D. The Mahaveer temple was built in the late 16th century AD is dedicated to the 24th Tirthankara of the Jain community. The exquisite interior with meticulousness in architecture and the magnificent marble stone carvings is a sight to admire. I was awe struck at the the carvings on the ceilings and the pillars. I have never seen such a feat of human craftsmanship anywhere else. The job must have been very painstaking and scientifically executed. When I once visited this place in the early seventies I was in middle school the temple had little restrictions. I did not have a camera then but those who had freely took pictures. But when I visited the place again in 1997 I had my camera along but alas, photography was disallowed. I returned with memories alone, much of which has faded by now.

Incidentally, as the legend goes Abu derives its name from Arbuada the powerful serpent who bailed out the sacred bull of Lord Shiva, Nandi when once trapped in a gorge. A beautiful temple of Arbuada and a magnificent marble image of Nandi could be seen at the Gaumukh Temple where Goumukh (Gau meaning holy cow and mukh means mouth) A natural spring flowing through a sculpted cow head gives the shrine its name. The famous sage Vashishtha, the self-controlled, the son of Brahma and also the family priest of Dasharatha and (his son-in-law) Rama is believed to have performed 'yagna' here.

A mile long lake in the heart of the plateau on Mount Abu is what breaks the monotony of the uniform mountain range that are stacked against each other. For tourists it is a place that provides relief activities. Be it boating or a walk along side or spending some moments in solitude watching the blue waters of the lake is mystifying indeed. A temple dedicated to Shri. Raghunathji—a famous Hindu preacher, is situated near this 'Nakki' lake. The Adhar Devi temple dedicated to Goddess Durga is yet another favorite tourist spot situated at a distance of 3 km to the north of the city. As it is built out of the rocks one has to crouch under the rock to enter the temple. This temple is regarded as one of the important pilgrimage sites of Mount Abu. This is also a good site to get a panoramic view of the valley.

The state adjoining Rajasthan in the south is Gujarat. This is one of the very colorful and culturally vibrant states if India. But I would come to it a little later may be close to the end of this book. Before that it would be better if we covered an important state which is also called the abode of the Gods or Dev Bhoomi the state of **UTTARAKHAND**. This is a small mountainous province constituted in year 2000 as the 27th state of the union of India after its separation from the then the largest state of Uttar Pradesh. Uttarakhand is described as "a region of outstanding natural beauty. Most of the northern parts of the state are part of Greater Himalaya ranges, covered by the high Himalayan peaks and glaciers, while the lower foothills were densely forested. They were denuded by the British log merchants and later, after independence, by the Indian forest contractors. Recent efforts in reforestation, however, have been successful in restoring the situation to some extent. The unique Himalayan eco-system plays host to a large number of animals (including snow leopards and tigers), plants and rare herbs of rich medicinal worth".[16] Uttarakhand is also the source of two of India's mightiest rivers the Ganga and the Yamuna.

Uttarakhand could broadly be said to have two regions the Garhwal region and the Kumaon region. To give a brief account of history that I have gathered, the Chands arrived in Kumaon from Jhansi sometime in the 8th and began its reign in Champawat. King Som Chand's kingdom later came to be known as Kumaon. After having fought many a battle and also having driven out of their land for several centuries by the indomitable Khas rulers they finally regained their lost territories in the mid 1500 and established their new capital in

[16] S. S. Negi [(1991). Himalayan Rivers, Lakes, and Glaciers. New Delhi: Indus Pub. Co

Almorah, Garhwal. But the territories of Kumaon and Garhwal never remained at peace. Until the 1790 there were incessant attacks by the Rohillas, Tibetians, the Sikhs and also from the Marathas in the south. All these years the Garhwal and Kumaon had put up a brave front and protected their land before they gave in to the Gurkhas in 1803 bringing an end to almost one thousands years of the Chand dynasty. In 1948, we witnessed it accession with independent India. They formed the two districts of Uttar Pradesh, namely the Garhwal and Kumaon. In 2000, Garhwal and Kumaon were integrated to form a new state of "Uttaranchal" later re-named as Uttarakhand.

From the ancient times this region has been considered as Dev Bhoomi or abode of the Gods. Uttarakhand has a multitude of temples and places for Hindu worshippers—so many that it is not possible even to remember how many out of the several left out that one might have seen while traveling the region. The most sacred and spiritual of all is the 'Char Dhaam Yatra' or journey to the four most hallowed shrines. They are the Deities Gangotri, Yamunotri, Badrinath and Kedarnath—collectively called the Chardham (char meaning four in Hindi). As far as the Hindu legends go, a visit to all these four places leads one to salvation. I have not been able to decisively trace the origins of this Char Dham but grouped together by the great 8th century reformer and philosopher Shankaracharya (Adi Sankara), into the archetypal All-India pilgrimage circuit to four cardinal points of the subcontinent were four important temples—Puri, Rameshwaram, Dwarka, and Badrinath. Pilgrims begin their journey from Haridwar ('Hari' meaning the Almighty and 'Dwaar' means door connotes thereby gateway to the abode of the Gods). The journey if undertaken under a tight schedule and without much rest it would take about ten days to cover. A slightly stress-free progression with halts at some of the wonderful spots on the way with local exploration at different locations this tour could be covered in a fortnight. My wife and I visited two of the Dhaams—Badrinath and Kedarnath in 1992 when we covered the journey in about 10 days (from Rishikesh and back). At Haridwar one can find innumerable temples, Ashrams and Dharamshalas. But the most visited place in Haridwar is the Har-Ki-Pauri ('pauri' signifies ladder). This is a sacred Ghat (embankment), which marks the departure of the Ganga from the Himalayas onto the plains. This place is said to have been constructed by Vikramaditya the 1st century legendary king of Ujjain in memory of his brother Bhartrihari that later came to be known as Har-Ki-Pauri. Bhartrihari's life was legendary in the sense that he transformed himself from a ruler obsessed in lovemaking, to a wise man who later scripted the immortal 'Shataka Trilogy', (comprising of Shringara (adorn to charm), Neeti (wisdom) and Vairagya (renunciation) Shatakas).[17]

Each day the journey was arduous but the breathtaking view in the evening would relive us of all pains. Situated in the banks of the Ganga and seated amidst the cosmic mountains and the woods is the holy city of Rishikesh. It is also the place of learning and meditation towards enlightenment. Yoga, another faculty of spiritual learning and attainment could be learnt here. The place gets its name from Hrishikesh an incarnation of God who was invoked by Hrisabh Rishi (saint) out of his deep meditation. Rishikesh is the launching point for the pilgrimage to the Char Dham. Over the Ganga River in Rishikesh one can walk over the hanging footbridge called 'Laksman Jhoola'. Laksman Jhoola is a hanging

---

17 'Encyclpopaedia of Indian Literature' By various writers. Published by Sahitya Akademi, 1992. ISBN 8126012218, 9788126012213

bridge ('jhoola' means hanging) named after Laksmana the younger brother of Lord Rama who arrived here to worship the Gods for their blessings he received in winning the war against King Ravana. The bridge that spans over the 450 meter wide stream of the Holy Ganga is not the original one that is said to have been made of jute fiber and used by Laksmana to cross over. The present one constructed in the mid 1930's is made of metal and concrete and does not quite align with the serenity of the natural environment. Mahatma Gandhi had once expressed "Lakshman Jhula was, I saw, nothing but an iron suspension bridge over the Ganges. I was told that originally there had been a fine rope-bridge. . . . I am at a loss to say anything about the rope-bridge as I have never seen it, but the iron bridge is entirely out of place in such surroundings and mars their beauty".[18] About twelve kilometers away at an altitude of about 5,200 feet is the famous Neelkanth Temple. Neelkanth is another name of Shiva. (Neel kanth literally means 'blue throat'. Shiva, in order to save the earth from getting perished by the fall of a deadly poison had swallowed it himself but in order the he him self did not get harmed held the poison to his throat when his throat turned blue—thus the name also synonymous to Lord Shiva).

Gangotri and Yamunotri are dedicated to the two of the famous and revered rivers namely Ganga and Yamuna. It is said that Goddess Ganga when first descended to Earth in most pristine state was received and collected by Lord Shiva in his tangled locks to save her from the impact of fall from heaven. The sources of the four holy rivers here form the four places of pilgimage. They are River

[18] Gandhi An Autobiography: The Story of My Experiments With Truth by Mohandas Karamchand (Mahatma) Gandhi, Mahadev H. Desai, and Sissela Bok. Beacon Press Boston. (Nov 1993)

Ganga at Gangotri, Yamuna from Yamunotri, Mandakini from Kedarnath and Alaknanda, which originates from Badrinath.

Passing through Rishikesh and Rudraprayag, we reached Gaurikund which is the foot of the hill and end of the motorable road and from where begins the 14 Km high altitude trek to the Temple of Kedarnath. Gauri Kund is said to be the place where Ganga actually comes out of the hair mesh of Shiva at Gauri Kund and begins her flow across the entire stretch of Northern India and merges into the sea at Bay of Bengal. Gaurikund (named after Maha Gauri the incarnation of Goddess Durga. It is said that while observing sacrament on earth the body of Gauri became dirty on earth when Shiva cleaned her with the waters of Ganga. Then on her brilliance came to light and she came to be known as the Maha Gauri). Located at an altitude of about 2000 meters there can be seen a temple dedicated to Maha Gauri and also two tanks with flowing natural springs one with hot water another with cold.

Covering a distance of about 140 km on our way up from Rishikesh we had our first halt at Rudra Prayag. Here one can find the temples of Jagadamba (Goddess Durga) and Rudranath. But the place finds its name from the confluence of the two rivers Mahananda and Alaknanda (prayag generally connotes meeting point or confluence of rivers). Here on as it flowed down towards Rishikesh, the river is called Alaknanda that flows down through Srinagar (107 Km from Rishikesh) to Deo Prayag (70 Km form Rishikesh) where it meets the River Bhagirati. It may be of interest that there are five important confluences (prayag) of Alaananada the river that flows down from Badrinath. These are Vishnuprayag (meeting point of Alaknanda and Dhauli-Ganga rivers) Nandaprayag (21 km from Karnaprayag, at the confluence of Alaknanda and river Mandakani), Karnapryag (on the way to Badrinath (on the confluence of Alaknanda and Pindar) Rudraprayag (situated at the second confluence of rivers Alaknanda and Mandakani.) and Deoprayag (the confluence of river Bhagirathi from Gaumukh and Alaknanda from Alkapuri glacier to form the Ganga). It is believed that after having killed Ravana Lord Rama had come here for penance. The Raghunath temple with a tall image of Lord Rama is built to commemorate that happening.

We climbed the 14 Km stretch from Gaurikund to Kedarnath on a mule. Slowly and gradually we tread to the top. Many people prefer to walk it up all the way. Some say to appease God one must take the pain of climbing on foot so as to inflict pain on oneself. What if one is not pained enough to reach the top? Does he have to find new means of inflicting pain? This is not my excuse of not taking the walk but I have a different perspective of thought. I do not wish to hurt any soul by challenging his belief and so I have never argued with any one ever on this. But if one were to take the pain to satisfy God then one should rather walk not just this 14 Km stretch but the entire 1400 Km stretch from home. My purpose of visit here or for that matter to any religious destination is not to appease the deity but to honor the God and pay my deepest respect to the power and the overwhelming might of that divine-being on which the faith of mankind has been so deep-rooted over the ages. I bow here to this supremacy before which I am infinitesimal, timid and utterly ignorant. I pray before this omnipotent entity to show me the course of well-being and righteousness. Afterall whoever and wherever I offer my prayer I believe it is meant to reach the indefinable omnipotent supreme authority from whom all the powers of all known deities across the world are drawn and who maintains the equilibrium of nature that confines the universe and beyond.

At Kedarnath the Temple is dedicated to Lord Shiva. That comprises of a cluster of five temples. Other for being Kalpnath, Rudranath, Madhy Maheswara and Tunganath temples, Similarly, there are five kunds in the neighbourhood named after Brahma, Vishnu, Rudra, Saraswati and Gauri. Ten minutes walk from the main temple is another temple dedicated to Bhaironath who is believed to be the protector of all evil. It is also believed that when after Diwali (generally falls in the months of Oct—November) when the temple closes due to extreme cold and snow and no body stays around it is Bhaironath who protects the temple and deity of Kedarnath. There is also a memorial of Aadi Shankaracharyya near the temple compound.

After a staying here for two nights we set off for Badrinath. Coming down hill to Gaurikund to spend the night before we proceeded towards Joshimath, our first halt on way to Badrinath which is 175 Km of mountainous track from Kedarnath. Joshimath is also a place of religions importance. It is here that Aadi Shankaracharyya attained enlightenment. Aadi Shankaracharyya who is said to have lived on this earth possibly between 788-820 AD was a philosopher monk with extraordinary knowledge and spiritual understanding. He has not only made remarkable elucidation of Hindu scriptures (Vedas & Upanishads) and restored their pristine purity and glory, but had also in the process contributed immensely to the growth of Hinduism at a time when disorderliness, superstition and prejudices was rampant. He was born in Karala to parents who were childless for long. The parents are said to have worshipped Lord Shiva who satisfied with their prayer appeared before them and assured to fulfill their wishes to have a child. Lord Shiva gave them an option. Whether they would like to have a mediocre child with long life or a short lived but exceptional child with extraordinary intellect.

Both parents opted for the later, and so the celebrated saint and philosopher 'Shankaracharyya' descended on earth. It is thus believed that Shankaracharyya was also a re-embodiment of Lord Shiva.

Amongst others is a temple of Lord Narasingha, (an incarnation of Lord Narayana who appeared from the pillars of a palace to save a devotee Prahlada from the ferocious demon Hiranya. This epitomizes that the almighty exists everywhere and that total submission to the almighty can releave mankind from all perils). Also one can find temples Vasudeva (father of Lord Krshna, later the king of Mathura a virtuous and truthful person never uttered a lie in his life-time) and of Durga in Joshimath.

Reaching the shrine of Badrinath (dedicated to Lord Vishnu) is not as difficult as reaching other sites in the region. The entire stretch upto the temple is motorable. It is situated on a picturesque mountaintop called 'Narayan Parvat' at an altitude of over 3,100 meters near the confluence of Rishi Ganga (a stream that flows from Neelkanth mountains) and Alaknanda. Before we went to the temple we cleaned our body with the water of the Tapt Kund ('tapt' meaning hot, 'kund' implies the pit of a spring). Nearby is Narad Kund. This kund is sacred because it is here that the Aadi Shankaracharyya discovered the idol of Lord Badrinath that is installed in the temple and is worshipped with gaiety. Around this place there are several sacred entities that have ancient religious incidence. They are in the form of rocks (pancha shilas meaning cluster of five rocks) or five streams named Pancha Dhara (meaning five streams), a pair of lakes, a group of caves and so on. During the day we went to a village called Mana. This village is the last place of human inhabitance on the Indian side of the Indo Tibetan border. As we walked that 4 Km stretch my wife and I realised from the hustle-bustle and the congregation that some event was on. We did not know still what significance it had but it was a rare celebration when the deity of Lord Vishnu carried from the Badrinath temple to the village in a palanquin thronged with priests and disciples singing and chanting sacred hymns. Some said we were lucky to see the Lord making a journey outside the temple and return after a small ceremony at Mana. Indeed that opportunity allowed us to see the deity from a closer proximity and for a longer time than we could have seen while seated inside the temple. After spending a satisfying and much contented visit to the shrine as well as natures mysterious beauty we started to descend the next morning.

On way is another marvelous place of religious importance. This is a Gurudwara (Sikh temple) the famous Hemund Sahib on route to the Valley of flowers at an altitude of nearly 4,400 mts. Located beside a glacial lake where it is said that the 10th Guru of the Sikhs once meditated on its banks one of his earlier incarnations. Surrounding the environs are seven snow-clad mountains called Saptrishi (seven monks) peaks that bear witness to all the happenings. This place is of importance not only for the Sikhs but all Hindus and all worshippers who believe in the happiness of devotion. There is also a small temple of Lakshman (youngest brother of Lord Rama) nearby.

Located on the eastern side below Badrinath and at a height of 1638 metres, is Almora, yet another picturesque location that was once the capital of the Chand dynasty. Golu Devta was consecrated general of Chand dynasty. A temple amidst a fur and pine tree forest is situated here with his idol inside. Devotees offer metallic bells of different sizes that could be seen tied on to the railing and the wall around the periphery. Golu Devata is known to be a quick dispenser of justice and thus many devotees submit written petition even on stamp papers and tie it to the canopy which they believe will be read by the God and justice will be delivered.

An hour's drive from Almora brought us to Ranikhet, (literal meaning 'the queen's fields') other beautiful place situated nearly 2000 meters above the sea level. The thick forests cover of deodar and pine trees over the mountain provides an immaculate view with unending Himalayan range in the background. Situated here is Jhoola Devi Temple dedicated to Goddess Durga and at an altitude of 2480 metres is the temple of Bindeshwar Binsar Mahadev as it is also called is said to have been built some time in the 9th century by a king called Pithu in memory of his father Bindu. Idols of Ganesha, Har Gauri and Maheshmardini adorn the precincts of this well architectured temple.

I have visited Gharwal several times, of which the first was in December 1997. I alighted from train at Dehra Dun and proceeded to Mussoorie, which is one of the many attractive tourist places of the Gharwal region in Uttarakhand (then Uttar Pradesh). After spending a couple of days here I set off for Dhanaulti a magnificent village at an altitude of 2286 meters and a couple of hours drive from Mussoorie on way to Chamba. Covering another ten km from Dhanaulti I reached a tiny village of Kaddu Khal the foothills of the Surkanda Devi Mountain. On top of this mountain is the temple of Surkanda Devi dedicated to Maa Durga. To reach the temple I had to take a 2 km of steep uphill trek over the rocks to cover a height of nearly 1000 meters. It was 31st of December 1987. As I reached the peak there was hardly anyone around. The view was totally different. This hallowed plateau was dark with dense forest and covered with a foot deep of snow. I was running out of breadth while I witnessed this unexpectedly breath taking appearance of nature's yet another dimension. I was wonder struck and indeed felt somewhat desolate. I had a realization there. I felt myself to be so timid and insignificant before the might of the mountains the nature and of course the repository of knowledge that exists on earth and beyond. I thought how meek and meager I was that I could be incited by greed. I realised that animals that we slaughter too love to live and roam around freely just as I do. So I decided thence that as long as there will be plants and vegetables I will not eat any animal or living being so that no life is lost to satisfy my greed. From that day I turned a vegetarian and today I am happy having done this least.

Across the southern boundary of Uttarakhand begins the state of **UTTAR PRADESH** that was once the largest state of India when the present Uttarakhand was included in it. Apart from its ancient historical significance this culturally rich province is one place of extreme religious importance and also of religious turmoil as witnessed in recent times. Ganges the holy river flows through almost the entire streatch of the state from northwest to the eastern end where it crosses over to the state of Bihar. One of the most sacred places is thus the city of Banaras or Varanasi is said to be the oldest living city in the world. Mention of 'Kashi' as the city is also known as could be found in the Upanishads and the Puranas (ancient philosophical inscriptions about religions insights and worldly creations) are said to have been composed here since 1000 BC). It is said that Lord Shiva and Parvati discovered this place when they alighted from heaven after their marriage to live on the earth. They had decided to reside in Kashi with nearly 350 other Gods and Goddesses. Ultimately of course he returned to his rightful abode in the Himalayas. Thus was founded the temple now called The Kashi Vishwanath Temple dedicated to Lord Shiva and in which is enshrined the Jyotirlinga of Shiva ('Linga' is a formless symbol of Lord Shiva). Jyotirlinga has a special significance in Hindu Mythology. There are only 12 such jyotirlingum located in 12 different places spread across the length and breadth of the country (that we will be exploring as we go along), and each has a special name that are components of prayer wordings. It is said that all the names pronounced daily in a defined order and mode helps the worshipper get absolved of all sins and attain a higher state of being. The Kashi Vishwanath Temple is visited by innumerable devotees round the year and during special occasions one gets to see huge congregations when pilgrims arrive to get the special blessings of the Lord. All great religious scholars of all times have all considered this place to be a place of compulsory visit and prayer at least once in a life time. When I visited Varanasi I wondered why the surroundings and the premises of this place that is one of supreme sanctity as considered by Hindus is kept is such a shabby and untidy manner. The narrow lane that leads one to the temple is utterly inadequate and often crowded. The passageway and the surroundings are unclean and unhygienic with filth and wastewater spilling around from open drains. The bulls that are considered holy stray around to eat garbage when they should be kept in suitable confines so that devotees could feed them with ease. This is prevalent from time immemorial and I am sure many do not like it that way. It reminds me of Mahatma Gandhi's observation about the banks of the Ganges at Rishikesh "the way in which men were using these beauty spots was far from giving me peace. As at Hardvar, so at Hrishikesh, people dirted the roads and the fair banks of the Ganges. They did not even hesitate to desecrate the sacred water of the Ganges. It filled me with agony to see people performing natural functions on the thoroughfares and river banks, when they could easily have gone a little farther away from public haunts".[19] I also wonder if there is a master

---

[19] An Autobiography or The Story of my Experiments with Truth. B*y Mohandas K. Gandhi, translated by Mahadev Desai.*

plan towards which we must know we should be working so that the dignity of the place is raised to the level of sanctity that we apportion to it. The priests, devotees the local inhabitants, the state administration are all very enlightened people but would surprise me if told that are ignorant of the teachings on cleanliness that are also enshrined in the doctrines of Hinduism. It is not only here but in many or most places of pilgrimage in India. I think a change of mindset is obligatory. By the side of the city flows the Holy river of Ganges. My head bows down more with shame than with reverence when I see the plight of this river of pride. Considered as an epithet of life that bestows purity to the living and salvation to the dead the river today is rendered to a state of sufferings by the very people who glorify her. But after sunset when the place is dark and illuminated by the lamps it gives an impressive view. Especially during the performance of the evening 'Aarti' (ceremonial prayer offered to any deity) the sight is spectacular. The priests holding the fire lamps and the chanting the mantras carryout an immaculately orchestrated drill facing the Ganga offering the prayers and gratitude for the life that it gives to this blessed land. The riverfront is paved with stones and the steps alongside leads to the waters edge below (called Ghats). These rows of steps are segregated by different names each having a religious significance but all are places for bathing in the holy river. Important amongst the many ghats are 'Man Mandir Ghat' (man meaning mind. mandir is temple and ghat is an embanked portion from where people access the river) where pilgrims pay homage to Someshvara the lord of the moon, 'Dusashwamedha Ghat' ('dus' means ten, 'aswa' imeans 'horse) where Lord Brahma sacrificed ten horses. It is said that blessings could be obtained by taking a dip here. Pictures of Varanasi often display activities of this area where priests sit lined up on wooden platforms beneath bamboo umbrellas and render ecclesiastical consultation to visitors. 'Manikarnika Ghat' also known as 'Mahashamshana' ('maha is great and shamshana is place for burning the dead) or the Great Cremation Ground of the universe where it is considered a great honor if one gets cremated after death.

While there has been repeated mention of Shiva and Shankar and the Linga in the above readings I would like to share with my readers here a passage that I came across in a news paper recently, written by one Prafulla Pant who has elucidated the whole thing very lucidly. Although written in the context of Maha Shiva Raatri an auspicious accassion that falls every year and dedicated to the Lord Shiva when devotees observe fast and other restrictions in daily life before offering water and prayer to the Lord in the evening. The article is entitled "Shiva the Supreme and Shankar the Deity" and goes to state that 'there is a subtle difference between the Supreme Soul Shiva and Shankar the deity. The Supreme has been worshipped in the oval or egg shapped form of the Shivalinga. The Linga Purana says that the one who destroys the world and re-establishes the same with Divine Power is called 'Linga'. In Shiva temples throughout India—including at Amarnath, Somnath, Kashi Vishwanath and Ujjain's Mahakaleshwar—and Nepal's Pashupatinath, He is depicted as the Linga, an elliptical representation in stone.

According to legend, Lord Rama invoked Shiva at Rameshwaram and Lord Krishna offered prayers to Him at Gopeshwar in Vrindavan. Shiva temples have been erected here honouring that memory. Shiva temples have been erected here honouring that memory. Shiva is worshipped as the Supreme Father of all deities and of Rama and Krishna.

Shiva's representation as linga is to show His incorporeal nature. He does not have any male or female human-like form like the deities. He is the incorporeal point of light. The 12 renowned Shiva temples in India are also known as Jyotirlinga Maths, signifying His form of Light. Incorporeal Shiva is also known as Trimurti, the creator of the three subtle deities—Brahma, Vishnu and Shankar.

The three lines marked in the Shivalinga symbolize His triple characteristics of Trimurti. Trinetri—the one with the third eye of wisdom, Trikaldarshi—the one who sees the three aspects of time, and Trilokinath—the Lord of three worlds. Shiva is also known as Shambhu or Swayambhu and Sadashiva meaning that Shiva is the eternal Soul who has no creator above Him.

Swami Dayanand Saraswati says Shiva is the "One who is bliss and the giver of Happiness to all'. Supreme Soul Shiva brings liberation or mukti and salvation or jeevan mukti to all.

In south India, Lingayats believe that Shiva is the Supreme God. The Ishtalinga worn by the Veerashalvas on their body is technically a miniature of Linga and is considered to be an amorphous representation of Shiva, which also proves that Shiva was worshipped in the oval-shaped figure. It was much later Shiva and deity Shanker came to be presumed as one. In Vaishik Darshan and Vedanta, Linga is mentioned as the image of the body-less Supreme God. It is free of personal characteristics.

The ignorance about Shiva is on account of confusing Shankar with Shiva. Deity Shankar has an angelic body whereas Shiva is oval shaped and worshipped as Shiva Linga. Shankar has a human form residing in the subtle world region called Sankarpuri; he is responsible for destrictuion of the old world order. In some paintings and sriptures, Shankar is shown meditating in front of the Shiva Linga, which also indicates that the two are different from each other.

The festival of Shivratri symbolizes the divine incarnation of Shiva on this earth. The night indicates the moral degradation in souls that sets in due to ignorance in this world. The true fasting (upvaas plus close company) on Shivratri is that we link our intellect with Shiva and stay in his company. The true 'Jagran' or awakening means to awaken from the slumber of ignorance and to protect the self from the negative influence of vices such as lust, anger, greed and ego. Absolute formless God, 'Sadashiva' appeared in the form of Lingodbhav Moorti exactly at midnight on Shivratri'.[20]

"The word 'Shiva' means 'that which is not'. Why we use Shiva and not some other form of God is because the other forms seem to be good people and you can easily get attached to them. It is difficult to get attached to Shiva. In Tamil Nadu it is said you shouldn't keep Shiva's form in your house. He is the Maheshwara, but he has no space in your home, why? Maheshwara means he is beyond all Gods. If he is there, his very form is such that all your attachments will get destroyed. You have made big investments in your attachments and even though they have brought you very painful dividends, you still can't throw them away".

"The egg-shaped Baana Linga reminds us that 'Isvara' has neither beginning nor end, like the sky. (Isvara is indicative of the almighty and the all powerful supreme infinite being called God) Looking at the horizon we feel that the sky and the earth meet at a particular point. But try as we might, we can never reach that meeting point. This point will still be as far away as it was from the place from which we first looked at the horizon. We may circle the earth and return to the point from which we started without coming to the point where the sky and the earth

---

20 Article 'Shiva The Supreme And Shankar The Deity' by Prafulla Pant appeared in appeared in the Times of India, Kolkata Edition on 6th March 2008

meet. The Linga symbol brings the unknown within our comprehension"[21].

It may be surprising why I chose Varanasi first when it is the last of the main cities where the Ganges passes by before entering the state of Bihar. I chose this because I felt that Varanasi is the most significant amongst the sacred places here and also is one of the oldest living cities that we know of. To go by some ones imagination one can quote Mark Twain who once wrote, "Banaras is older than history, older than tradition, older even than legend, and looks twice as old as all of them put together".

About six kilometers north of Varanasi is Sarnath a Buddhist Pilgrimage point. The place displays the reminiscence of Buddhist monasteries and temples that disappeared in the 13th century and later excavated in the late 18th century. Discoveries that continued until about a hundred years back have revealed monuments that date back to as early as the 1st century, of the time of ruler Chandragupta II (376-414 AD), of Harshavardhan reign (606-47 A.D) till about 1114-1154 AD of the Gahadavala dynasty (that originated in Varanasi in Uttar Pradesh who later made Kannauj their main center for political activity). A significant reminiscence at Sarnath is a 3rd century column which had four lions engraved. This momento was erected by King Ashoka when he visited the place after he surrendering to the philosophy of Buddhism and eventually becoming a Buddhist himself. History is witness to the fierce battle at Kalinga a fertile land that King Ashoka desired to possess. He thus waged a war against the defendants and wanted to win over. He won the war but in the process left thousands dead and wounded. When he witnessed the battle field after the war

21 Article by Paramacharya, Kanchi Kamakoti Peetam [appeared in the Times of India, Kolkata Edition on 6th March 2008]

he was awe strck at the calamity that his army had caused. Moved by the bloodshed and distressed by the grief of the defeated clan the mighty king got miserably depressed and turned remorseful. He was dawned by the light of self-realization and vowed that he would never wage war ever. He disarmed himself and chanting "Buddham Sharanam Gachchaami" (meaning I depart to submit to the Buddha) he walked away. Thereon he is believed to have piously capitulated to the principles of Buddhism—that of kindness, charity, goodness, purity and truth). This four-lion symbol was later adopted as the emblem of the modern Indian Republic signifying the same philosophy of state policy. But the importance of Sarnath lies in the fact that it was here that Lord Buddha preached his first discourse after attaining enlightenment at Bodh Gaya in Bihar and there by set into motion the 'Wheel of the Dharma'. From then on his teachings began to flow. To mark the spot where after attaining enlightenment Buddha gave the first sermon to his five disciples, King Ashoka built an edifice in commemoration—the Dhamek Stupa. This monument or 'Stupa' (a mound) that now stands nearly 44 meters tall and 28 meters in diameter was enlarged in stages over the years. The initial teaching as is believed to have professed by Lord Buddha is that sufferings are inevitable but the cause of sufferings could be removed if one followed the "Eight-fold Path. They are "Right speech, Right action, Right livelihood, Right effort, Right mindfulness, Right concentration, Right attitude and Right view".

About a 125 Km west of Varanasi is Prayag. It is said that in order to perform a sacred 'Yagna' (a sacred fire ceremony) Lord Brahma chose the confluence of the three rivers—the Ganga, the Yamuna, and the Sarswati. This confluence is called Sangam. Though the two rivers Ganga and Yamuna can be identified by the variance in color, river Saraswati is mysteriously hidden. Some believe it flows beneath the earth. In 1575 AD the great Mogul king Akbar had visited Prayag. He later founded a new city in the name of the almighty Allah that is now known as Allahabad. During certain auspicious times of the year sacred Hindu ritual are held along with month long fairs (Kumbh Mela) and festivals when Hindu saints from different parts of the country congregate and hold discourses on religion. The Sangam is considered sacred and pilgrims attend this place to take a holy dip at the point of confluence. It is believed that one who takes a dip at this auspicious meeting point of the three rivers where Lord Brahma himself performed 'Yagna' all his sins will vanquish and he will be purified once again. I too have taken a dip here but that time I was too small in school and had hardly accumulated enough sin to wash. Thus could not make it serve its purpose to the full.

Lucknow the thriving capital city of Uttar Pradesh is situated on the banks of the Gomati River about 650 Km west of Varanasi. The Gomati river that arrives from the mountains in Pilibhit (from a large lake called 'Gomat Tal' east of Pilibhit. 'Tal' means a lake) in the north of Uttar Pradesh. Gomati is considered holy as she is believed to be the daughter of Sage Vashistha and had brought prosperity to the plains of Avadh. Lucknow was a part of the Awadh province that was under occupation of Humayun in 1526. During the rule of Aurangazeb there was rampant disorder and corruption with atrocities on peasants and disobedience amongst the officers. Thus after the death of Aurangazeb (in 1707) the Nawabs of Lucknow asserted their autonomy over the region. The last of the Avadh Nawabs was Wajid Ali Shah who was succeeded to the throne in 1847. Unlike his father Amjad Ali Shah and grandfather Muhammad Ali Shah who ruled effectively and peacefully, Wajid Ali became famous more for his love of art, music and poetry than managing of the kingdom. This made the kingdom vulnerable and impelled Governor General Dalhousie to annex the state to British East India Company in 1856. Incidentally, the first encounter of the Company with Avadh was under the rule of Shuja-ud-Daula at Buxar in 1764. Though the British army had won the war they decided to retain Shuja-ud-Daula in power to rule as their representative because the territory under the British was becoming seemingly large and unmanageable but for this Shuja-ud-Daula had to pay a hefty amount as compensation. After Avadh was finally annexed to East India Company in 1856 the irresolute Wajid Ali Shah proceeded to Calcutta, to place his representation before the Governor General and seeking the intervention of the Queen in London. But all this inevitably went in vain and Avadh remained under the mighty British rule for nearly a century thereafter.

My travel and visit to the reminiscence and the monuments in Lucknow inspired me to learn a bit about the history of the place. I found that the chronology of historical events that took place since the time of Sultan Iltutmish dating back to 1330s the various invasions, crisis, rebellions and reoccupations the history is indeed quite complex but very interesting and would go out of context if elaborated here. However it is for sure that the city has all along been popular for its royal mannerisms and ostentatious etiquettes. When as a child I visited Lucknow with my parents I remember we had toured the desolate town on a chartered 'Tonga' (horse drawn carriage). Twentyfive-years on when I again visited the place as a tourist I found that the city had grown and populated. It appeared much dissimilar to olden days with motor-driven three-wheelers zooming all around. I was in a state of dismay but was determined to find a 'tonga'. From Hotel Taj Avadh where I had put-up, I boarded my car and asked the driver to find me a 'tonga. He was a bit perplexed, 'Tonga? When you have the luxury of a car to move around'! We went from place to place and finally got one at the railway station. I asked my car to return to the hotel and traveled around the city's historical places on the crude carriage hearing the clip-clop all my way.

Built in January 1967 is a very gorgeous temple of Lord Hanuman near the banks of River Gomti. As the iconic lord of physical power, an ardent devotee of Lord Rama and a symbol of loyalty and assiduousness, Hanuman is much admired and worshipped more in this part of India. It is believed that petitions placed before the lord here would be heard and the he will provide necessary relief to his worshippers. It is for this reason that the Lord is also called the diety of 'Sankat Mochan' (problem eradicator). There was an old temple in the same place earlier but a flood in 1960 washed away most part of the temple leaving behind the six fool tall idol of Hanuman. Later a larger temple was built around the idol, which now adds to the beauty of the riverbank.

But of all the other things that fascinated me the most when I visited Lucknow during the childhood days were the two 'Imambaras' (place of Muslim congregation and worship). When I saw it later in life I was intrigued by the engineering feat and the concept of design that prevailed 250 years ago. The main hall of 'Bada Imambara' is one of the largest of its kind in the world. An 80 square meter hall has a ceiling that hangs column-less over it 15 meters high. There is no support from below in the form of any beam or girder. It rests on the twenty feet walls that are fifty meter apart on the sides and sixteen meters to the rear. These walls, which curve inwards to form the base of the ceiling, are made of interlocking brickwork. I guess in order to reduce the weight of the walls and to provide a cantilever type support the wide wall has been hollowed at the top. The hollow has turned out to become a maze of convoluted passages. This passage design with over a thousand corridors has culminated into what is also popularly known as the 'Bhool Bhulaiya' (where you are destined to get lost). No wonder entry to this area is restricted and one who enters the Bhool Bhulaiya is destined to get lost and can be retrieved only by the help of a guide). An architect by the name of Kifayat-ullah designed and built this 1784 monument during the time and rule of Nawab Asaf-ud-Daula.

Another breathtaking structure built by the third Nawab of Avadh is the Husainabad Imambara also known as the Chota Imambara built in 1837 by Muhamad Ali Shah in memory of his daughter. The mausoleum contains exquisite collection of chandeliers made of Belgian glass collected from different parts of the world. The exterior of the structure is equally majestic. It has a glittering golden dome with ornate façade that makes it look immaculate from a distance. Beside the monument is the Jamin Mosque that was completed three years later in 1840.

Moving northwards from Allahabad in the district of Faizabad is the holy town of Ayodhya where Lord Rama, the seventh incarnation of lord Vishnu is believed to have born. Situated on the banks of river Saryu, Ayodhya is not only sacred to the Hindus but also to Jains, Buddists and Muslims alike. Lord Rama is the personification of a Perfect Man or Lord of Restrictions. "Rama, the ancient idol of the heroic ages, the embodiment of truth, of morality, the ideal son, the ideal husband, and above all, the ideal king, this Rama has been presented before us by the great sage Valmiki. No language can be purer, none chaster, none more beautiful, and at the same time simpler, than the language in which the great poet has depicted the life of Rama." said Swami Vivekananda. Here once lived the emperor of Khosala kingdom King 'Dasharath'. King Dasharath had four sons out of his three wives. The eldest of them all was 'Rama' who is said to be the seventh incarnation of Lord Vishnu. The other three sons of Dasharath were Lakshmana, Shatrughna, and Bharata. Rama was married to 'Sita' the adopted daughter of king 'Janaka' of 'Mithila' (now in Nepal). Sita is believed to be the incarnation of Goddess Lakshmi the consort of Lord Vishnu in heaven. At the time of Rama's coronation, mother of 'Bharat' and the youngest queen of Dasharath asked the King to carry out his promise that was pending for Dasharath to fulfil. Dasharath agreed to fulfil what ever she would ask for and told her to submit her wishes. She said that her son 'Bharat' be made the king of Ayodhya and 'Rama' be sent away to the forest for 14 years. Helpless and reluctant, the King acceded as he was commitment bound. Then on began the term of exile for Lord Rama. He wandered in the forests and mountains accompanied by his wife Sita and his loyal younger brother 'Laxmana'. It was during this period in exile when 'Ravana' the Demon King of 'Lanka' (now called Sri Lanka) and also a staunch devotee of Lord Shiva abducted Sita and flew her over the sea to his home to Lanka. This was followed by the rescue operation that led to the historical war between Ravana on one side and Rama assisted by the monkey woriers led by 'Hanumana' on the other. The army of the apes constructed a walkway across the sea by putting boulders into the water. (A chain of sandy elevation of the bottom the sea as seen from space streaching across the Palk Strait between India and Sri Lanka is believed by many to be the geological evidence and the reminiscence of the 'Rama Setu' built by the army of apes for Rama to reach the Ravana Kingdom to rescue Sita). The entire army walked over to the other side and attacked 'Lanka'. After a fierce battle Ravana was killed and Lord Rama came out victorious rescuing 'Sita' from captivity. After the fourteen years of exile ended Rama returned to Ayadhya and gained his rightful place as the King of Ayodhya.

It is here in Ayodhya where once stood the 16th century Babri Mosque. It is believed that Babri Mosque built by order of Babur the first Mughal emperor of India. Hindu fundamentalists demolished this monument on 6th December 1992. Assuming that it infringed into the place of birth of Lord Rama, the community wanted to get rid of the mosque so that a majestic temple of Lord Rama could come up in its place. There are several temples of worship around the place but non-except this one carries the aura of mythological magnificence. Chitrakoot perched on the Vindhya Range of mountains deserves a mention here as it carries special mythological significance. It is here that Lord Rama spent eleven of the fourteen years of exile with his wife Sita and brother Laxmana.

Moving from the land of Rama we now enter the land of Krshna that is located closer to the modern capital city of Delhi. About a 150 Km from Delhi Mathura is the birthplace of Lord Krshna one of the eighth and the most complex of incarnations of Lord Vishnu. The grand temple at the Katra Keshav complex is believed to be the real spot of the Lord Krshnas birth some 3,500 years ago. A stone slab now marks the place. There was a chamber earlier in the temple where as legends go, was a prison cell within a walled compound in the kingdom of King 'Kansh'. It is believed that the king was very fond of his sister 'Devki' and always loved fulfilling her wishes. He got her married to a very respectable boy named 'Vasudev'. Unfortunately on the day of the wedding he came to know from a clairvoyant sermon that the eighth male child that will be born to his sister would put his dynasty and his life to an end. Perturbed by the sermon he ordered that Devki and Vasudev be taken into custody and be put in the prison cell where the guards and he himself could keep a close vigil. Over time as Devki would give birth to a child Kansa would come to the prison cell and kill them there by smashing the tender body against stone slabs. After the first six sons of Devaki were killed, Lord Vishnu's script on the next happenings came to light. What was witnessed next was actually the prelude for the reincarnated birth of Lord Vishnu himself as the eight son of Vasudeva who would later be known as 'Krshna'. Here 'Yogamaya' said to be the 'Goddess of Sleep' also played an important role. After Devaki conceived for the seventh time Yogamaya took the embryo from Devaki's womb and transferred it to his other wife Rohini's womb. The maids guarding Devaki told Kansa that she had miscarried. Rohini in Gokul later gave to 'Balrama'.

After Devaki concieved for the eighth time Kansh was perturbed, not knowng how and under what circumstances his death would occur. Devaki too was terrified fearing that her cruel brother would kill this one too. Dusk gave way to a dreadfuly stormy night with the sky splitting apart with wrathful rains. At midnight a sudden calm decended and was broken by the sound of a crying child. The voice of the devine then spoke to Vasudev asking him to pick the child up in his lap and carry him across the River Yamuna to the kingdom of Gokul. There his friend 'Nanda's wife 'Yashoda' had just given birth to a daughter. Voice of the Oracle asked Vasudev to reach his son there and exchange him for Nanda's girl child and return forthwith to the prison before anyone comes to know about all this. This put Vasudev in extreme dilemma. On the one hand he was keen to do anything needed to save his child and on the other he feared how he would go unnoticed and unscathed. But to follow the devine advice Vasudev decided not to loose the chance.

To his utter surprise all the sentries were in a state of hypnotic sleep. As he reached the prison gate with the child in his arms the door opened on its own to give him way. The raging river too calmed down as he stepped into it to cross by foot. But the rain was pouring with terrible gust. But now he had no option but to move forward. He had meanwhile picked up a basket in which he put the child and covered with whatever cloth he had on his person. But that was bearly enough to protect the child from getting wet. As he waded through the river with the basket on his head Vasudev saw a huge black snake raising its head from the water behind him. Vasudev was terrified at the magnanimous size of the beast and thought there was no escape now. It was a multideaded serpent that crawled from behind and positioned its hood like an umbrella over his head as if to save the child from rain. He then realised that this was no ordinary snake but a God sent saviour to escort them through. Indeed this was no ordinary snake. It was the Snake-God called Sheshnag of Lord Vishnu himself. And who in his incarnation lay quietly in the basket on Vasudev's head. Who now could have hindered his way when the Lord himself was charting the course. After reaching the opposite bank he entered the village of Gokul and entered the palace of king Nanda. He found Yashoda sleeping with her newborn baby girl by her side. Vasudev took baby girl in his other arm and placed his son next to Yashoda. He returned to the prison with the girl-child and laid the baby by Devaki's side and went to sleep.

After a while the guards were awakened by the cry of the child. The news of baby's birth reached the ears of the prison guards and in no time it was conveyed to Kansh. Kansh was apprehensive and nervous too not knowing of the immediate cosequence. Cautiously he entered the prison cell where the child and the parents' were confined. Devki then was unaware of the happenings that night and knew nothing about the swaping of the babies. When she found that the child was a girl he prayed to his brother to have mercy and spare the child's life.

But for Kansa his own life was dearer and would not take any chance for it. Kamsa snatched the baby from Devaki's arm and as he did to the other children chucked the child against the wall to kill. But the baby instead of getting smashed to the wall flew up and got suspended in the air. The next moment the child took the form of the eight-armed Goddess of Durga and said to Kansh that his demolisher was now out of his bound. He would appear before him very soon and those would be last moments of life. After this warning to Kansh the Goddess disappeared into oblivion.

Gokul meanwhile were making merry celebrating the arrival of new baby. Nanda named the dark-blue cloloured child 'Krshna'. Thus was born Lord Krishna, the supreme God, the saviour, the philosopher, the teacher and the pathfinder for mankind in every age. Out of the foetus transferred to the womb of 'Rohini' was born a son who was named 'Balarama' who later in life always stood by the side of Krshna at all trying times. Krshna with his brother Balaram later went to Mathura and killed his maternal uncle the atrocious Kansh. He thus freed the people from anguish and established tranquility in Mathura by bringing Ugrasen (Kansh's father) back as king.

Born in approximately 3200 BC as the eighth and the absolute incarnate of Lord Vishnu, Krshna grew up in the cowherd family of Yashoda and Nanda. The gopas (cowherd boys) and gopis (cowherd girls), who were greatly fond of him. While all the gopis played with Krshna, Radha was deep in love with Him. This attachment of Radha epitomises the eternal bond of an individual soul with God while 'Rasa Lila', the dance of the gopis to the tune of Krshnas flute absorbed in love with Him signifies blending of the human with the divine,. This blissful ecstasy of the soul as it unites with the divine is the supreme ecperience of surrender . . . He who is awakened to the love of Lord responds to the divine call of the flute and finally gets absorbed in the tranquility of liberation.

The birthday of Krshna calculated by the lunar Hindu calender falls on the eighth day of month of Shravana.

Over the ages this day is being celebrated as the festival of "Janmashtami' ('janma' means birth and 'ashtami' means eighth day). This commemorating occasion is also known as 'Gokul-ashtami' or 'Krishn-asthami'. It is believed that whenever in the world the evil becomes unbearable, God himself decends on the earth in disguise and over whom not even the mightiest of the evils can prevail.

Mathura in later times witnessed the Buddhism monasteries flourish in the city under the benefaction of King Ashoka the great. Recorded history goes back to 2500 years when Buddha did his preaching here. Several Chinese travelers like Fahien and Xuan Zhang are reported to have visited Mathura between 400 AD and now. Later Mahmud of Ghazni who came from Afghanistan in 1017 and Mughal emperor Aurangzeb too plundered the city. Finally in 1757 Afghan Ahmad Shah Abdali's brutal outrage burnt the entire city to ruins.

The city has indeed been an ill-fated one. When I came here in Mathura some time back (mid 1990s) I was taken aback by the scale of security arrangement that was around. The temple appeared like a fortress. Uniformed police and gunmen in large numbers were deployed all along the temple site, on the walkways, staircases and on top of the monuments. This arrangement was in anticipation of any possible outrage of violence or communal disturbance as worship sites of two religions Hindu and Muslims lay almost overlapping each other and both contesting the existence of each others sanctity. The likelihood of this mosque meeting the same fate as the Babri Mazjid loomed large and its possibility is yet not ruled out. One can now find the Jama Masjid on the ruins of Keshav Deo premises. This temple was destroyed as evidenced by history and the mosque was built there in 1661 by Abd-un Nabir. Nearby, on the main road in Mathura is the Gita Mandir (again built by the house of Birlas) where on the walls are inscribed the text of the holy Bhagwat Gita. Coupled with Mathura is a nearby town Vrindavan that are called the Braj-bhoomi or the land where the Krshna grew-up amidst performance of cosmic miracles. Here one can find the imposing Govind Dev Temple built in 1590 Raja Man Singh of Amber. Raja Man Singh was a trusted General of Moghual King Ashoka and a great devotee of Lord Krishna. He is believed to have spent ten million rupees to build a seven-storied temple in Vrindavan in honor of Lord Krshna. Man Singh also received patronage from Akbar himself who allowed red sandstones to be brought here for the pupose. Aurangazeb later demolished most of this structure.

Sri Ranganatha Temple is another of the sacred temples of the Hindus, which is said to have been built in 1850s. Others amongst the more than 5000 temples in the vicinity are Madan Mohan Temple (Built by a follower of Lord Chaitanya named Kapur Ram Das of Multan—now in Pakistan), Jaipur Temple (built by Sawai Madhav Singh, Maharaja of Jaipur, in 1917), Shahji Temple (built by a wealthy jeweler from Lucknow), Banke Bihari Temple (built in the year 1864 by Swami Haridas a saint-musician of Dhrupad style of classical music devoted to Krshna and consort Radha), and Shri Krishna-Balram Temple (Built by the International Society for Shri Krshna Consciousness or ISKCON).

Vrindavan is also the abode of many an unfortunate women who have been widowed (many at a young age) or deserted by their husbands. They live in 'widow houses' beside Meera Bai Ashram where they congregate at different times of the day. Left at the mercy of Lord Krshna the ashrams are funded by the rich that takes care of the maintenance of the houses and their inmates. Women like one can find in any other part of the world have been left deprived and discriminated. But here it is bigotry to the extreme setting a glaring example of the shameful and insane act of manhood of the recent times. Women especially of Bengal who were rendered helpless having lost their husband or chastised were left here to lead the entire life in mourning and restrictions that is devoid of adornments or amusements. These women who having devoted their entire lives serving the family surely deserved to be accommodated and understood on reaching this unfortunate state. Instead they were discarded to live on their own as if they were never a part of their families. Likely claim to property by these ladies and their maintenance and other liabilities were the main causes for putting these women in such state of incarceration.

The Indian National Commission for Women in a study[22] has brought out some painful facts about these unfortunate women thus "... a young woman rendered a widow is barred from marrying even if she is only in her teens. She has to control her emotions and feelings and live like a recluse all her life and die as a widow. This rule that widow should not remarry is even more atrocious than that of 'Sati', as sati at least puts an end to her tragedy immediately. But if the widow is living, her life is socially, culturally and emotionally dead. She has to live all her life facing the slings and arrows of society as a widow. The laws of the religion, as interpreted by the men in the society, prohibit a widow from remarrying even if she has never experienced the pleasures of a married life. Though remarriage is not forbidden in the religious books as stated earlier that the Rig Veda has a direct connotation on widow remarriage, such teachings are conveniently

---

22 "Status of Widows of Vrindavan and Varanasi"—A Comparative Study *By* The Guild of Service *Supported By National Commission For Women* Research Analysis by Dr. V. Mohini Giri Ms. Meera Khanna.

not read by the religious leaders". The study further enumerates "... during our survey, the majority of the women whom we interviewed were found to be from West Bengal. After having conducted a detailed study of Vrindavan we shifted our attention to Varanasi where at least 10000 out of these 33 million Indian widows reside. We found widows sitting on the banks of the river Ganga at the entrance of the Vishwanath temple holding a small broken bowl in their frail hands begging for alms". Such is the plight to which the 'the brave men' had reduced their own family women.

West ward about 25 Km is the holy hill of 'Govardhana'. This mountain existed during the times of Krishna too as believed. The hill is considered sacred, as Krishna believed so. The young Lord Krishna once held 'Govardhana' on the tip of a finger for 7 days and nights to protect the Braj dwellers (braj-vasi) from an intense downpour that could have washed away the entire village into obscurity.

South of Mathura is the historical city of Agra. Famous for its Taj Mahal the city has a vivid history until the recent times. It is said that the place refered to 'Agravana' in Mahabharata and even before as 'Arya Griha' is this same city now known as 'Agra'. Reference is often drawn to one Raja Badal Singh ascribing him to be the founder of this city in 1475. Subsequently, Sikander Lodi, Sultanate of Delhi and later Ibrahim Lodi ruled the place from 1504 to 1526 till Babar (the founder of the Mughal dynasty) overthrew in the famous battle of Panipat. Later his grand son Akbar who came here in search of a saint "Salim Chisty' to seek his blessings for a son found the Chisty in Fatehpur Sikri about 40 km from Agra. Soon thereafter he was blessed by a son. Akbar named him Salim after first name of the Chisty. Salim later came to be known as Jahangir (literal meaning—'Emperor of the World'). In reciprocation of the favour and in gratitude for the wish fulfillment Akbar build a magnificent city called Fatehpur Sikri, the reminiscence of which exhibits the splendor of architectural fondness that these Moghul rulers had in them. Similarly, Agra under the Mogul rule also got the name 'Akbarabad' and gained prominence not only for becoming the headquarters of the reign but also because of all the beautifications it received. Like his great-grandfather who built beautiful Persian styled gardens; Jahangir too had a fascinatioin for landscapes and flower gardens and ultimately Shah Jahan whose creative knack in architecture found expression in the form of the world's most wonderful heritage site called The Taj Mahal in 1648. But as fate would have it his own son, Aurangzeb, dethroned this extraordinary person and had him arrested and rot in prison till death. Aurangzeb ushered the dawn of the decline of the Moghul Empire. After the death of Aurangzeb in 1707 several claimants to the throne began to emerge. During the course of the next about a hundred and fifty years there was chaos and infighting amongst the Moghul kinsmen all of whom claiming superiority over the other. Finally in 1858 the British Imperial forces took over the reigns of power and the dynasty of the Moghal officially came to a disgraceful end.

Agra, which is popularly understood as the seat of Muslim culture, has places of worship for all religions. Prominint amongst them are the St. John's Church, St. Peter's Church and St. Mary's Church for the Christans Arya Samaj Temple, and several Hindu temples. Important Hindu temples are the Mangaleshwar Temple, Bhageshwarnath Temple and Shri Krishna Pranami Temple. Sacred places of worship for the Muslims are the Moti Masjid, Jama Masjid and the Akbari Masjid. Also in Fatehpur Sikri there is a 1570 AD Dargah of Salim Chisty by whose grace Akbar was blessed with not one but three sons. People of all faith and religion come here to pray and seek wish fulfillment particularly wish of having a child.

Towards this they tie a holy thread on the lattice walls around the Dargah.

Controversies have since arisen as to the history of the place. Excavations near Fatehpur Sikri have discovered remains that relate to Jain religions like temples, idols utilities etc that date back to tenth and eleventh century AD. It is also believed as revealed by research that Taj Mahal itelf was a Shiva Temple that was destroyed and restructured to give it the present shape. This belief appears interesting to me and would surely like to know the historical facts if some body could bring forth the truth. But fanaticisms do not quite prejudice me. There are many and enough temples of Lord Shiva all across the country many of them are not ever well looked after. If there was one here it would never have brought the glory that the Taj Mahal of today has brought to the country. Thus I would like to put the controversy to rest.

A few miles north of Agra is mausoleum of Akhbar in a place called 'Sikandra'. This tomb was built by his son Jahangir and represents a symbol of secularims in one way as it has four gates dedicated to different religion.

Though it is not a place of worship, The Taj Mahal is indeed something that the world can never afford to ignore. That is why I am inclined to place for reading an excerpt about the spledid monument and its history taken from the 'World Heritage' document of the UNESCO that describes The Taj Mahal as an 'immense mausoleum of white marble, built between 1631 and 1648 by order of the Mughal emperor Shah Jahan in memory of his favourite wife Mumtaz. Taj Mahal means "Crown Palace"; one of the wife's names was Mumtaz Mahal, "Ornament of the Palace". The Taj is one of the most well preserved and architecturally beautiful tombs in the world, one of the masterpieces of Indian Muslim architecture, and one of the great sites of the world's heritage. The Taj has a life of its own that leaps out of marble, provided you understand that it is a monument of love. The Indian poet Rabindranath Tagore called it "a teardrop on the cheek of eternity", while the English poet, Sir Edwin Arnold, said it was "Not a piece of architecture, as other buildings are, but the proud passions of an emperor's love wrought in living stones." It is a celebration of woman built in marble and that's the way to appreciate it. Despite being one of the most photographed edifices in the world and being instantly recognisable, its physical presence is awe-inspiring. Not everything is in the photos. The grounds of the complex include several other beautiful buildings, reflecting pools, and extensive ornamental gardens with flowering trees and bushes, and a small gift shop. The Taj framed by trees and reflected in a pool is amazing. Close up, large parts of the building are covered with inlaid stonework. There is an apocryphal tale that Shah Jahan planned to build an exact copy out of black marble on the opposite side of the river. But his son after murdering his three elder brothers overthrew him to acquire the throne. This foiled all his plans. Shah Jahan is now buried alongside his wife in the Taj Mahal'.

[http://whc.unesco.org/pg.cfm?cid=31&id_site=252]

Travelling further to the east is situated the State of **BIHAR**. This state has recently been bifurcated into two parts Bihar and Jharkhand. Bihar and Buddhism are synonymous as it is here the Siddhartha Gautama achieved enlightenment and became the 'Buddha'. Buddhism and Jainism are two of the most well known religious orders that took off from Bihar. Perhaps the oldest of the temples is also here beside the 'Bodhi Tree' in Bodh Gaya. The Bodhi Tree is the blessed tree under which the Siddhartha Gautama meditated to acquire 'Maha-pari-nirvana' the luminous knowledge of understanding (bodh). It is believed that the Maha Bodhi temple situated nearby to have been built in the 3rd century BC by the emperor Ashoka to idolize of the revered Buddha. King Ashoka took to Buddhism after the war of Kalikga and there after never inflicted cruelty not to speak of waging a war ever. This place later became the center for learning of Buddhists teachings. Hindus too consider the place as sacred as Hindus consider the Buddha as reincarnation of Lord Vishnu. After attaining 'Nirvana', Lord Buddha is believed to have met his council in a cave known as 'Saptaparni'. The cave could still be seen in Rajgir that is about a 100 Km from Patna the capita of the state of Bihar. Rajgir was then the capital of Magadh. (Rajgir comes from the words 'Raj' meaning 'kingdom' and 'griha' meaning residence or seat). Buddha inspired the Mauryas (the ruling dynasty) to follow the devine path that he preached and thus the spread of Buddhism became more overwhelming and far reaching. Buddists from Japan have built a majestic Buddha Temple here on a mountaintop that could be reached by a ropeway. This ropeway is very old perhaps the oldest in this part of the world. If I remember it correctly I climbed the mountain on that ropeway way back in 1966. Near Rajgir, tourists are generally shown a place called the 'Jarasandh Akhara' where Jarasandh had fought 'Bhim' (one of the Pandava brothers of Mahabharata epic) over a period of fourteen days but was defeated. To provide a glimpse about Jarasandha it could be said that he was a demon but a devotee of Lord Shiva. The surprising thing about him is that he was born in two half in the womb of two queens of a king of Magadh. As this was a peculiar happening the two queens threw the half bodies in the forest. This was later discovered by a female demon named 'Jara' who accidentally put the two together and the child came alive. She brought the child to the king who was too happy and named the child after the demon and thence he is called Jarasandha. Jarasandha lived in Magadh (now Bihar). He picked up a fight once with the Panadavas when they had disregarded his hospitality. He decided to fight with Bhim because he thought the other brothers of the Pandavas were too timid. He is said to have lost the fight to Bhim out of sheer trick (conspired by Krshna) and not by physical of strength.

Lying in silence a few miles near Rajgir is an excavation of the ancient university and perhaps the oldest seat of organised learning called Nalanda. This university was established in the 5th Century AD where over 10,000 students who came from far away land. Hiuen Tsang the famous Chinese scholar lived here during the 7th century and disseminated his learning. Ashoka and King Harshavardhana too patronized these monasteries at different times. Recently a Centre for Buddhist Studies was established here in 1951. Nearby is a sacred temple of the Jain community called 'Pawapuri. The temple made of marble and located in the middle of a lotus pond provides a unique look. People of Bihar who celebrate 'Chhatt puja' with much pomp and giety is dedicate to the Sun God a sacred temple known as th Sun Temple is located at Baragaon nearby. Bihar Sharif which fall on the way to Rajgir is a place of Muslim pilgrimage and situated here is the sacred 'dargah' of Malik Ibrahim Baya. The capital city was later shifter to Patna by a Magadh ruler named 'Ajathshtru' 2500 years ago when the city was named Pataligram later Pataliputra and now Patna.

Important temples in Patna are the Sher Shah Masjid the oldest mosque in the entire region built in 1545 and architectured by the then ruler Sher Shah and Hari Mandir Temple built by the great Sikh ruler Raja Ranjit Singh at the birthplace of Guru Gobind Singh is one of the four most important pilgrimage spots for Sikhs.

My memories of Patna will always remain unforgettable. I spent the most enjoyable of times of my life there—the childhood days. I lived at a time when life was different. It was peaceful, abundant and people were wise. I still recall Patna of those days as a land of milk and honey. I studied in the famous St. Xavier's school located between 'Gandhi Maidan and the illustrious of all monuments 'The Gol Ghar'. History that dates back to the sixties and the mid seventies was one of fun and frolic. The only pain that interfered was in studies and homework from which there was no escape. Patna of those times was a small and a lousy place but thanks to our school that made good for all the boredom. Established by missionaries from the American Chicago Province of the Society of Jesus our school provided us with the best of sports facility and accessories apart from quality education. We had one of the finest and well-maintained swimming pool, hardcourt tennis court and handball arena. The concrete basketball court was constructed very methodically under the careful supervision of Father Faulstich right in front of us. St. Xavier's school Patna, "established in 1940 . . . became a cricketing center not only for those who studied here but for all those who played cricket in Patna . . . No speculation needs to be made about who was responsible in planting cricket in St. Xavier's. Who else could it be but Father Kevin N. Cleary, S.J.?"[23] Father Cleary was our class teacher for three years till 1973. After that we went to class X when Rev. Paul J. Faulstich, S.J took us over. Father Cleary died in February 1994. Father Faulstich returned to the U.S. in 1995 and was missioned to Loyola. As far as I could retrieve, he is now (at the time of my writing this book) the Registrar of Loyola Academy North Shore of Chicago and also serves as the Chicago province assistant for records and research. These two teachers amonst the many others who taught us had immense contribution

---

[23] Autobiography of an Unknown Cricketer By Sujit Mukherjee. Published by Orient Longman, 1996. ISBN 8175300019, 9788175300019. 168 pages

towards our up bringing. Their role was not in teaching alone. They worked towards innovating method for imparting knowledge. More importantly they focused on improvement of the school infrastructure for the students to benefit. They worked silently for us. Least did we realise then, but now when I look back I find that they were so dedicated and devoted towards us. 'Good Manners of a School Boy' a small booklet written by Father Cleary is still with me and I still love going through those simple pieces of advice. Each time I read it I enrich myself so much more. I can still remember Father Faulstich had set-up 'casual library' where there were several books of interest for those who loved to read. This was apart from a very large library and reading room that our school had equipped us with. The library had a diverse collection of books and journals, which very few schools in the country had. We also had very effective 'Students Council' that organised various events round the year. Extra curricular activities like debate, elocution, drama, drill, audio-visual, crafts etc along with studies that kept us occupied all day. Excursions and fete were few of the annual events that the school organised for us. Looking back I find it surprising that in those days our school organised sex-education sessions when specialist lecturers would come and impart this education in small batches. As ours was a boys' school then, we were provided opportunities by the school to socialize with girls of other schools. This was organised in the form of a party after school hours and was a part of the schedule of activities where participation was obligatory though not compulsory. All these and much more that I have grown up with has had an invaluable impact on my character and person as a whole. May be that I could not acquire all of that or was not capable of making full use of everything that was provided but the very fact that every bit was displayed and put forth before us helped in raising our level of cognition and comprehension. My school has taught me not only this but the essence of all that goes into the understanding of things. I truly acknowledge that whatever I have achieved in life and what ever I could accomplish I attribute it to my school my respected Teachers and the reverend Fathers most of whom were American and Europeans. After completing my schooling in 1976 I left the town with my parents. Eversince I never had been there. I have come to know that the city has grown and must have become very crowded and surely very filthy because that city (and the state) is known today as a capital that has developed the least in every respect. During the last five years or so I am told it has improved much. I imagine that the green fields and the woods that were there all over must have been converted into concrete jungles and the beautiful old buildings must have got ruined and crumbled. And above all the people must have changed like in all places towards the worse and become more fake than innocently genuine as they used to be. I would never like to go back here lest the picture that lives in my memory till today gets ravaged leaving me upset and saddened.

But for those who wish to know more it might be of interest that while the present day Bihar is often looked down upon and many in India make fun about the place and the people it is actually the place from where the shoots of the present day Indian civilization has sprouted. The earliest form of religion that existed before Hinduism emerged was called the 'Sanatan Dharma'. This practice (the eternal religion) is deeply associated with Bihar. Also Bihar has the distinction of having been the abode of many an event of solemn mythological significance. All this actually should command admiration of all instead. The story of 'Rama and Sita' the most admired and holiest of couples worshipped by people in the sub-continent was a happening of this locale. There is a place in Bihar by the name of 'Sitamarhi'. This is the sacred place where

Sita the daughter of King Janak was born and who later became the wife of Lord Rama. 'Janakpur' the capital of King Janak was the place where Lord Rama and Sita were married. Valmiki Nagar is where lived Maharishi Valmiki (regarded as the author of the epic, Ramayana). Here was the unique forest of 'Champa' (magnolia) that emitted the mystic fragrance of purity. The place is now known as 'Champaran' (from the words 'champa and 'aranya' mean forest). It is here that the founder of Buddhism gained enlightenment, where Jainism was spread and Sikhism flourished. Magadh that the place was known in ancient times witnessed the foundation of one of the oldest kingdoms about 800 years before the birth of Christ. The land also witnessed the foundation of the Republic of the Licchavis, the growth of the Maurya dynasty and the rule of the Ashoka—the king extraordinaire. The earliest systems of state administration, judicial methodology and division of power were first put into practice in this land in the Republic of Licchavis. Great political thinkers like Chanaky, the mentor of Chandragupta Maurya and who authored the tenets of Military Science and Defence Management, Kautilya whose transcript of Arthashastra treatise forms the basis of modern science of Economics lived and accomplished on this blessed land. Around 270 B.C it was King Ashok who was the first to formulate firm tenets for the governance. This place also was the first where empowerment of women and their participation in the affairs of governance could be found. 'Megasthenes' an emissary of Alexander's General, Seleucus Necator and Hiuen Tsang the famous Chinese scholar are amongst the several foreign travelers who came here with a serious purpose. Even during the times of the Mughal Bihar remained under a Bihar born ruler Sher Shah Suri who was not only a challenge to the mighty Moghuls but was able to extend his kingdom from the Indus in the west to Bengal in the east. His rule witnessed excellent administrative regulations, efficient revenue, agricultural and tax collection system and acts of land reform. These methords were later adopted by the Moghuls and even by the Britishers. Even during the struggle for India's independence Bihar came into prominence with many brave and dedicated men from this land joined to the clarion call of great leaders from different parts of the country. It was from Bihar that Mahatma Gandhi launched his civil-disobedience movement, which ultimately led to India's independence. Great leaders too were born here who led the freedom struggle from the forefront. Even post independent era witnessed one of the biggest peoples movement led by an eminent person from Bihar known as Jay Prakash Narayan whose contribution to modern Indian history was substantial and was responsible for changing the face of Indian politics once and for all. Also in Bihar were born many /legendry writers like Raja Radhika Raman Singh, Shiva Pujan Sahay, Divakar Prasad Vidyarthy, Ramdhari Singh Dinkar, Ram Briksha Benipuri, amongst the many luminaries who contributed to the blossoming of Hindi literature. But the city established by King Ajatshatru around 5th Century B.C., at the confluence of the rivers Sone and Ganga and that witnessed the grandeur of life in Patliputra ever remained wretched and the people desecrated.

The state of Bihar has lately been split into two. The portion in the north remains as Bihar and the tribal forest belt in the south is now called **JHARKHAND**. Capital of the new state is Ranchi. 'Jhar' and 'khand literally mean 'forest—portion' or jungle zone. This region predominantly remained tribal dominated without much interference or influence of the various rulers who came and went in the neighboring urbanized areas. Earliest references reveal that Jarasandha the king of Rajgriha (now Rajgir, referred above) had this territory under his rule. Later during the Moghul period emperor Akhbar had dominance over this region. But there was little direct interference of these rulers till the days of the British reign when a system of forced labor and imposition of taxes were introduced. Out of the growing discontent amongst the Mundas and the Oraon tribes grew a reformist leader in 1895 by the name of Bisra Munda. To protect the cause of righteousness and the interest of his people this spiritual leader became revolutionary in his actions and soon resorted to arms struggle. Birsa was arrested and jailed where he later died in 1900. Birsa's will perhaps be known as a socio-religious leader who stood for the cause of the ignorant and the helpless against an adversary to whom they were no match. He considered that the land they cultivated was reclaimed from the forest and hence belonged to the people who cultivated it. Therefore the imposition of tax by those who had no contribution in it was incorrect. Inspired by Birsa Munda's teachings and his acts of bravery, the tribal community gained consciousness. In the later years the region and the community contributed immensely to the freedom struggle and participated in several movements led by Mahatma Gandhi.

About an hour and a half drive through the hills and forests is a famous temple of Rajrappa. Here Goddess Kali is worshipped in the form of the deity of 'Chinnamasta' (literally meaning 'severed head'. It is believed, as also scripted in the Rig Vedas that the consort of Shiva once chopped her head by her own hand to let flow the 'vital essence' in order to quench the eternal thirst of all beings. It is said that the stream of blood that flowed from her chopped throat represented 'Soma' or 'Madhu'—the nectar of immortality. This incident happened at the instance of his two attendants of the Goddess named Varnani and Dakini who were nagging her in hunger. She then chopped her head and the two were fed with her blood that flowed from the headless torso). This is symbolic of the Cosmic sacrifice that preaches that we must remove all of our desires and attachments thereby destroy the illusion (or Maya) of Universe and then qualify to drink her blood). Here Goddess Kali is also denoted as Prachnda Chandi (infinite infuriation) or the Goddess that represents power. This temple situated at the confluence of Damodar and the Bhairabi Rivers is amongst the fifty-two Pithasthans (explained before).

Another famous pilgrimage place in Ranchi is the Jagannathpur Temple built in 1691. Situated on a hill top about 10 Km away from the city center. The temple organises the chariot festival every year like the one held at Puri. In the vicinity one can find the temple dedicated to the 'Sun' called the Surya Temple. Also located nearby is a Shiva temple and Ram, Sita, Hanuman and one Lakshman temple situated at Muri.

But of the religious places in Jharkhan the most popular and most visited is the temple of Baidyanathdham in Deoghar. The premises forms a cluster of 22 temples dedicated to the Hindu god Shiva, here called Baba Baidyanath. It is believed that Lord Viswakarma who is considered as the architect engineer of the Gods originally built this temple. While this place is one of fifty-two Peethasthana, the diety form is also one of the twelve Jyotirlingas sacred to Hindus. As narrated by some Hindu believers that after 'Ravana' the king of Lanka (now Sri Lanka) became all powerful by the blessings of Lord Vishnu, he decided to carry Shiva from the Himalayas and install him in his kingdom in Lanka. While Shiva was reluctant so were other Gods. The deal was finally agreed to on the condition that he would have to carry Shiva in one go without rest midway. It so happened that Ravana got confused on his way due to the tricks of the lesser gods and he almost lost his way. Bewildered he put Shiva down from his shoulders and put him on the earth the place now called Deoghar (or house of God). Once on ground Ravana's vow got breached and Shiva could not be picked up again. The Lord thus stayed on in the form of 'Baidyanath' as he is worshipped till today. Some believe that Lord Vishnu had himself installed Shiva in this form and thus the presiding deity here is worshipped as Baidyanath Jyotirlingam. The origin of this temple is not quite clear as the reference of this place is found in various texts dating back to the Maurya dynasty of 320 BC. Several rulers at different times have set claim to have been the builder of this temple. Some even had removed earlier inscription and put their name instead to take credit. But what appears evident is that the temple was built in parts at different times in history which goes to establish that the temple and the deity was so well honored and valued throughout that every body who had authority contributed in his own way for its betterment. It is one of those fortunate places that never faced the onslaught or disregard of any ruler of a different faith. I was surprised to learn that Pilgrimage to Baidyanath was well recognized in the Muslim period also. It is said to have an appealing description in muslim writings of the late 17th century when the dominance of the muslim rule was all pervasive. A locally known Muslim priest by the name of 'Data Saheb' was a devotee of Lord Baidyanath. It is said that perhaps because of the prohibition and not to distract the staunch Hindus, Data Saheb used to hand over flowers and 'vilva' (vilva patra, or vilva leaves is Bel leaf and considered as a sacred offering to Lord Shiva) to the priest who in turn offered them to the Lord in Data Saheb's name. Even the East India Company after the battle of Plassey in 1757 appointed a special officer an Englishman to look after the betterment of the temple and the devotees. But in order to maintain the sanctity of the place and avoid direct interference he handed over the control to the priests of the temple so that the orderliness of the management of the shrine could be maintained.

Believers consider that the 'Baidyanath Jyotirlingam' has a great power and the deity never refuses to fulfill the wishes of 'Bhaktas' (devotees). It is also said that the Lord too is obligated to fulfill every devotees' desire. There is a story that a once a British jailor was posted at Deoghar when he heard the news of his son's disappearance in mid sea while he was travelling in the ship. Devastated at the news he kept following up on the whereabouts. But no news of his discovery ever came. Following the advice of his Indian staff he took to meditating before the Baidyanath. This gave him peace of mind and some solace that allowed him to overcome the distraction at work. While he had lost all hopes a miracle happened during the course of his prolonged meditation before the Lord. News arrived that the ship in which his son was traveling could be retrieved and his son was recovered alive. Then on he introduced a custom in Deogarh Jail of offering flowers and Vilva Patras to Lord Baidyanath in honor of his gratitude.

This place is also a place of congregation for those who practice 'Tantra'. The Shakti Rup (power projection) of Shiva is depicted in the form of Durga or Kali. And one of the ingredients of attaining closeness to this Supreme Being is through the practice of Tantra. This practice could be found being performed in the vicinity of the temple. Not that one can see it being performed like a stage drama but sense or get a glimpse of certain acts being performed in places. Tantra in simple language as I understand is a discipline of performing ritualistic worship following the true principle of execution as laid down in the Vedas and which a true knower of that knowledge could only enumerate. Generally people have an impression that this is occult to the extent that it involves nasty things like meditating on a corpse or doing sacrifices causing bloodshed and indulging in sexual acts or performing gestures that are peculiar to look at and so on. But all this is only a part of the entire course of the process or curriculum that takes years to accomplish. Some also think of Tantra Yoga as magic and witchcraft and performance of a mysterious formula that causes miracle that are at times harm causing. But all this is far from the truth. Tantra as I understand can be undertaken by Tantra Yoga practitioners who must have purity, humility, devotion, and courage. Dedication to his Guru, cosmic love, faithfulness, contentment, dispassion, non-covetousness, and truthfulness are the other requirements.

I'm absolutely unacquainted with this spiritual understanding and have no knowledge whatsoever about Tantra. All that I know of is that there is a path of attaining certain cosmic goals and Tantra is one such. By practising Tantra in the right spirit, one 'sadhak' (practitioner) may be able to merge his inner consciousness with cosmic force. As I have learnt, Tantra is concerning Tattva (Truth or Brahman) and Mantra (mystic syllables). Hence it is called Tantra. Coming across a reading I found that a renowned Saint Paramhans Swami Nikhileshwaranand has explained, "Tantra is the process of intensification of our peculiar inner potentialities so that we can command this atomic arrangement which in other words is known as 'Siddhi'. The flow of energy is going on ceaselessly in the environment and when your own inner energy becomes capable of influencing the external ones, nothing will remain impossible for you and this is the science of Tantra . . ."[24]

Similar practice of meditation is also prevalent in 'Tarapith' in Bengal. The state of **WEST BENGAL**, which is adjoining Bihar and Jharkhand in the west, is a

24 'Mantra Tantra Yantra Vigyan, International Siddhashram Sadhak Parivarm Jodhpur April 1994 '5'

region that has been the crucible of history. The wide and long history of Bengal can neither be summarized here nor will it be doing justice if I did attempt to do so. Bengal is famous the world over for its love of creativity, its attainments in art and culture, for being a repository of knowledge and a place where religion and politics have been explored to the limit. It has been a hub of trade and industrial activity, the epithet of power. It is also a land that is gifted with the enormous diversities of nature. Be it the snow capped high mountains or the sea, the abundance of water bodies and rivers or the world's largest mangrove forest or large expanse of arid landmass you have it all in Bengal. I feel elated, as I was fortunate to have been born in the capital city of Calcutta now renamed as Kolkata. But as I said before I spent my childhood days partly in Maharashtra and mostly in Bihar. Later I returned here to pursue my college education. I joined the St. Xavier's College in Calcutta in 1976 and completed my graduation with Economics and Political Science in 1979. Subsequently I completed my Masters Degree, Management and Law from this celebrated city's most reputed university called the Calcutta University. This University incidentall is trhe oldest in this side of the globe. It was set up in 1857. During the early days its catchment area extended from Lahore (now in Pakistan) to Rangoon (Mayanmar / Burma). The first Chancellor was Governor General Lord Canning. The first graduate was Bankim Chandra who went on to become a Deputy Magistrate and was later conferred the Order of the Indian Empire in 1894. But Bankim Chandra is remembered as an usherer of literary renaissance in India whose partiotic writings stirred freedom fighters across the county to drive British rule out of the country.

Apart from the several historical monument and locations that this city is home to there are some very important places of worship and divine pilgrimage for several religions of the world.

The most significant and well known is perhaps the temple dedicated to Goddess Kali located in the heart of the city of Kolkata in a place called Kalighat. Situated in the banks of a stream of the Ganga Kalighat Temple is regarded as one of the fifty-two Peethasthans where the toes of the right foot of Shakti or Sati is said to have fallen.

The present day shrine is merely 200-year-old, built in 1809 but it history dates back to ages. As the story goes one entity by the name of Attaram once saw a beam of light radiating from the water in the stream. On coming close he found that a deity half submerged in the mud under the stream water wanting to be brought out. Thus was discovered, the dark and fearful deity with three large eyes and protruding an enormous tongue that still adorns the temple and accepts the offerings from its devotees giving her blessings in return. Her terrifying form is only a symbol of caution for the perpetrators but is bliss for the virtuous. The deity here has been an idol worshipped by not only the people of Kolkata but by devotees all across the globe.

Similarly there is another temple devoted to the Kali that is situated in the north of the city at Dakshineswar also called the Dakshineswar Kali Temple at Calcutta. The widow of Babu Rajachadra Das built this temple between 1847 and 1855. Babu Rajachadra Das was a wealthy 'zamindar' of Janbazar. ('Zamindar' meaning Landlord. 'Zamin' in Persian means land and zamindar as applicable in the olden days connotes possessors of proprietary right over large expanses of land and having right to collection of rent). His widow named 'Rani Rashmoni' was a dynamic leader and true philanthropists. She was also a devout of the divine Mother Goddess Kali. It is said that in 1847 on the night before the day she was to set sail on a pilgrimage to the sacred Hindu city of Kashi (now Varanasi) Goddess Kali appeared in her dream and decreed her not to proceed with her journey rather build a temple on the banks of the river Ganga and install a Kali idol in it. The majestic temple that now stands on the banks of the Ganga at Dakshineswar near Kolkata is the manifestation of that dream. In the context of this Temple mention must be made of three outstanding individuals whose actions culminated into one of the greatest missions of the country that the world takes recognition of. And it is for this reason that I take the privilege of briefly narrating about their lives and deeds. Rani Rashmoni (born in 1793) a lady of those olden days when the ladies in India never dared to come to the fore. Their lives were restricted to managing the house hold and bearing of children. But the Rani was exceptional. After she was widowed she not only held the reigns of business and management of the huge estate efficiently but also faught for the cause of underprivileged and the weak. So much so that she took on the British to withdraw taxes of the poor fishermen who lived by the river. For this she even went to the extent of obstructing the transit of ships on a part of the Ganga River. The British were finally compelled to concede. Her benevolent deeds are visible even today. For the convenience of those who bathe in the Ganga and perform ceremonies on its banks the Rani constructed a series of Ghats (embankments) in facilitation. Nimtala Ghat, Ahiritola Ghat and Babughat Ghat (built in memory of her husband Babu Rajachadra Das) are a few that people from across the country visit and make use of even today. She had also built roads for pilgrims in different places and generously carried out charitable work that came to the service of innumerable human beings several years after her death in 1861. But of all the things she did one that she did though unknowingly turned out to be the most eventful and that was the engagement of Sri Ramakrishna as a priest of the Temple of Dakshineswar

Kali who later turned out to be one of the greatest spiritual monks of 19th century India. Ramakrishna then known as Gadadhar Chattopadhyay was inducted after the death of his elder brother who was the original priest of that temple.

Sri Ramakrishna was no simple priest. The miracle at his birth and the phenomenon prior was indicative enough to suggest that a spiritual leader was destined to ascend on earth. In February 1836 a child was born in Kamarpukur to a poor Hindu Brhamin family who was named Gadadhar. Gadadhar who later came to be known a 'Ramakrishna' and after his enlightenment was addressed as 'Ramakrishna Paramahansa' later became one of the greatest scientific spiritual saints leaders of 19th century Bengal and the whole of the sub-continent. He was a saint with a difference. He was a non-conformist and questioned existing beliefs and conventions. He did not preach the worship of any deity or profess any religion rather he spread the message of the harmony of religions and questioned the worship of stone idols. He said that different religions are not contradictory rather they complement each other. Ramakrishna did experimentation also with other religions. He became a Christian and studied the Bible. He also read the holy Koran and once converted to Islam. Likewise, he became a Tantric and spent many lonely nights, meditating in cremation grounds with human skulls as props. He was one who provided spiritual enlightenment to the people of Bengal and played a key role in the social reform movement in Bengal in 19th century. After having practiced the spiritual disciplines of different religions he came to the realization that all religion lead to the same goal. Upon this he proclaimed that the path to the almighty are as many as there are faith (religions) amongst humanity. In other words 'all roads lead to the same destination—the abode of the almighty'. Ramakrishna emphasized that the absolute goal of all of mankind is the realization of the existence of God and to this end religions were only the means to reach the Absolute. His teachings inspired the spiritual leaders, philosophers and political thinkers as much as many men and women of that time who became his followers and disciples. But the most illustrious of his disciples was one Narendra Dutta, who later became 'Swami Vivekananda' and subsequently the first known Hindu Sage to reach out to the western world where he introduced Eastern-Thought at the World's Parliament of Religions, in connection with the World's Fair in Chicago, in 1893. He was also the one to have introduced the philosophy of Yoga and Vedanta to Europe and America. Later he founded the 'Ramakrishna Mission' named after his Guru Ramakrishna Paramhansa. Ramakrishna Mission is today the world's largest charitable relief missions and runs a monastic order that is the largest in India called the Ramakrishna Math. The worldwide Headquarters of the Ramakrishna Math and Ramakrishna Mission is situated in Belur Math where Vivekananda lived and attained 'Maha Samadhi' (utltimate stillness ie when the soul of a saint departs from the body) on 4th July 1902. At Belur Math located on the West Bank of the Ganges one can see a magnificent temple and prayer arena where hundreds of devotees congregate each day to worship. One of swami Vivekananda's disciples Ms. Hellen Rubel contributed a large sum of money towards the building of this temple. The math is an embodiment of universal brotherhood that Sri Ramakrishna Paramhansa preached and stood for.

Calcutta or Kolkata as it is now renamed and once the capital of undivided India was one of the few places where Industry flourished and as a cosequence people from all across the country with diverse faiths settled around wide and large. Thus there are innumerable places of worship. This cosmopolitan city has a large community of Jains. The Jains are generally engaged in trade and business.

They had migrated to the city in large numbers during the time of the East India Company. They are God loving and followers of the Jain Tirthankara. In honor of the 23rd Jain Tirthankar a magnificent Pareshnath Jain Temple stands in North Kolkata built in 1867 by Ray Bahadur Badridas. Dedicated to Lord Mahavira, the last Tirthankar is a shrine on the further north. These temples have been built with utmost care and adoration that is evident from the magnificence displayed in the interiors of the temple and the well-maintained garden around it.

Like in other cities as we have seen and will see as we go further, here too the House of the Birlas' has erected an all-marble temple with rich Rajasthani engravings. Located in south Kolkata and inaugurated in 1996 it is popularly known as the Birla Mandir. Designed on the pattern of the Lingaraj Temple of Bhubaneswar it houses the idols of Goddess Laxmi and Lord Narayan. Thanthania Kali temple where the deity of 'Siddheswari' (incarnate of Kali as a wish-fulfiller) is worshipped is one of the oldest shrines said to have been built in 1703 by a rich Bengali named Shankar Ghosh.

St. Paul's Cathedral built by Major W.N.Forbes of the East India Company in 1847, the Agni Mandir or the Fire Temple of the Parsee community, the 17th century Armenian Church built by the Armenian community of Kolkata, Chinese Temple that dates back to the 18th century. This temple and the grave of its builder Tong Achi a Chinese businessman who lived in a place now called Achipur. Built during the times of Warren Hastings in the 1780s this memorial is visited by many Chinese during the Chinese New Year. A Jewish place of devotion—the Kolkata Jewish Synagogue built in 1884, the Nakhoda Mosque built in 1926, largest and also the most beautiful place of worship for the Muslims. These are essentially Kolkata's important places of worship that also displays the diversity of the population living here.

About 35 Km from Kolkata on the banks of the Hooghly is an important place of Shia Muslim pilgrimage at Bandel. Built in 1861 by one Haji Mohammad Mohsin has quotes of the holi quoran inscribed on its walls. There is a 35-meter tall clock tower. Though the clock is dysfunctional today the gigantic clock apparatus is still intact inside the tower above.

The Chinese community in Kolkata is an important and inseparable component of the city's heritage. They have lived and grown with the city contributing greatly to the culture that is Kolkata. The cuisine, the tannery their skilled carpentry works have all made this city gain out of their presence here. Chinese families who arrived in India and settled in Calcutta arrived during the Kuomintang-rule, the 2nd World War and time of Mao's revolution. Most of the Chinese population living in India are 'Hakkas' or those engaged in leather tanning and shoe making. Other two known categories are 'Cantonese' who are mostly carpenters and restaurateurs, and 'Shanghai' who run laundries. A good number of Chinese made a living out of dentistry and school teaching. The Chinese celebrate their festivals with passion and fervour. The only festival that the Chinese are seen to observe is their New Year. This is celebrated with dragon-dances, traditional music and firecrackers. This apart they are now seen involved also with the local community observing the Indian festivals Durga Puja, Diwali and Christmas. Some celebrates Buddhism, and Confucianism too with much gaiety. San Chu or whole pig form an important part of their festival when a pig with a curly tail is roasted in whole and served to the Gods as a part of the ritual.

St. John's church is the first of the British built church in Kolkata.a and is historical in that sense. Built in the year 1787 St. John's church is also considered as the first Anglican Church of India. Painting of a renowned German painter Johann Zoffani's 'The Last Supper' could be seen inside this church and in the premises lies the grave where the founder of Kolkata Job Charnock lies in eternal slumber. But one of India's oldest churches the Roman Catholic Church is in Bandel very close to Kolkata. This Church was built by first European settlement in West Bengal sometime in 1599. The Portuguese rebuilt this church in 1640 after the Mughals destroyed it during Shahjahan's rule. The statue of our Lady of Happy voyages in the bell tower was considered auspicious by the oceangoing Portuguese of those times. Influence of Bengali culture on some European individuals has also been remarkable. One such instance is of Hensman Anthony a man of Potrugeses origin who is said to have arrived in Bengal in 1810. He lived in Chandannagore not far from Kolkata. He was greately influenced by the religious songs devoted to Goddesses Kali and Durga. His deep connect with the Hindu mythical world stirred him to renounce his ancestry and marry a Hindu Bengali widowed devotee of the Goddess. He went on to learn the Bengali language so well that his compositions of Bengali devotional songs find place in the various collection of songs sung during the performance of religious rituals. He had a temple of Kali built in Bowbazar Kolkata where religious rites and puja are still performed with utmost reverence. This temple came to be known as the Firinghi Kalibari (Foreigner's Kali Temple).

Kolkata is one of those unique places where numerous embankments (called Ghats. Ghats refer to places along a river front or a water body where an artificial landing has been erected to access the waters) have been constructed during different times alongside the river to facilitate diverse purposes. Be it to facilitate movement of goods and passengers or facilitate trade and commerce or bathing or carry out religious ceremonies including immersion of holy idols or a memorabilia or be it a sought after rendezvous point the Ghats along the Hooghly have been of significance for the residents of Kolkata. Some of the important names are Outram ghat dedicated to the memory of a brave British general named Sir James Outram, The Princep Ghat built in 1843 commemorates James Princep a learned British researcher and the Armenian Ghat constructed by the Armenian people to facilitate cargo transshipment arriving from foreign shores apart from a few others built by Rani Rashmoni.

The attachment of the habitants of Bengal to the Nobel laureate Rabindranath Tagore is no less devine than any religious attachment. A Bengali could be an atheist but can seldom fall short of being a staunch follower of this famous poet. Rabindranath Tagore lives in the heart of every Bengali and in fact any human being who has interacted with him personally or through his literary work.

Before moving to the other parts of Bengal where innumerable locations of worship awaits us we will have a peep into the Sunderbans Situated about a 100 Km from Kolkata on the lower end of Gangetic West Bengal is the largest impenetrable mangrove forest in the world where 'Bon Bibi' is the ruling deity. Sunderbans extends over an area of over 10,000 sq km and is home to the fearless man-eating Royal Tigers of Bengal. Sunderbans is also a part of the world's largest delta formed by the three mighty rivers Ganges, and Brahmaputra (from the Indian side) Meghna (through Bangladesh) that merge into the Bay of Bengal. A characteristic tree called 'Sundari' is perhaps from where the tract gets its name or is it derived from its literal bengali meaning 'beautiful forest' ('sunder' meaning beautiful and 'bon' meaning forest). The former seems more appropriate as there is nothing there to feel so beautiful about. Rather the place is uncanny, mystical and intensely untamed. As the soil there is not conducive to cultivation the inhabitants of the fifty-four odd islands depend on on forest products and fish. As Amitav Ghosh the author of the international bestseller "The Hungry Tide"[25] has rendered, life for the settlers here is extremely precarious. Attacks by deadly tigers are common. Unrest and eviction are constant threats. Without warning, at any time, tidal floods rise and surge over the land, leaving devastation in their wake. When people go into the forest, there is a kind of an invisible line they recognize. They know that on the other side of the line is the land of the tiger. For them venturing into the forest is de rigueur because that is where there livelihood lies. Thus before they proceed into the forest not knowing whether and in what state they will return they will say prayers and perform rituals before the forest goddess, 'Bonbibi' whom they consider as their savior who will protect them from harm. Bon Bibi is a crude deity made of clay and installed in a bamboo shack. On the one side a soldier flanks image of Bon Bibi who is seated on a tiger, and on the other is a strong human figure wearing an Islam look. Bon Bibi or Deity of the Forest May 10, 2007 one A.K. Sircar a member of the photo.net community puts the legend as follows: "Once upon a time, Ibrahim of Medina was blessed by the Archangel Gabriel, to be the father of twins. The girl was named Bon Bibi and her brother Shah Jongli. After reaching adulthood, they were sent by the Archangel to the shores of Bay of Bengal, now known as Sunderbans. A demon named Dakshin Roy ruled this marshy land and terrorized human beings. Bon Bibi & Shah Jongli defeated Dakshin Roy and saved the humans. The legend is now modified to suit the modern times. The Royal Bengal Tigers, which devoured the humans, is called Dakshin Roy. Dukhey represents the fishermen and bee-collectors.

---

[25] The Hungry Tide: A Novel By Amitav Ghosh. Published by Houghton Mifflin Books, 2005. ISBN 0618329978, 9780618329977. 333 pages

Large number of settlers, who enter the dense forest for collecting honey, and fisherman, who catch fish in the rivers and creeks, worship Bon Bibi & Shah Jongli as their saviours. Bon Bibi thus has come to stay as the resident forest deity of Sunderbans".

Some 80 Km westward of Kolkata is a well-known temple of Tarakeshwar. The temple dating back to 18th century and built by Raja Bharamalla is dedicated to Lord Shiva. It is believed that the temple of Tarakeshwar is the manifestation of a dream experienced by the Raja. He located the spot where cows and goats would empty their udders of milk. He had the place dug up and discovered a Shiva-lingam. And on that very spot he had a temple built. Today this temple draws scores of people from all across the region. Hindu believers congragate in large number during the month of 'Shravana' (July-August) to decant water and milk on the idol and worship for their wishes to come true. Many devouts take the pain of covering the journey on foot from their homes, some fifty-miles away or more to carrying with them a pair of water filled pitchers, which they would empty on the 'lingam'. Taking this pain, they believe would surely draw the attention of the Lord who in turn will be sympathetic and generous in giving his blessings.

But one of the most sacred of temples in Bengal is the Ma Tara Temple at Tarapith in the district of Birbhum. Ma Tara is the consort of Lord Shiva in the form of intense feminine energy and a compassionate mother. Ma Tara of Tarapith is another of the fifty-two 'Pitha-sthans'. Here Ma Tara depicts a form of Kali having two hands with snakes garlanding her and has Shiva lying in her left lap like a child sucking her breast. But this theme image is hidden behind the idol of Tara Ma that is placed in front. The original image is kept concealed in wake of a divine message that the common visitors may not understand the significance. But this original image is displayed only on certain occasions when special worshippers assemble. It is said that during the 'Sagar Manthan' (meaning churning of the ocean which is an event in mythology when Gods were obliged to resort to churning the ocean. During the course of this churning emerged a pot of poison that was so deadly that if it spilled it could perish the entire world. In order to save all beings Lord Shiva drank the poison but did not swallow. It stayed in this throat keeping Shiva unharmed. As a result his neck turned blue. He is thus also called 'Neelakantha' where 'Neela' means blue and 'Kantha' means neck or throat). At this time it is said that the affectionate Mother Kali in order to extinguish the Lord Shiva's sufferings from his burns and pains due to engulping the poison fed him her breast milk. Mother Kali in the form of Tara Ma has significance in Tantrik cosmology where phonetics of words, forms, music and mantra, are considered to be the very source of the cosmos.

Incidentally, the reference of Tara, which means Star in Sanskrit, could be found in many ancient religious findings across the world. Buddhist tradition believes that Tara is actually much greater than a goddess—she is a symbol of extreme enlightenment, enormously capable and compassion. It is also thus reflected in the Tibetan pantheon through which it has also passed into the countries of the west. A Native American Cheyenne tribe refers to a Star woman who descended from the heavens who became the source of nourishment and wisdom. Research of Z. Sitchin tells of IshTar who came to earth from another planetary system and instructed her people to inter-marry with earthlings, making them capable of many things. Ishtar the Mesopotamian God depicted in by a sacred symbol of eight-pointed star. Similar to the ones stated before but not as magnanimous and vivacious there are at least ten 'Pitha-sthans' in Bengal.

In the western part of Bengal is a beautiful place called Bishnupur in the district of Bankura. This place close to Kolkata about 140 Km away also called the land of terra-cotta, is famous for its clay art, terracotta temples and artifacts. The historical monuments and temples for which Bishnupur is famous date back to the 14th century to the rule of the Malla dynasty. Ari Malla founded Malla rule in Nepal in the 12th century after the fall of the Lichchhavis. It is said that Mallas were tribal inhabitants of the region that is now bordering Bihar and Nepal during 6th-4th century BC (time of Buddha). The terra-cotta temple structures that could be seen here are now more important as places of tourist interest than of worship. Noteworthy are The Shyam Ray Temple, constructed in 1643, twin temples built in 1655 called Jorbangla Shyam Ray Temple, Radhey Shyam of 1758. These temples are dedicated to the Lord Krishna and the times he spent frolicking with the 'gopis'. Such depictions and those of the social life and warfare could be seen painted on the walls. Sarbamangla temple and the Chhinnamasta Temple are other prominent temples where religious activities have resumed later and rituals during the festival times are followed with much gaiety. The monuments and structures of Bishnupur reveal that the Mallas apart from religious inclinations had immense adulation for culture and music. A temple of Goddess Durga is perhaps the most visited and the annual celebrations too take place with great festivity. But one of the most ancient of the modern Durga temples is situated in Jamboni about 13 km from Jhargram in west Midnapur district of West Bengal. The deity here is called Devi Kanak Durga that shows the Goddes with four-arms and three-eyes. Once upon a time even human sacrifices were offered at this Temple.

Moving northwards from Kolkata into the district Nadia we will reach Mayapur the land of the 'Vaishnavs' or worshippers of Lord Vishnu or Lord Krishna. Vaishnavism is the identification of Vishnu or Narayana as the one Supreme God from whom all Gods are derived. Mayapur situated on the confluence of the rivers Ganges and Jalangi is often associated with Vrindavan because it is the birthplace of Lord Chaitanya Mahaprabhu who is believed to be the reincarnation of Lord Krishna and Radha. Chaitanya was born here in 1486. Four hundred years later another saint named A. C. Bhaktivedanta Swami Prabhupada though born in Kolkata and who later took 'sanyas' and became a Vaishnava sadhu (monk) spent his years of preaching here in Mayapur. Prabhupada spread the message of Chaitanya Mahaprabhu of promoting universal harmony and brotherhood in the English language and therby influenced the westerners to take to this path of wisdom. He later founded the International Society for Krishna Consciousness (ISCKON) that has its headquarters here and has branches all over the world. The place is also home to Gaudiya Math—organisation was formed in 1918 to spread Vaishnavism throughout the world. Though Mayapur was peaceful across the river Nabadwip was a relatively eventful place. In 1201 Muhammad Bakhtyar Kilji a loyal lieutenant of Muhammad Ghori occupied the place with an advance party of 20 Turkish horsemen, and laid the foundation of Muslim rule in Bengal.

Moving to the extreme north towards the mountains in Bengal we can find two popular places that are of tourist interest as much as they are religious—Kalimpong and Darjeeling. Until 1865 Kalimpong was under the kingdom of Bhutan later following the Anglo-Bhutanese War it came to be merged with Darjeeling. Kalimpong has a Tibetan influence and the Gompas (Tibetan Monastries) are important religious shrines of the place. But interestingly Christianity and Hinduism closely co-exist with Buddhism and thus Hindu temples and Churches could also be seen in the vicinity. Durpin Dara Monastery built in 1970 and sanctified by the Dalai Lama is an important Buddhist shrine in Kalimpong. Thongsha Gompa built in 1630 during the Bhutanese period is the oldest gompa around. St. Theresa's Church and Manga Temple are two other religious site in the town. Ghoom near Darjeeling, which is famous for having the highest railway station in India and until recently the highest in the world at nearly 2200 meters, is also famous for having one of the holiest monasteries. Built in 1875 by Lama Sherab Gyatso the statue of Maitreye Buddha is the deity of worship here. Another shrine the Dhirdham Temple built in the style of Pashupatinath Temple of Kathmandu was actually built by Dhir Shamsher Rana of Nepal.

Darjeeling was until 1835 a part of the then Royal Kingdom of Sikkim. Sikkim became of the Indian Union on May 15, 1975 and became the 22nd state then following a special referendum held in 1975 when 97 percent of the populace expressed their opinion in favour of merging of Sikkim with India. Sikkim has since got annexed to the Republic of India and forms a state of Sikkim that lies beyond Darjeeling and shares its northern borders with China. History of Sikkim dates back to the pre-historic times. What comes to light is that some of the Lepchas who came from the east (probably from Garo and Naga hills) to migrate towards Nepal came to settle here. By nature the people here are peace loving, innocent and their love for nature is immense. They are also deeply religious. Most inhabitants being followers of Buddhism, a good number of Monasteries could be seen here. Most important amongst them is the Rumtek monastery in which a ten feet large statue of Sakyamuni Buddha is installed amidst beautiful decoration of silk banners, large paintings and several sacred ancient texts. It is at present the seat for the exiled 16th Karmapa of Tibet. The 9th Karmapa named Wang Chuk Dorje originally constructed this in 1740. Amongst important temples of Hindu worship are Ganesh Tok (at an altitude of 6500 meters) and Hanuman Tok dedicated to Lord Ganesh and Lord Hanuman respectively.

Adjoining this state is a narrow passage in the state of West Bengal that opens into a large territory that comprises of six beautiful sister-states of India, collectively called the **Northeastern states** or the NE Region. Tucked away behind Bangladesh these are some of India's extremely potential but least attended states. Be it agriculture, tea cultivation, petroleum reserve these states reign supreme. Having the potential to become destinations for international tourism these states are blessed with immensely spirited human resource whose potentials remained dwarfed due to lack of proper and timely application of resources as availed constructively by the states in central India. To makeup for the lost time and attention these states have lately been given special status and attention for their development. In earlier times there was only one conglomerate state of Assam that was later subdivided. Nagaland, Mizoram and Meghalaya were tribal dominated regions subsequently brought under the British reign. Manipur and Tripura were princely states like Sikkim later annexed to the Indian Republic. Today **ASSAM** is a separate state and a constituent of the republic of India and is the largest amonst all states in the NE rgion People here pronounce Assam as 'Ahom'. It is understood that 'Ahoms' were Tai Mongoloids who came here from around present-day Yunan Province of China in around 1200 AD. They ruled this territory most of Brahmaputra valley till the arrival of the British in 1826. This is one place in India where the Mughals received repeated set-back in their endeavor to conquer. Rather it is believed that had the great Ahom king Rudra Singha (1696-1714) not died prematurely he, as planned would have invaded the Mughal Empire. Such was the might and strength of the Ahoms. Assam has witnessed migrants coming from different neighbouring regions. Chinese,

Burmese and from other Southeast Asian locations have all contributed to the unified cultural richness of the entire region. These locations have a long history that dates back even to the prehistoric times. Stone Age human footprints are also said to have been found in this land. Evidences of prominent human activity are traced back to 200 BC. History shows that Huen Tsang, the great Chinese traveler, visited this region in the 7th century. Mention of the names of the present time places are also found in the epics of Ramayana and Mahabharata. King Naraka of 'Kamrup' (a name still in existence) participated in the Kurukshetra battle when he sided with the Kauravas. 'Hirimba' queen was a 'Kachari' (inhabitant of 'Kachar', now a district known as Cachar and located in southern part of Assam near Mizoram). She married 'Bhim' (one of the Pandava brothers in the epic of Mahabharata) and their son 'Ghatotkach' fought for the 'Pandavas' in the battle of Kurukshetra.

Ancient history of this land makes it obvious that the place would have some significant holy places and temples. On of the most visited places is again a 'Pitha-sthans' located in Neelachala Parvat or Kamagiri a hilltop in Assam near the capital city Guwahati. As the legend goes and narrated in earlier sections 'Pitha-sthans'are locations where the severed body parts of 'Sati' fell. Atop Neelachal it was the reproductive organ of Goddess that fell to make it qualify to become a 'Pitha-sthans'for the Hindus and thus the Temple. But the temple as believed by many has a different story behind. There lived a beautiful Goddess by name of 'Kamakhya' with whom a demon named 'Narakasur' fell in love. He was so desperate to possess her that he would not let her stay in peace if she wouldn't marry her. But the 'Kamakhya' was unwilling and being a Goddess she would never marry a demon. But 'Narakasur was desperate. Finding no option the Goddess chalked out a plan of giving 'Narakasur' an impossible task, which he would fail and thus give up his intentions of marrying her. The Goddess told that she would marry him if in one night he could build a temple for her on the hilltop. 'Narakasur' agreed and on a decided evening started to build the temple. To her utter surprise he had almost completed the building by late night. The Goddess then played a trick. She sent a rooster to crow to announce the dawning of the day before the last stone could be laid. Thus the condition to which 'Narakasur' had agreed failed and the Goddess was relieved. It is said that the temple that stand today is the same one that 'Narakasur' had built then.

But a more realistic estimate is that around 1665 a 'Khasi' (inhabitant of neighboring state of Meghalaya) devotee rebuilt the temple over an ancient site that lay demolished by Muslim invaders. The large dome of the temple as seen from the outside does not give any impression that the actual deity is located in a cave inside a few steps underneath in a dark moist rocky cavity. Inside flows a natural stream of water There is a sculptured image of the sacred 'yoni' (genitals) of the Goddess signifying the holy passage that is kept covered with a colored cloth and decorated with flowers. It is perhaps for this reason that the festival of 'Ambubasi' is celebrated here as a cyclical annual event. It is believed that during a certain time the mother earth undergoes her menstrual period when for three days the temple is kept closed. These days are unfavorable days when no believer would do any thing that is auspicious like plantation or starting a new construction or signing of an agreement etc. On the fourth day when the temple is opened the festivity begins signaling the beginning of life afresh.

When I visited this temple for the first time in 2001 my host told to me that if the Goddess commends you and your visit she will call you thrice within a short span and whatever you may pray this time or next will not be heeded to. Only your prayer made on the third visit will be fulfilled. I only smiled at him thinking that neither shall the Goddess ever appear before me nor will I hear any clarion call. My smile, I am sure did not satisfy him. I returned home to Kolkata the day after and all was forgotten. A few months later I was assigned to report at Guwahati again to meet a very senior officer arriving from Delhi to review of our on-going projects there. I reached Guwahati. The next morning the same host offered to take me to the temple. I did not decline, as it was a matter of honoring the ruling deity of the place. A few months later when my wife and I were pondering over the idea of going on a holiday trip to some mountainous location far from the crowded metropolis we decided on Shillong. The closest airport being Guwahati we arrived there and decided to spend a day before taking the onward journey by road to Shillong. My host this time suggested that because my wife was visiting for the first time we pay a visit to the temple of Goddess 'Kamakhya' before we set off. We gladly complied. I later realised that the surmise of my host on my first did carry strength. Perhaps God was pleased at my presence during the first visit so all the three visits culminated in a shot span and all happened effortlessly as he had believed it would happen. Now when I look back I reaslize that my life had indeed under gone a change for the better and got elevated too ever since.

The river Brahmaputra that flows by the side of city of Guwahati and most of Assam is a holy one. It is considered that Brahmaputra is the son of Lord Brahma ('putra' meaning son) who is the creator of the entire universe. There is a legend to this. The son of Brahma was borne out of a disciple by the name of Amogha when she and her husband had been to Mansarovar (in Tibet) to worship Brahma. After his birth Brahmaputra was placed amidst the mountains where it formed a large water body called Brahmakund that always remained full to the brim and where the Gods and Goddesses used to swim. This captive water content later got released when a saint named 'Parashurama' slashed its embankment on the eastern side with the help of a magic axe that he used to carry. The gush of water began to flow through the gorges and over the cliff down the mountains at torrential speed washing away everything that came its way. Covering over 800 miles eastward and having descended about 5000 meters it enters the land that is now Arunachal Pradesh. The river that is called Tsangpo in Tibet is now named Siang and after a short while when a few other streams converge it takes the name Lohit. Here on the river begin to widen and upon entering Assam where it actually acquired the epic name Brahmaputra and attains deadly proportions. Brahmaputra is considered a male river. A river of sorrow that some compared to a monster. Every year it takes a heavy toll on the human and cattle life, boats capsize in its fury and floods devastate miles of land washing away villages and crop along its way. The entire stretch of Brahmaputra valley is inhabited by a civilization that narrates tales of epics and several tales of mythological upbringing. It is natural therefore that innumerable temples too have been set up in different parts of Assam. Not all are of equal importance in terms of their legendary significance but are worshipped with immense respect by those residing in the vicinity.

Asvakranta Temple at Guwahati, Vishnu Temple at Shibsagar, Barpeta Satra, the 16th century Hayagriva Mahadeva Temple at Hajo are some dedicated to Lord Vishnu. Similarly, Negrit Temple, Sib Dol Temple, at Shibsagar, Sukreswara Temple, Tamresvari Temple, Vasisht-Ashrama Temples are dedicated to Lord Shiva. Others like Hatimura Temple at Silghat, Kamakhya Temple at Guwahati, Devi Temple at Shibsagar, Ugra Tara Temple are dedicated to Mother Shakti and there are other temples like Navagraha Temple (temple of nine planets),

Sun Temple at Goalpara are dedicated to incarnations of God in planet forms. Many of these temples display immaculate craftsmanship of the bygone era. The exquisite murals, wooden engravings, sculptural work on stone, and paintings in many of these temples are very old and treasured pieces of art. Guwahati also has a Balaji Temple, built at the initiative of His Holiness Sri Jayendra Saraswati, Sankaracharya of Kanchi who felt the need of it for peace and prosperity of the North Eastern parts of the country. Spread over a three-acre land the temple complex is an extremely ambient place with lush green landscaped gardens surrounding a beautiful temple structure that houses the replica of the original deity of Lord Tirupati Balaji that is installed in Tirupatti in the state of Andhra Pradesh.

Between the Brahmaputra valley and Bangladesh to the south lies the hilly state of **MEGHALAYA** (abode of the clouds, 'megh' meaning cloud and 'alay' means abode of). Earlier, a part of the state of Assam, Meghalaya gained autonomous statehood in January 1972. The entire state is a land of pristine natural beauty with placid lakes, thick woods and exotic flora and fauna. Incidentally the wettest place on earth is located in this state in a place called Cherrapunji. Meghalaya has been the homeland of a number of tribes, namely the Garo, Khasi and Jaintia. Today Meghalaya is the home of the Tribals especially the Garo, Khasis, Jaintias, Cacharis and Mikirs, It is said that they colonized here prior to the Christian era. Their evolution came about through the process of migration by inhabitants from Chinese, Burmese, the Mon-Khmer and Austro-asiatic family. [26]. When I visited here I came

[26] Jenner, Philip N., Laurence Thompson and Stanley Starosta (eds.). 1976. *Mon-Khmer Studies*. Volumes I & II. Honolulu: University of Hawaii Press.

across only one place of worship and that is the Shillong Cathedral built by the British. There is also a Durga Temple that is 500 years old but I was told it was quite a distance away from the capital. The main occupation of the inhabitants like many other parts of the country has been farming and agriculture. Their primitive faith has rested on the God of harvest. The Wangala Festival usually celebrated in the Winter Season at Garo Hills is a proof of that expression to display their gratitude to the God for the splendid crop that it blesses them with each year. The Sun occupies a prominent place in their worship of the almighty. Most of the Garos in recent times have turned Christians but their religion and faith is based on nature worship and worship of the supernatural. As I have understood since there are no scriptural or other religious teachings or specified doctrine one can say the religion here is a combination of Hinduism and Pantheism(the belief that the material universe and God are one and that God is omni-present thus worship many deities). I regard such a practice as superior due to its distinct advantage in the modern world where the cord of harmony amongst different religions bruised and battered. Deep rooted religious beliefs give rise to secetionism and fanaticism as noticed in recent times particularly in India, leading to radicalism that culminates into animocity, unrest and chaos. The resultant events that follow as a result of such hatred are neither ascribed nor preached in any religion. In fact they are utterly anti religious and tend to retard the process of progression towards welfare. Meghalaya apart from the slight feeling of dissociation in the past has never been belligerent. They are peaceful, educated, hard working and extremely honest in their approach.

Extreme northeast of northeastern India is the state of **ARUNACHAL PRADESH**. It is highly mountainous and extremely treacherous terrain. For this reason my exploration always remained restricted. But whatever

I have explored I have discovered beauty beyond imagination. Most Indians have never visited this state or for that matter any state in the Northeast except Guwahati and are thus oblivious of the knowledge even basic information about these regions. Arunachal Pradesh is very thinly populated state. Only about a million people occupy a total area of about 90,000 Sq km. The population comprises of more than 20 tribal races that are broadly covered under three cultural groups namely Monpas, Singphos and Membas. The Monpas dwell in the Twang region and follow the Mahayana sect of Buddhism where as the Singphos who are of Thai and Burmese origin now live mostly in the eastern part of the state follow the Hinayana sect of Buddhism. The Membas and Khambas are also Buddhists who live mostly in the higher regions of Siang. The communities are progressive. They maintain decorated shrines in honor of the Gods, they celebrate festivals that coincide with agricultural cycles, and many of them are also pastoral. They rear and breed cattle particularly Yak and mountain Sheep. Located in Bomdila is a replica of Tsona Gontse Monastery of Tibet later consecrated by His Holiness, the 14th Dalai Lama. This monastry was built in 1965 by the 12th reincarnate of Tsona Gontse Rinpoche in 1965. But the largest of its kind in the country and 2nd largest in Asia is the Tawang Monastery situated at an altitude of 3200 meters above sea level. The large three storied building is fully equipped with a large hall, quartes for students, monks, Lamas and visitors. It has its source of water supply and school to educate the pupil. In the middle of main hall is a large statue of Lord Buddha and on the wall is a painting in Thankas art of the main deity of the monastery—Goddess Sri Devi ('Palden Lhamo'). It is said that the Thanka was painted with blood drawn from the nose of the 5th Dalai Lama. Palden Lhamo is a female deity who is comparable with the Hindu Goddess Kali. Both are Black, both garlanded with skull, flaming eyes, wears tiger-skin skirt, etc. She also has moon disc in her hair like Shiva. Legends also associate her with Saraswati and Ma Tara. It is also said and believed that she once lived in Sri Lanka where she was the queen of a monster king who used to sacrifice humans. She was against this practice and decided to run away from the kingdom as the king was incorrigible. The king on seeing her flee shot an arrow that hit the hind of the mule she was riding on. She promptly turned around and pulled out the arrow leaving a slit in the mule's haunch. This slit became the eye through which she could see the eternal world that Buddha has preached about. This splendorous monastery is also a Centre for Buddhist Cultural Studies.

A step southward will bring us into **NAGALAND**. This state is bordered by Burma (now called Myanmar), and the Indian states of Arunachal Pradesh and Assam. A state with a dozen tribal races those are immaculately artistic and skilled in handicraft and colorfully woven fabric. They are also good worriers and hunters. Display of their weapons could be seen in their motifs and adornments. When I visited the place there was animosity brewing for political reasons. My movement was restricted due to security reasons. So I could not explore much of the state. Most Nagas being dependent on agriculture their festivals tend to revolve around agriculture and harvesting. Although there is a Church in the capital Kohima, the Nagalnd people are believers not in any deity or religion rather their rituals are indicative of the faith they have in the Supernatural that is beyond the realms of religious conviction. In a village called Shangnyu located in the north of Nagaland is called where a large wooden monument could be seen. This, people believe was built by the angels who arrived from heaven. Some stones and pebbles that lie before it are reminderd of the ancestors who sacrificed their lives for the people. A similar memorial but more elaborately laid out is the one close to Kohima that is maintained by the Commonwealth War Graves Commission. Set up on the slopes of Garrison Hill on what was once the Bunglow and tennis court of Sir Charles Ridley Pawsey, the then Deputy Commissioner Naga Hills and where much of the battle was fought. It was in April-June 1944 that the British and Indian troops under the British regime countered the Japanese Army that had entered into India and were contemplating to overthrow the British from India. It was a turning point and also a decisive turn in World War II. Unable to sustain the onslought of the British army and starved of all supplies the Japanese were compelled to give in. Earl Louis Mountbatten then the Chief of Combined Operations of the British Army (Mountbatten was a British admiral and statesman. He was the last Viceroy and first Governor-General of independent India and First Sea Lord. Mountbatten was later assassinated in 1979 by the Provisional Irish Republican Army, who planted a bomb in his boat) had described the battle at Kohima as "probably one of the greatest battles in history" till then. The battle witnessed the death of about 5,000 soldiers on either side.

South of Nagaland and surrounded by Myanmar (Burma) in the east and south, Cachar (Assam) in the west and Mizoram state in the southwest is the state of **MANIPUR** (means a jeweled land). The inhabitants here are mostly Vaishnavites ie followers of the Vaishnav sect and disciples of Lord Krshna. The beautiful Govindajee Temple built by King's of Manipur with shrines of Krishna, Balaram and Jagannnath is an indication to that. It is said that sometime in the 15 Century AD a King Medingu Senbi Kiyamba ruled the state. He and the King Pong (Shan Kingdom, central Myanmar) were good friends. Pong during one of his visits to Mainipur presented Kiyamba with a Pheiya (sacred stone image of

God, which meant the Almighty and having divine power) and a little spear contained in a golden box. Kiyamba later constructed a temple structure in honor of his friend Pong and worshipped the stone gift with great respect. During that tme then there was no system of deity worship in the kingdom until a Brahmin (upper caste Hindu) arrived from Cachar (in Assam). On seeing the stone image (the gift of Pong) he said that in order to usher in good luck to the king and the kingdom this deity should be offered boiled rice mixed wth cow milk. The kingsmen complied with this prescription. Happenings that followed pleased the king and the Brahmin was appointed as the state priest. He declared that the stone image that was gifted to the King was actually the idol of 'Vishnu' and so did all believe it. People of the state then on became the worshippers of 'Vishnu' and the followers of the priests came to be known as Bishnupriya i.e. lover of Vishnu. Gopinath Temple is one of the biggest temples in Manipur and worshipped by many.

Manipur today is famous for its cultural richness and the exotic lifestyle. They have a very decent sense of application of colors on clothing, apparel and decorations. Manipuri dance is a classical dance form that depicts the life of Lord Krshna and his consorts. This is one of the most admired from of performing art recognized the world over. This dance form emanates from the devotion and worship of Krshna an incarnation of Lord Vishnu. Visiting Manipur yet remains my distant dream. Twice I attempted to visit the place but was debarred by my local companion who did not dare to take me out of fear of insurgency. All I learnt of this state is from conversation and reading books. I hope to be there once situation normalized.

The state of **MIZORAM** located between Bangladesh and Myanmar is a repository of natural splendour. It is a mountainous terrain engulfed with green vegetation and streams of water flowing through innumerable rivulets. I have traveled to some of the villages neighbouring the capital city of Aizol. What is fascinating about the place is the youthful character of the people of this tribal populace. Music and dance are the favourite past time for all ages alike. Having interacted with the youth I discovered that unlike most Indian states the literacy rate and the cognition level of youth is far superior and modernized. The Mizos also do not practice any form of discrimination on the basis of caste or cred as practiced in other parts of India. 'Tlawmngaihna" is an ethnic virtue that they follow which preaches kindness, cmpassion, selfless service to others and being hospitable to all. It is thus believed that no specific religion or deity worship ever came into practice there till the advent of the British in the late 19th century. Mizos in early times believed in one Supreme Being whom they called 'Pathian' and their religious rites were centered around wading away Ramhuai (evil spirits). Perhaps by the influece of the British missioneies that a system of education was introduced in the region and a value system got introduced. Mizo thereafter adopted Christianity as their religion. Though it is believed that like many other tribes in the northeastern states of India are decendents of th Mongoloid race that decended from China and entered through Burma there has been a belief spread by a few that some Mizos (and Manipuri) tribes are actually decendents of an Israeli tribe. Influenced by such preachers a section of the Mizos even adopted Judaism after being convinced that they were originally tribes of Israeli origin. Though no tace of any authentic evidence has been found but it is said there are some rituals amongst the two communities that have some commonality. The Chief Rabbi of Sephardic Jews in Israel had also authenticated this belief and even agreed to take away Mizos after their Jewis conversion in India. By the time several hundered Mizos had migrated there were several diplomatoic high drama amonghst the two nations after which the issue was finally laid to rest. Meanwhile the wishes of the several thousands who aspired to migrate to what they presumed was more prosperous a land oblivious of the fact that they would trade off their peaceful survival with a harrowing existence in Gaza and the West Bank, fortunately remained unfulfilled. Presently the four majour Churches in Mizoram are the Roman Catholic, Salvation Army, Presbyterian Church and the Mizoram Baptist Church. Aftre a long drawn spell of insurgency and militant upserge Mizoram became a State of Indian Federation on February 20, 1987. Today it is one of the most peaceful, enlightened and promoisnig amongst the states in the country. The people are mainly occupied in agriculture and forestry and all their festivals, Chapchar Kut or Spring Festival celebrated after clearing of jungle for 'jhum' operations, Mim Kut or Maize Festival or Pawl Kut the harvest festival is symbolic of their agricultural endeavors.

Adjacent to Mizoram is **TRIPURA** a state of the Indian territory that appears like a landmass jetting into Bangladesh like a bay. Not unlike the inhabitants of other northeastern states people are of Indo-Mongoloid origin. But the history of Tripura is somewhat different. It was under the dynastic rule of the Manikyas. The name Tripura perhaps came from the fact that the British called it the Hill Tippera. By the wishes of the then Monarch of Tripura the territory of the kingdom accede to the newly independent country of India in 1949. Later in 1972 it became a full fleged state of the republic of India. Tripura has had a gtreat influence of Bengal over it and this is reflected in its froms of religion and pattern of living. Today apart from its communist influence as in Bengal it also has a large Bengali speaking population and the influence of Bengali festivals and life style is widespread. Also the diversity of religious faith is evident of the civilisational transitions that the region must have undergone. Thought the majority of the population is Hindu, followers of Buddhism, Islam, Sikhism, and Christianity also exsist in large numbers.

Tripura again has one of the Hindu 'Pitha Sthans'. As described earlier the portion of the Devi's body that fell here was the right foot. The temple is well adorned but the exact dates of the formation of the deity (in fact there are two deities) could not be accertained even by the archiologists as I have gathered. But the temple that is said to have been constructed by Maharaja Dhanya Manikya in 1501 A.D, records of its maintenance and renovation by the royal kingdom are quite evident. Located on a hillock near Udaipur, the earstwhile capital of the Manikya kingdom, at a distance of about sixty kilometers from the capital city of Agartala the temple is called the 'Tripur Sundari Temple' housing the image of 'Choti Maa' (younger mother). Here the idol Maa Kali made out of 'reddish black Kasti pathar' (black granite) is worshipped here in 'Soroshi' form. (As is enshrined in the Purana, Soroshi is one of the ten Mahavidya—divine knowledge, that Maa sati was equipped with). On the east side of the temple is a large lake called 'Kalyan Sagar' where it is considered sacred to feed the fish. Thus no fishing activity takes place here. But one of the most unique places of worship in Tripura is the Chaturdasha Devata Temple where the heads of fourteen Gods and Godessess are aligned together and are brought out in the open for worship during the occasion of the seven-day festival called 'Kharchi Puja' (earth festival in recognition of the enourmous resouce that mother earth gives to mankind).

Located near the old Royal palace of Maharaja Govinda Manikya beside the river Gomti in Udaipur is the Bhubaneshwari Temple that was constructed during 1660-1675 A.D and now a major tourist attraction. Another famous Kali Temple is situated beside the Kamala

Sagar Lake situated about thirty Kilometers away from Agartala. This is a sacred temple where large number of dvotees congragate during the annual celebrations. It is the holi temple of Godessess Kali and is thus also called the 'Kali Bari' (meaning house of the Kali). All these temples are located in the vicinity of of Udaipur, which is why perhaps the place had once become the capital. Reminiscance of of old Vishnu and Shiva temples and deities dating back about 500 years excavated later could also be found in Udaipur. Within the city of Agartala the present capital the most important and prominent of all is the Benu Bon Bihari a Buddhist temple that hoses a beautiful metal statue of Lord Buddha.

If one could take a few kilometers walk westward through Bangladesh then one would reach back to the main land of India and enter West Bengal. West Bengal and Bangladesh were one and the same when it was called Bengal. The region was large and territory of Bengal included the present day West Bengal, Bangladesh, Sikkim, Assam, Tripura, large parts of Bihar, Orissa and Madhya Pradesh. The first partition of Bengal was carried out in 1905 during the time of Lord Curzon when a new province called East Bengal was carved out and some parts of Hundu populated regions on the west of Bengal were swaped between Bengal and Central Province (now called Madhya Pradesh). During the 19th century Bengal witnessed a sudden spurt of resurgence, with the birth of several creative intellectuals, reformers, scientists, writes all of whom contributing towards what could be described as the Bengal Renaissance. In fact it all started with Raja Ram Mohan Roy in late 1700. This resurgence also contributed to the awakening of the entire subcontinent and the shaping of modern India and its struggle for freedom. The images of these intellectuals are still held in high esteem all across India particularly in Bengal and are highly regarded not only for their contribution in their respective fields but also for the road map of idealism that they had charted for the ignorant and oppressed Indians. Be they the spiritual and social exponents like Vivekananda and lswarchandra Vidyasagar, Ram Mohan Roy or powerful writers like Rabindranath Tagore, Madhusudan Dutta, Bankimchandra Chatterjee and others or persons of artistic brilliance like Nandlal Bose Abanindranath Tagore, Gaganendranath Tagore, Jamini Roy and others they all contributed towards bringing about a transition from the 'medieval' to the 'modern'. For this reason they are remembered like semi-Gods and worshipped with great reverence for their exceptional virtuosity.

From the south of Bengal begins the 14,000 Km long coastline of India and the state next to Bengal along this coastline is the ancient land of **ORISSA**. On this land is inscribed an anthology of very rich and significant historical happenings. From the days of the Mahabharata, the rule of the Nanda Kings in the pre Christian era, the Mauryas till the 1st century and later the Marathas in the 5th century to the visit of Huen tsang in 630 AD Orissa remained a place of pilgriamage from the very ancient times. It was in 1110 AD during the rule of Somavamsis several temples of worship were built. King Mahasivagupta of the Somavansi is also believed to have constructed a cluster of 38 temples for Lord Jagannath at Puri. But it is gathered that the main temple of Lord Jagannath at Puri was actually constructed by Raja Ananta Varman Chodaganga Dev of the Ganga dynaty in 12th century A.D. (history records that king Yayati Kesari I of Kesari dynasty built the original structure of the Jagannath Temple at Puri in 795 AD. Later after about 450 years this was rebuilt and the structure is altogether different from the old one) Jagannath as the Name suggests ('Jagat' meaning Universe and 'Nath' means the Guardian) is considered the Lord of the Universe and also comprises as one of the 'Dhams' of the 'Char Dhams' (four notified / sanctified places of pilgrimage) for the Hindus. As far as the Hindu legends go, a visit to all these four places leads one to salvation. I have not been able to decisively trace the origins of this Char Dham (concept) but grouped together by the great 8th century reformer and philosopher Shankaracharya (Adi Sankara), into the archetypal All-India pilgrimage circuit to four cardinal points of the subcontinent were four important temples—Puri, Rameshwaram, Dwarka, and Badrinath. After the Ganga reign came the Suryavamsi Gajapati rulers who were vaisnavits (Believers of Vishnu) had great influence of Lord Chaitanya Mahaprabhu and for all these reason several Jagannath temples were build across the kingdom in different places. Thereafter with the advent of the Mughals there was more chaos than orderliness and growth. The Marathas invaded and then came the British rule in the late 18th century.

The Jagannath temple today occupies one of the most important pilgrimage centers for all Indians. It is said that Buddhists, Jains, Christians and even Muslims had all shown faith in this deity. So much so that a Muslim named Salabega consecrated his life to the devotion of Jagannath. In his memory a tomb still stands on the path of the Chariot-festival bearing testimony to his devoutness. It is a location of supreme religious fusion. Jagannath is also denoted as 'Purushottam' (meaning superlative amongst all beings). It is perhaps from this nomanclature that the place got its name Puri. Inside the temple are the idols of Jagannath (Krishna personified. Here the deity's hands are missing)—Balabhadra and Subhadra—(Balabhadra and Subhadra are the brother and sister respectively of Jagannath).

The legend behind the built up of this pilgrimage is that Deva Dharma (designated God in-charge of the underlying orderliness of nature and all lives in the universe. It is said that he was born out of the right breast of Brahma and father of Yudhisthir of Mahabharata. For this reason Yudishthir is also called 'Dharma Putra' or son of Dharma) once discovered the image of Jagannath in the form of a brilliant jewel stone at the foot of a sacred fig tree. The radiance of the stone image was so dazzling that he had it buried in the earth. A king by the name of Viswabasu (the son of Jara) worshiped 'Nilamadhab' (the idol of Krshna that was actually the same image of Lord Jagannath) in privacy. Indradyumna, the king of Malwa some how sensed the presence of this idol and wished to liberate the idol from captive worship and have it installed in a public temple where all could visit and worship. Then followed a sequence of several events over the ages after which the God 'Nilamadhab' himself was convinced that Indradyumna would fulfil His wishes. Thus the God decided to disappear and so he disappeared. But the devotion of His disciple Indradyumna compelled the God to appear in his dream and disclose that He would come at the mouth of the river Banki in the form of a log of wood. Indradumna then set off for Puri with his soldiers and convoy of elephants and finally succeeded in locating the sacred log. But to his utter dismay he was not able to pull out the log from the stream even with the strength of all the men and elephants that he had. Seeing his pitiable condition Lord Jagannath appeared before him again in his dream and said that his show of strength and rigor in picking up the log would not work. He has to show tenderness and humility in carrying the log to its rightful place. So did it happen and the log could thus be carried easily to the temple. Then came the most difficult of all challenges, that of carving the idol out of the wood. Many artisans came and went but their chisle could not chip even a bit of the wooden log. Then came an old frail and unassuming man who offered to do the task. Left with no option the king Indradyumna and queen Gundicha agreed. But this old man laid down a condition that for 21 days the doors of the room where he would work must remain closed and the door shall not be opened for any reason befor the period of 21 days was over. The king agreed but wondered how this was possible to survive for days without food, water and air. After fourteen days had passed the queen was unable to bear and from the scilence she assumed that the old man must have died. They broke the door open and were awe struck. The old man was not there but the image was carved though part completed. It was believed that the old man was God himself who appeared in human form to create the image He wished peoploe to worship. None the less God was pleased with the performance of king so far and again appeared before him to ask for a wish. The king in his humbleness asked for a simple wish and that was to make his creation of the temple a heritage site that would never become a private property and be visited by people at all time through the ages. It was perhaps this wishfulfilment that everyday visitors from all across the country and abroad pour in every day to offer their prayers and take away the sacred 'Prasadum' (God's blessed food) that gets disseminated to far off places. The prasadum is very filling and has always been captivating and sought after for its immaculate flavour, which has remained the same through the decades. This temple incidentally has one of the largest kitchens in the world where this prasad is cooked. The kitchen is capable of cooking food sufficient to fill a hundred thousand stomachs on any day. Also dry prasad is prepared that lasts for weeks and which the pilgrims carry to far away places to their home for distribution to friends and neighbours.

Puri being a coastal town and having a lovely climate it has become a place of tourist arrtaction as well. People from all across the globe and the country visit this place for different reasons. People from neighbouring Bengal particularly frequent this place and stay here for days together to enjoy the calmness and tranquil surroundings. Pato-chitra paintings and the Odessy dance forms have emanated from the culture and devotion of this place and have made this place even more popular and fascinating. Another attraction of the temple is an annual ritual called the 'Ratha Yatra' (or the 'charriot journey') Also popularly known as the car festival when the deities are taken out of the temple for a seven-day excursion on a chariot to a place nearby Gundecha temple that symbolises Lord's maternal aunts place.

The Chariot festival in Puri is preceeded by a huge preparation that includes the construction of three wooden chariots from the large tree trunk that are brought from the forest. After the sixteen-wheel chariot is completed it would reach a height of nearly fifty-feet and weigh over sixty-five tons. These chariots and the respective canopies would then be painted in accordance with the colors that are specified for each deity—red and yellow for Lord Jagannatha, green and red for his brother Lord Balarama and for sister Subhadra its red and black. Similarly, the diety of Jagannatha is painted black representing faultlessness, white color of Balarama denotes enlightenment, and goodness is represented by color yellow of Subhadra. It is very peculiar to imagine that the chariot of Jagannath that is pulled by thousands of devotees at times gets stopped and would not move however amount of force is applied. The worshippers and sometimes the Minister would have to come and pray for penance after which the chariot would again begin to roll. This chariot is used only once for the festival that lasts seven to eight days after which it is abandoned. But quite sensibly the chariot is put to another good use. The chariot is dismanteled and broken down and the wood is used as fuel for the large kitchen which would have used wood anyway. It is said that he who will pull the rope of the chariot and broom the road over which the chariot will pass will be blessed by the Lord and the Lord will be with him to help him attain victory in his endeavours in life. It is even believed that the physical potency of Jagannath could liberate the blessed from the shackles of the cycle of life and birth. But sweeping or brooming the floor has gone out of pratice perhaps a hundred years ago. Now-a-days the king (for name sake) inaugurates the ceremony along with other senior priests'—one of the ritual being a symbolic dusting of the chariot with a golden broom. The discontinuance of brooming the road also has an interesting tale behind. Once upon a time when Purusottama Dev the then king of Puri was to get married to 'Padmavati' the daughter of Maharaja Sallwo Narasingha of Kanchi he invited Sallwo Narasingha to attend the famous Ratha Yatra festival. The Maharaja of Kanchi being preoccupied at that time depiuted one of his Ministers to attend the festival on his behalf. When he reached the temple that morning of the chariot journey he found that Purusottama Dev was performing the menial job of brooming and sweeping the road. After he returned to his kingdom he conveyed this to the Maharaja of Kanchi who immediately called-off the marriage. Hearing this Purusottama Dev got furious and decided to wage a war against the Maharaja and rob his daughter away from him. He gathered his troops and set of for the battle. Unfortunately the king of Puri got badly defeated. While on his return he took shelter in a cottage that belonged to one of the devotees of Lord Jagannath. The devotee on hearing this inferred that his defeat was inevitable, as he had not taken the permission and consent of the Lord before he went for the battle. The king realizing his mistake rushed to the temple and cried before the Lord asking Him to forgive and grant him relief from the grief of this shameful defeat. That night the Lord appeared before him and directed him to prepare his army once again for the battle with the Maharaja of Kanchi when he would find himself in accompaniment of Jagannath and brother Balarama. The King prepared himself again but was in doubt as to whether the Lords will actually be with him or whether this was just a illusionary psychosis that was instigating him towards further disgrace. Amongst the Kings army went two of his soldiers, one riding a black horse and another on a white horse. But they were not noticed by anyone. Near Chilka Lake (still existes a few miles away from Puri) as the soldiers rested to have some food these two soldiers went to a nearby stall to buy some milk porridge. After consuming the milk porridge when the stall owner asked for money they said they did not have any. So the soldiers handed over a precious jewel ring and said she could exchange this for money from the King. The lady who was named Manika then went to the King and handing over the ring asked for payment for the milk porridge that the soldiers had. The King on seeing the ring was astonished. The ring that the lady gave her was 'Ratnamudrika' ring worn by Lord Jagannatha. The King was overwhelmed and instead of paying her for the milk porridge bequeathed the entire village in her name. (the village named Manikapatna still exists in the vicinity). The King then marched with confidence and without much effort broke through the fortified fortress of the King Sallwo the Maharaja of Kanchi and took his daughter 'Padmavati' away. Though Purusottama Dev brought the dame to Puri he still wouldn't marry her as his revengeful heart still fumed with fury. Back in his kingdom he declared that that the princes though beloved to him would now be married to a sweeper but a respectable one so that the insult that her father inflicted on him could be settled. Some time later when the Ratha Yatra was about to take place again Purusottama Dev took to his broom as usual and began to swep the floor. The Nobels who gathered around watched him perform the sacred ritual and said that he himself now seemed to be the most respectable sweeper of all and was indeed the best match for the princes. Succumbing to the wishes of his well wiseres Purusottama Dev married Padmavati. It is said that their child later became Maharaja Prataparudra, a very pious king who is said to have played a central role in Sri Chaitanya Mahaprabhu's life.

There is also a consecrated insinuation into the performance of the Ratha-Yatra. It is said that the Ratha Yatra actually personifies the situation when Lord Krshna while living in Dwarka decided to come over to Vrindavan to satisfy his thirst of love for the residents to whom he is so beloved and particularly to Radha his consort. He thus went to Kuruksetra accompanied by his brother Balarama and sister Subhadra. There he met the folks of Vrindavana and also his beloved Radha. Mesmerized by this reunion he slithered into a state of 'Mahabhava' (meaning the supreme echelon of sensitivity for love) "In that state, His eyes dilated like fully bloomed lotuses, and His hands and legs retreated into His body. In this way, the form of Lord Jagannatha is called 'Radha-viraha-vidhura', the separation from Radharani, and also 'Mahabhava-prakasha', the manifestation of 'Mahabhava' for Radharani"—Stephen Knapp [http://www.stephen-knapp.com /rathayatra_festival_at_jagannath_puri.htm]. Thus the both hands of Lord Jagannath in the deity that is installed in the temple at Puri are also missing.

A little away from the town of Jagannath Puri is a temple of Sakshi Gopal ('Sakshi' meaning witness and Gopal is a synonym for Krshna). It is a deity replicate of the Lord in Vrindavan that had once become manifest on seeing the plight of his devotee. He appeared to offer witness in support of the cause of righteousness that his devotee stood for. The legend that passed down the ages is a story of two Brahmins (Brahmin in Hindu culture is a caste of highest order who are generally agents/performers of sacred rituals for and on behalf of the other casts). The two Brahmins from Rajahmundri (a town on the banks river Godavari in what is now the neighbouring state of Andhra Pradesh) set off on pilgrimage to various religious sites in northern Inda. Of the two one was a young lad and the other elderly and affluent. As a matter of courtesy the young lad showed obedience and affection to the elderly partner and helped him immensely during their painstaking entourage. The elder one pampered the young and kept him in good humour to ensure that he did not desert him and made him do all the arduous tasks all the way. On their visit to the temple in Vrindavan they were mesmerized by the magnificence and the glory of the deity of Gopal. Overwhelmed by the site and overtly satisfied the elder Brahmin committed to the lad that he would give his daughter to him in marriage. This created a further bondage for the young one and extracted more service from the young one till they reached back home. Then when time came for the elderly to fulfill his commitment he realised that his family was not agreeable to this proposal as the groom he had chosen was a poor guy and was not as respectable to match their clan. So he said to the young boy that while I did make the commtment then, 'I had put a caveat to it that perhaps you did not register'. It was that 'I woud give my daughter to you in marriage only if Gopala of Vrindavan stood as witness'. On hearing this, the young lad was crest fallen and bewildered. He had no answer to this as he saw his dreams and wishes shrinking and fade into oblivion. It then came to his mind that as this commitment was made before the Lord at Vrindavan he should visit that temple again and narrate his plight to the Lord to see if he could give him some relief. So he did. Praying before the Lord he saw the lord appear before him saying not to worry, He would accompany him to the place where where he needed Gopal to present himself as witness. But Gopal's only condition was that he would walk behing the lad and the lad would never look back at him during any point in the journey. If he did that would be the place from where on Gopal would not proceed any further. As he walked he heard the string-bells of Gopal following him. Each day he would wait to cook rice for the Lord and himself as they kept doing the journey. Then one day he felt the sound of the bells fade. Suspecting that the Lord was withdrawing he got too curious and wanted to be sure and so he turned back. But to his utter surprise he found that the Lord was as close as he could imagine. The Lord looked with a smiling face at him as he got reminded of breaching his vow. The Lord would now move no further. The Young boy rushed to the neighbouring and called all people to show them the Lord and told everyone of the story behind. This happening now compelled the brhamin to surrender and the marriage took place as he had conditioned before the Lord as a witness. The Lord Gopal of Vrindavan thus fulfilled the young boy's wishes and saved him from the humiliation. It is believed the temple of Sakshi Gopal was then built to remind people that the Lord is where the innocence of truth exists. The present temple was built sometime in the 19th century inside which the idol of Sakshi Gopal depicting Lord Krishna with a flute and Radha standing on his left is worshipped.

The attraction of travelers to Puri is for many reasons. There are several places of tourist interest like one at Chilka, which is the lagest salt-water lagoon in Asia. Spread over an area of a thousand kilometers it is a resting place for a large variety of migratory birds. It is also a wonderful place for adventure and past time. Amidst the lake there are a few islands. On one of them is a temple dedicated to Goddess Kali.

Similarly, there is another seaside attraction at Konarak where the famous Sun-Temple is situated. Though this is called a temple but there is no deity inside or any worship conducted. It is actually a monument that was constructed sometime in the 13th century by Raja Narasingha Dev-I of the Ganga Dynasty and stands as a memorial of the supremacy that he enjoyed during his time and to celebrate his victory over the Muslims. Later however, an envoy of the Mughal emperor Jahangir desecrated the structure. The monument is dedicated to the Sun God—thus the name Konarak, ('kona' means corner and 'Arka' meaning the Sun). Although the temple was bult later but the significance of the place as an abode of the Sun is also found in the Puranas and other religious texts where the existence of a sun temple is stated. It is also said that the Sun who is also believed to be the healer of all skin desease has its powerful influence of cure here and that 'Sambha' (the son of Krshna) who was cured of leprosy here by Surya (meaning the Sun).

Whatever be the history this temple is a piece of mgnificent archtecture. The design and symbolism is a testimony of the immaculate skill of the sculptures of that era. It is rightly said that monuments is actually poerty on stone. Nobel Lauriet and poet Rabindra Nath Tagore one said that the language on stone here has surpassed the language of humans. From the pristine chisel work that embellishes the large chariot wheels to the erotic enunciation that are carved out on stone. It is a display of profound expression. It portrays a remarkable carnival of passionate lust and full-blooded exhilaration in enjoyment of the supreme pleasure that can arouse between woman and man. The reasons for the prsence of these erotic elements in the temple are not known. Some say it is to convey the third 'purushartha' (objects of life) of 'Kama' (others being Dahrma, Artha and Moksha) while other believe it relates to Upanishadic doctrine of delight as experience through unification of 'Atma' (the soul) with the 'Brahma' (the creater of all beings). Some also are of the opinion that such sculpture would attract people to this place. But I would like to believe that this is basic education that teaches men and women of the natural and divine phenomenon of making love, which the orthodox societies like ours are starved of and also debarred from being well informed about. Whatever be the reason I honor the artisans who sculptured the temple to such high degree of perfection.

The road from Puri to Bubaneshwar passes through the mountain of Dhauli called Dhaulgiri ('giri' denotes mountain) that is witness to the butchery and bloodshed of the Kalinga war. It was in the 3rd century BC when King Ashoka in his persuit to expand the great Mayrian empire (that he had inherited from Chandragupta Maurya his grand father and Bindusar his father) to the south of the country when he encountered the brave army of the Kalinga kingdom. This led to a gruesome battle and the young king Ashoka emerged victorious. But on witnessing the horrific bloodshed and calamity caused by the war he was deeply distressed. He underwent a psychic transformation and derelicted war for the rest of his life. He laid down the weapons of violence and adopted a life of Ahimsa (non-violence) in the form of Buddhism. To immortalize this event and in remembrance of the realization of the supremacy of non-violence the Japanese Buddhists have lately built a majestic temple called Shanti Stupa (peace pagoda) here on a hill top at Dhauli. This monument now visited by tourists across the world stands as a testimony to the wisdom of lasting peace and happiness.

Other attractions on the way are the 2nd and 3rd century BC Spartan caves of Udayagiri ('uday' signifys sunrise, 'giri' is mountain) and Khandagiri ('khanda' means fallen to pieces) built under the rule of Jain king Kharavela of the Kalinga dynasty. These are evident of the Jain and Buddist influence in the region during that time.

A slight detour from the Puri-Bhubaneshwar road is a unique temple of 'Chattris Yogini' (Chattris means

figure 36. Yogini is a supernatural feminie being possessing cosmic energy who have manifested out of the Goddess Durga) This 9th century circular roofless (hypaethral) temple also called 'Durga paatha' meaning the sanctified place of Godess Durga, at Hirapur is said to have been built by Queen Hiradevi of Brahma Dynasty to glorify the rare invincible force of feminine energy. The idols here are a depiction of the sixty-four Yogini who are not only subservient to Durga but are divine un-detachable forms of the Great Goddess herself. Durga as the chief Yogini is placed in the core of this legion and represents the epitome of an enlightened energy called 'Shakti' (meaning Power). It is this sacred force that was convened by the mightiest of Gods to annihilate the indestructible demon 'Raktabeeja' or 'Mahisasur' who terrorized all Gods and threatened to destroy the Heaven. There are three other similar yogini temples—one at Titilagarh in Bolangir district of Orssa itself and the other two in Khajuraho and Jabalpur in Madhya Pradesh.

On reaching Bhubaneshwar one can easily see the 120 feet lofty conical dome of the hallowed Lingaraja Temple from a distance. Lingaraj temple is devoted to Lord Shiva (Lingaraj means 'the supreme amongst the of Lingas', the icon of Lord Shiva worship). Bhubaneshwar is a land of temples and sacred legends. It is believed that over 7000 temples were built in this city since the 800 BC. Some of these temples still remain while many have perished with time. Amongst them all the most prominent and the most visited one is the 'Lingaraj Temple', which was completed in the 10th century. The construction statred in the 7th century by Yayati Keshari III of the Keshari dynasty king and later said to have been completed by his son Lalatendu Keshari. Incidentally Yayati Keshari III was also responsible in making Bhubaneshwar the capital of his kingdom that was later shifting to Cuttak by Nripati Kesari in the 10th century. The large temple premises estimated to be around 250,000 sq feet comprises of about 150 other temple structures like the nata mandir and the bhog mandir that houses the various other deities. The temple is equally devoted to Lord Vishnu as evident from the worship of the Saligramam idol. Also at the main gate one can see the image of Vishnu's Chakra (rotating wheel ammunition) along with the trishul (spear) of Lord Shiva . . . Amongst the other temples in Bhubaneshwar the oldest is the Parasurameswara temple built about 150 years before the Jagannath temple was completed. It is believed that Parvati (consort of Shiva) had visited this place at the instance of Shiva to whom this was a resort superior to Banaras. The Bindu Sagar Lake situated in the middle of the city was said to have been created by Lord Shiva to quentch the thirst of Parvati when she felt thirsty during the entourage. Once in a year during 'Rath Yatra' the deity of Lingaraj temple is carried to the Jala-mandir (jal means water and mandir means temple) situated in this lake for bathing and worship.

Other important temple sites in Bhubaneshwar are Mukteshwar temple, Parashurameshvara Temple, Siddeswara Temple, Vaital Deol Temple, Raj Rani Temple, Chandi Temple all of which are quite ancient and in good shape still. They also display excellent architechture and wonderful carvings that are worth the visit. These temples are dedicated mostly to the family of of Lord Shiva, with well carves figures of Ganesha, Kartikeya, Durga, Kali and others in thier pricints. The Jami Masjid, the Shahi Mosque and the mazar of Hazrat Ali Bukhari are places of Muslim worship. It is believed that Muslim settlers in Orissa are mostly decendents of soldiers of the invadors' side who had come here to battle. There are also muslim migrants from Bangladesh and Bengal. The Baptist Church and the Anglican Church, Roman Catholic at Cuttack are evident of the British rule and the influence of Christian culture during those times. The Sikh Gurudwara

Guru Nanak Datan Sahib on the bank of the Mahanadi is a pious place for tranquil communion with the almighty.

Adjoining the state of Orissa is a picturesque forest belt on the west that is inhabited with a large tribal population. This territory until recently formed a part of Madhya Pradesh that was earlier known as Central Province. In November 2000 this region was cut out to form the state of Chattisgarh. Although the name **CHATTISGARDH** sounds like tirty-six Forts ('chattis' means thirty-six and 'garh' meaning fort) but as I could not relate this to any such historical presence or events I doubted whether the name really got derived from that. After some exploration the closest that I could get to is derived from the term 'Chedi' of the Kalchuri dynasty who established their kingdom in Madhya Pradesh during 10th-12th century AD. This reference is also found in the local government publications. These publications also have included another probability found in the British Chronicle. According to this the name is derived from 'chattis-ghar (here ghar means house i.e., 36 houses). These 36 houses relate to some 36 families who settled here after Emperor Jarasandha drove them out from his kindom. Emperor Jarasandha ruled over 'Magadh' now in Bihar.

This tribal populace of Chattisgarh has its unique and glorious way of giving expression to their devotion and gratitude to the almighty. Most interesting and touching aspect of the innumerable festivals held here are a reflection of their innocence and honesty to the giver of good things in life. Thus the festivals celebrated here are in recognition of the nature's kindness. Like the festival of 'Charta' is the festival of harvest, when cereial from every household is collected and cooked together near a riverside like picnic. Similarly, 'Navakhana' is celebrated to celebrate the harvest of rice. 'Pola' festival is in adulation of the bulls that contribute in the process of cultivation. 'Hareli' is a festival dedicated to the almighty for assuring a good crop.

In worship of the Mother Earth are the festivals of 'Surhul' and 'Mati Puja'. Similarly there are various colorful festivals that are celebrated with much pomp and ferver. There are thus several related temples of worship. But the two-mportant places of worship are the Mahamaya Temple at Bilaspur and the 1100 AD Bhoramdeo temple situated 135 kms from the capital city of Raipur.

Mahamaya Temple is dedicated to Goddess Mahamaya who according to the Hindu mythology is Mother Goddess, 'Kali' also denoted as 'Maha-Kali'. She is considered as the Giver of Perception. The Woman's Encyclopedia of Myths and Secrets, 1986 associates "Virgin Kali as the creatress of earthly appearances, i.e., all things made of matter and perceptible to the senses. She also gave birth to the Enlightened One, Buddha. The same Goddess, called 'Maia' by the Greeks, was the virgin mother to Hermes the Enlightened One, who had as many reincarnations as the Buddha. Sometimes Maia's partner was Volcanus (Greek Hephaestus, the divine smith and fire-god). This was another mythic mating of male fire and female water. Hindus said Agni the fire-god was the consort of Kali-Maya, though he was periodically swallowed up and "quenched" by her. According to the Tantric phrase, the Goddess quenched a blazing lingam in her yoni". "Maya's name appears also in Greco-Roman (or, Classical) mythology. There was extensive commercial contact between India and the Mediterranean lands long before the time of Alexander of Macedon (ca. 350 BCE.) However, whether the Greek name had a different origin or not, is not as relevant as the fact that there, Maya or Maia was an earth goddess. Maia is usually explained as meaning Maker, for she is seen as the cause of the spring season when all that we have seen die away before winter now springs back to life. Therefore we have come to use her name to designate (in the northern hemisphere) May, the month of flowers—the time of rebirth."

The temple at Bilaspur has a statue of Mahamaya in Mahishasur Mardini (slayer of the ferocious buffalo devil) form and just behind is an idol of Goddess Saraswati. Though the temple is believed to have been built around 12th century AD, it is held that Kalinga king Ratna Dev performed the first prayer and offering cremony of Devi at this place in 1050 AD. Other deities of Mahakali, Bhadrakali, Surya Dev, Lord Vishnu, Lord Hanuman, Bhairav and Lord Shiva feature along the precincts. These and several other temple structures around that are even older are surely of rich historical and archeological value.

The 1100 AD Bhoramdeo temple near Raipur is a Shva Temple where in a sacred Linga is worshiped. This temple has resemblance the Sun temple at Konarak. People also relate it to the Khajuraho temple for the erotic sculptures carved on its outer walls. The different erotic postures of 'asanas' as depicted in 'Kama-Sutra' that epitomizes eternal love could also be seen carved on the stone-walls of the "Madwa Mahal" near the Bhoramdeo temple.

Thus a few hundred kilometers along the coast of the Bay of Bengal beginings a whole new region called south India starting with **ANDHRA PRADESH** on the east coast. Andhra Pradesh has an eventful history and the populace represents a diverse socio-cultural leniage. It is said that Lord Rama during his days in exile spent most of his days in what is now the state of Andhra Pradesh. History also mentions of the visit and preachings by Lord Buddha in Amaravati. In 300 BC the Greek traveler Megasthenes traveled as an emissary to the court of Chandra Gupta Maurya. From 100 AD the Pallavas, Kalingas, Ikshvaku, Golkondas, Reddys ruled during different times the different parts the land that is now Andhra. After 600AD during the rule of the Chalukyas several social and literary advancements happened. It is during this time that Telegu language originated and came into officaial usage. With the fall of the Kakatiya dynasty in the mid-14h century came the Muslim rulers. The colonial era began in 1753 with the control of the French and later in 1792 the British captured control over the entire territory and established its supreme rule here. The formation of the State of Andhra Pradesh began in 1953. In 1956 with the inclusion of Telengana region a composite Telegu speaking state was established with Hydrabad as its capital. The state preserves a large collection of historical tombs and places of revere. They depict the legacy of the diverse religious beliefs of its population that today lives in love and secular harmony.

One of the largest Mosques of the country the Mecca Masjid situated here in Hyderabad near the famous Charminar monument. It reminds us of the Mosque at Mecca. It has a capacity to accommodate about ten thousand worshiper. This Mosque was built during the times Aurangazeb in 1687. It is said that a hair strand of the Prophet Mohammed is preserved here.

Incidentally, the intricately carved graceful structure Char-minar (meaning four-minarets) built by Sultan Mohammed Quli Qutub Shah the founder of Hyderabad city in 1591 in honour of his wife Bhagmati is the popular landmark of the Capital.

The oldest mosque in Hyderabad is the Jama Mazjid, built in 1597 by Quli Qutub Shah. All these mosques are exquisitely built. The care and attention in its construction is evident from its architchture, planning and ornamentation. Other such places of pilgrimage are Deval Masjid built by Mohammad Bin Tughlaq, the Toli Masjid and the Chote Hazrat Ki Dargah Masjid constructed in the honor of Hazrat Ali, who was the son in law of prophet Muhammed. About 700 kms south of the capital city of Hyderabad (about 130 kms from Chennai) in the southern district of Chittoor is situated the worlds most visited deity of Lord Venkatapati Balaji residing in the famous temple in Tirumala. This temple is also considered as the richest among all temples in the country. Most Hindus throughout the world have either visited or aspire to visit this temple for its great power to give solace as well as fulfil the wishes of its real devotees. The Lord is again visited when the wishes are fulfilled. In fact as believed amongst the Hindus the Lord Himself desires and charts-out ones visit without his ever coming to know of it. Without his wishes the visit no aspirant can ever reach here and his wishes will ever remain a distant dream. I had visited south India several times particularly Chennai, which is so close. But as interpreted by many, my first visit was destined to take place sometime in 2002. And so did it happen. Perhaps by His grace the queue that sometimes takes hours or even days to reach the main deity took us only a couple of hours and we could return to Tirupati (at the foot of the Tirumala hills) the same night. The deity is so admired that the devotees surrender a large part of their wealth and earnings to the Lord believing that all of it has been gained by the blessings of the Lord and is part of the wishfulfilment granted by the Lord—hence the same is surrendered back to him. The Lord in turn gives him more wealth and prosperity. This temple, which is situated on the Venkatachala hill, could be reached from Tirupati by road. The temple is here from time immemorial and no authentic record of its history or any legend describing its coming into being could be found. But mention is said to be there in the Vedas and Purana. Kings of the The Pallavas of Kancheepuram (9th century AD), the Cholas of Thanjavur (a century later), the Pandyas of Madurai, and the kings and chieftains of Vijayanagar (14th-15th century AD) were all devotees of the Lord at the Tirumala Venkateswara Temple.

Sri Kalahasthi temple located 35 Kms from Tirupati along side the shores of river Suvarnamukhi is one of the very auspicious Siva temples in south India. It is believed that while creating the Kailash (in Tibet) a piece of Brahma's composite fell on the earth like an asteroid. This place later came to be known as the Dakshin Kailash (meaning Kailash of the south) and subsequently the Srikalahasti. Srikalahasti is named after the three patriot devotees of Shiva namely Sri (spider), Kala (serpant) and Hasti (elephant) where Lord Siva the merciful three eyed Lord manifests in the form of Vayu linga (representing the wind or 'vayu' element. (The five elements in Hindu scheme are called panchabhoot). Shiva as embodiment of these panchabhoot is represented in respective temples in the south. The other four are 'Agni (or fire located at Tiruvannamalai, Prithvi, (earth located at Kanchipuram) Jal (water located at Thiruvanikkaval), and Aakaash (space located at Chidambaram) respectively. This temple of which reference are said to be available in the Siva-puranam is believed to have actually been built during the Pallavas some time between the 7th and the 8th century. The white holy lingum in the temple is actually implies 'swayambhu' ie self made and not created by human hands. The belief of 'vayu' element that represents wind energy is corroborated by the flicker of the lamps inside in absence of any blowing wind.

There are several other important temples in Andhra Pradesh. To name a few, Simhachalam temple located near the town of Vishakhapattanum is an immaculate temple structure perched on a hilltop. The deity of this 11th century temple is Lord Narasimha—an incarnation of Vishnu. The 16th century Lepakshi Temple located in a small village by the same name near Hindupur in the Anatpur District and built during the regime of the Vijayanagar Empire is legendary in exquisite art form. The temple precincts has three major shrines dedicated to Lord Shiva, Lord Vishnu and Lord Virabhadra (Veerabhadra is a cult deity with the Siva lineage) is famous also for its architecture and murals that are still sought after. Kanaka Durga Temple located in Vijaywada is a powerful deity dedicated to Goddess Durga. Durga in this temple like else where is worshipped as the Goddess of rescue. Rescue from the demons and evil who purturb the sanctity of peaceful co-existance. Even today the world is infested with evil minds that may not appear to be so but they co-exist with all else. Their deeds are venomous, atrocious and tend to victimise those who are competent but humble. It is believed and so goes the faith that worshipping this deity will keep one and his dear ones protected against such unholy beings. Similarly the temple of Sri Ujjaini Mahakali near Hyderabad is dedicated for the cause of bringing repite from the curse of dreadful epidemics and ghastly deseases. It is the replica of of the Mahakali temple of Ujjain (in Madhy Pradesh) built as fulfillment of a vow made by a soldier Suriti Appaiah who prayed before goddess Mahakali at Ujjain to be saved from the epidemic that broke out in Ujjain where he was posted. It is said that in 1815 when he returned he was blessed by an idol of 'Manikyamma' while he was digging a well beside the temple that he had built. This deity is also installed here and worshipped with full fervor along with the main deity that adorns the temple. The main deity is of the mother Goddess in seated posture holding a damaru (sand clock shaped rudimentary sound instrument), spear, sword and a vessel of amrut (syrup of immortality) in her four hands. About 150 Km away from the capiltal city of Hyderabad is a place called Warrangle (means history) where the famous 12th century Thousand-Pillar Temple is situated. This temple with three shrines, called Trikutalayam is dedicated to the Gods Shiva, Vishnu and Surya was built in 1163 AD by King Rudra Deva (legendary Kakatiya kingdom) and dedicated to. The name 'thousand pillar' as it has come to be known is for its richly carved and intricately fashioned thousand black stone pillars that bedeck this unique temple. Here a superbly carved granite figure of Nandi (Shiva's bull) and sculptures of elephants adorn the surroundings of the main shrine. Ramalingeswara temple is situated in Palampet is located at a distance of 77 km from Warangal . . . Kakatiya King Kakati Ganapathi Deva's Chief Commander Rudra Samani built this temple in 1261 The architectural beauty was such that it also came to be known by the name of its sculptor archtect Ramappa. It is said that Marco Polo (the famous Venetian trader and explorer who gained fame for his worldwide travels) once visited here and expressed that the temple was the "brightest star in the galaxy of medieval temples in the Deccan".

One very prominent place of religious congragation in the modern times is 'Prasanthi Nilayam' or The Abode of Supreme Peace. This is situated in Puttaparthi a town in the Anantapur district of Andhra Pradesh. Here is the headquarters of the Sri Sathya Sai Seva Organization and the Sri Sathya Sai Central Trust. Here lived Bhagawan Sri Sathya Sai Baba. Sri Sathya Sai Baba was a "great spiritual Master, famed for His simple and sweet exposition of the greatest and most intricate of spiritual truths which form the fundamental teachings of all the religions of the world". On visiting the place one can see His numerous service projects, be it free hospitals, free schools and colleges, free drinking water supply or free housing projects. Indeed for a poor country like India where such basic neccessiites are unavailable to many theses services are of immense importance and valuable for survival. When I visited this place I did not intend to come here with a great sense of devotion. My main interest was to explore just another place. But on arrival and seeing the work for myself I was awe struck. Many in India talk a lot of things to dissuade attention from his deeds describing them as hoax. Many even resort to mockery. But I for one would like to say that he who has done so much for the needy, whether a spiritual minded or not, is undoubtedly a being who is closer to the Almighty and surely above many a human who lead a meaningless life. This "township is the destination for thousands of spiritual aspirants of varied cultures, faiths, races, languages and socio-economic strata from all over the world to behold His divine form and experience His pure love".

Chitoor where in Tirumala the temple of Lord Venkatapati Balaji is situated forms the southernmost tip of the State of Andhra Pradesh. Beyond its boundaries begins the thriving and holy land of **TAMIL NADU** and Pondicherry. The Tamilians have been the greatest of all temple builders in the country. Their history that is marked by enormous contribution to the glorification of Hinduism and the Gods and Goddesses of Indian Mythology is also discernible by extreme sense of dedication and ritualistic discipline towards such faith. The land that is now known as Tamil Nadu is of great relevance to human civilization. This is one of the few places on earth where man and women existed during which the Palaeolithic civilisations stages from about 500,000 BC up until around 3000 BC. The land that at most times in history remained independent of any foreign occupation also originated its own unique cuture, language and literature that proved helpful in the growth of other literary forms in different parts of the world. Tamilians who belong to the Dravidian race are also believed to be the earliest inhabitants of this country. They lived in the northeastern part of the country and later as reportedly revealed from the excavations of the Indus Valley civilization that they moved southwards with the advent of the Aryans. The most ancient dynasties recorded in history were the 'Chera', 'Chola' and the 'Pandya' dynasty who co-existed almost during the same times. Later during the third centuries the Pallavas emerged superior to all these three dynasties and they along with the Pandyas established their hegemony. Six hundred years later the Cholas reemerged and established their dominance and began to spread their kingdom. This empire in no time got spread from the present day Sri Lanka to Bengal in the northeasterly direction. But in the fourteenth century and with the Muslim invasion in India lot of transformation came about and the land came under the rule of the Vijayanagar dynasty of Andhra Pradesh in around 1600 AD and Telegu language gained importance in the official parlance. Later with the entry of the British trading companies the local rulers started loosing their grounds and finally the entire land came into the hands of the British East India Company. The British reigned here since almost 1765 when the Emperor of Delhi issued a 'firmaan' (decree) recognizing the British possessions in southern India till 1947 when India gained independence. But during all there centuries the rulers left behind their impressions of history in the great religious monuments and temples for the world to cherish. These ancient temples were built according to the prevailing culture of the times and using the resources that were available. Thus some are bullt of stone, some with brick and mortar and many (prior to the eighth Century) were scooped out of caves. Pallavas (900 AD) mostly built Stone temples. The Cholas (900-1250 AD) had constructed monumental structureswith ornate 'mandpams' (domes with Halls below) and some large towers. The Pandyas (Upto 1350 AD) too had a fascination for building huge towers and gateways. The Vijayanagar dynasty (1350-1560 AD) creations are marked by the artistic intricacies. The immaculate carvings on stone and monolithic pillars are the styles they signify. The Naik (who were the representative rulers of the Vijayanagar Dynasty in Tamil land during 1600-1750 AD) created places of worship with pillared halls around the main shrine that created large prakarams or circumambulatory paths around the shrine.

The oldest of the known temples in Tamil Nadu is at Mahabalipuram near the capital city of Chennai. This temple built between 300 and 200 BC was dedicated to 'Muruga' a deity popular in the south amongst Tamilians and not much amongst other Hindus in India. (The literary meaning of Muruga is the beautiful one. It actually refers to the ever-youthful bachelor God 'Kartik', son of Shiva and Parvati—their other son was 'Ganesh'). Kartik is known to have been the general of the demi-God army and had once lead the Gods to victory over dreadful demons Surapadmn, Tarakasur and their companions who wrecked havoc on the Gods. The Pallava rulers rebuilt this temple some time after 800 AD the excavations of which are all the remains that could be seen there. But the oldest temple in Chennai is the 8th century Sri Parthasarathy Temple that was built by the Pallava rulers. Parthasarathy (meaning charioteer, refered to Krshna who was the charioteer of Arjuna in the war of Kurukshetra of Mahabharat) temple is dedicated to Lord Krshna and is considered as one of the sacred abodes of Lord Vishnu. There is a story that Lord Krshna pleased by his devotion appeared before King Sumathi who was a great devout of Lord Venkatapati Balaji of Tirupati. The Lord appeared in a form as seen in Mahabharat war where he stood without any weapons and only a conch in his hand and wearing moushtach as a real charioteer would. As believed, ever since the parents of Sri Ramanuja performed ceremonies here and were blessed with a son like 'Ramanuja' who later grew up to become the great Sri Vaishnava Acharya who revived the 'Vishistadvaitha', it became a popular palce for childless parents. Here it is believed that offering ghee (butter) along with ritualisic ceremonies and then taking that ghee for 48 days a childless couple will be blessed with parenthood.

Yet another temple creation of Pallava kings in the 7th century is the Kapaleeshwarar Temple at Chennai. This one dedicated to Lord Shiva and his consort Parvati. The place where it is located is called Mylapore ('Mayil' in Tamil language means 'Pea-Cock'. Once Goddess Parvati taking the form of a Peacock worshiped Lord Shiva at this place, hence the name, it is believed). It is said that the original temple that was on the seashore, which was destroyed by the Portugese during the 16th century. Later Santhome Cathedral was built in is place. The Vijayanagara Kings rebuilt the present temple in the 16th century.

San Thome Cathedral built in 1504 is said to be the oldest church in Chennai where the remains of St. Thomas the Apostle still remains. Amongst the other important churches in Chennai are the 16th century Luz Church built by the Portuguese, St. Andrew's Church built in 1821 and the St. Mary's Church built during 1678-80. Another important and interesting place of worship is the Mosque of 'thousand lights'. Built on land donated by Nawab Wallajah and built by the Nawab of Arcot in 1795 it has also come to be known as the Wallajah Mosque. The mosque building displays lovely medieval architectural. What I admired most there were the tall spearing minerettes of the mosque. So imposing it enhances the historical and religious importance of the place. It is said that in earlier days it required a thousand lamps to light up the main assembly hall of the mosque. So is the name given to it.

One of the largest of the temples in Tamil Nadu is the Meenakshi Temple, as it is known in the town of Madurai. In fact this temple complex is a town within. Although created by the Pallavas people would still like to give credit to the Naik rulers for their cotribution in giving this place the magnanimous spread that it is known for. The Gopirum (the large Dom with a huge hall below and the circumambulatory paths around shrines) are said to have been contributions of the Naiks. Meenakshi ('meen' in

Sanskrit means fish and 'akshi' means eyes. That is fish like eyes. It is a hyperbole that signifys immaculate beauty. So was the lady who was born here to Malayadwaja Pandya, a king of Madurai). As the legend goes—the childless King Malayadwaja wanting an heir to be born performed deep prayers before the holy fire. Pleased by his devotion the king was gifted a daughter that emerged from the fire. The king was very pleased by getting the child but was somewhat upset for the fact that the child had three breasts. But in consolation he heard a devine voice that the third breast would diappear when she meets her real life partner. The girl grew up to be a very powerful warrior. She succeeded in many a battle but while in Kailash (now in Tibet) her ferocity subsided before the Lord. She, who was actually a form of Goddess Parvati realised that this was before Shiva the Lord—her devine life partner. As assured by the God the third breast of the princess disappeared and the two decided to get married. It is said that it was here in Madurai where the marriage actually took place and they has spent some time living here in the vicinity for a while then. The temple Meenakshi is thus dedicated to Parvati and Sundareswarar or Shiva. Surrounding these two sanctums that stand in the core of the walled premises are several tall shrines, in fact twelve of them with one mandapam (meaning canopy) having a thousand beautifully decorated pillars and another with musical pillars. Every location and every mandapum has a special significance and purpose that complies with the events that take place round the year. A holy tank is situated in the center of the premises where devotees take bath. All of these towering shrines have brightly colored murals on the outer walls that attract visual attention of all visitors. The festival of marriage is still celebrated here with much gaiety as an annual festival (some time in April-May) that lasts for twelve days. This temple is visited by thousands of devotees and tourists every day. I found this place humming with activity all day. Indeed it is this faith and the creation in antiquity that draws people from around the world has also become a source of livelihood for several thousands living there.

The other very large temple complex in Tamil Nadu and perhaps the whole of India is Sri Ranganathaswamy Temple in Srirangam in the Tiruchirappalli region. Covering an area of 155 acres the complex is boundered by the River Kaveri and the Kolladam stream. The temple is dedicated to Lord Vishnu and is considered as one of the 108 sacred abodes of Lord Vishnu. Out of these, two are outside this terrestrial world. Lord Ranganatha the deity here is a form of Lord Vishnu reclining on a great serpent. Sri Ranganathaswamy Temple is also one of the denoted 'Graha Sthal' (position denoting cosmic planets that govern the earth and its beings). This one denotes Venus. (The other such temple site that denote 'Graha Sthal' are: Suryanarcoil temple in Kumbakonam dedicated to the Sun, Tirupati Temple in Tirumala to the Moon, Murugan temple at Palani is to Mars, Planet Mercury is assigned to the Meenakshi temple at Madurai, the 3rd century Sri Subrahmanya Swami Temple of Tiruchendur located at Tuticorin relates to Jupiter, Tirunallaru Darbaaranyeswarar Temple, Keezhperumpallam Temple and Tirunageswaram Nageswarar Temple at Thanjavur dedicated to Saturn Ketu and Raahu respectively). The temple has about 21 'gopurams' (conical shaped temple-tops that are quite high), The Naanmugan Gopuram here is over 50 meters tall with intricate carvings on its outer walls. Apart from the murals painted on it there are also inscriptions that narrate history and mythological stories. This temple is also considered as ideal for doing self-realization exercise through meditation.

The island temple of Ramanathaswamy at Rameshwaram is situated in the Gulf of Mannar, about a 150 Km away from Madurai. Apart from being one of the twelve sacred Jyotirlingams this temple is famous for its popular legendary association with Lord Rama's victory in the Lanka war against Ravana—the blessed demon God and king of Lanka (now Sri Lanka). The island where it is situated is 40Km apart from Jaffna in Sri Lanka and connected to the mainland by the Pamban channel. Incidentally, the gulf of Munnar is considered as one of the richest coastal regions in Asia and protected as a bio-shpere reserve as it is home to several hard corals, sea turtles, dolphins and over 3000 spiecie of flora and fauna.

It is believed that the temple was built by Lord Rama himself after his return from war at Lanka and as atonement for having committed the sin of killing the demon king Ravana. This war occurred as a rescue mission. When Lord Rama accompanied by wife Sita and brother Lakshmana were in exile in the forest, Ravana the demon king of Lanka abducted Sita and fled to his kingdom and kept her captive. Living lonely in the forest Lord Rama felt isolated and helpless. It was then that Hanuman (humanoid-ape) appeared in the scene that restored Rama's confidence. Out of devotion for the Lord, Hanuman assured to deploy his 'banar-sena' (monkey-army) to invade Lanka. (Hanuman is recognized more as the prodigy of Vayu the Lord of wind than his actual parents Anjana and her husband Kesari to whom he was born after their offering deep prayer before Lord Shiva for a child. By the grace Lord Shiva, Vayu reassigned his male energy to Anjana's womb. Thus Hanuman was born. He is also considered by many as an incarnate of lord Shiva himself. Hanuman was a blessed child, blessed by many Gods who granted him immunity, power and comfort in life. Like from Lord Brahma he gained the power to induce fright amongst foes and annihilate fear from his friends, he was also blessed to be able to transform himself and travel easily wherever he wished to. Similarly other Gods gave him other blessings like immunity from hurt in any war, immunity from water, fire etc and so on).

The greatest obstacle then was of crossing the sea. This problem got resolved when the army under the commandership of Hanumana took the challenge on to themselves. They brought boulders and wood and layed them over the strait. This passage now made way for the Lord and the army to reach Lanka and invade the demon kingdom. The battle followed and Ravana was defeated and killed along with his brother Kumbha-karna and a whole bunch of armymen of the demons. Sita was recued. On his return Lord Rama rested in an island that is now called Rameshwaram. Now in order to express his gratitude and also his penance he decided to offer a prayer ceremony in worship of Lord Shiva. Thus the place got its name, meaning the God of Rama ('eshwam' means God of). There are two sacred Lingams (structure symbolic of Shiva) here. The legend says that Rama had deputed Hanumana to bring a Lingam from Kailash, which was to be installed before his prayers could commence. While all arrangements for the prayer was complete and the auspicious time for the prayer drew near there was no trace of Hanumana. Sita decided that before it got late she should assemble a Lingam with sand from the nearby sea and have it installed so that the prayer could go on. Finally, Lord Rama performed his puja with the Lingum made by Sita. After the ceremony was over Hanumana arrived with the Linga but was dismayed to find that his effort went futile. To console his loyal servant, Lord Rama declared that the Linga brought by Hanumana was sacred and should be installed before the one with which he performed his prayer. Thus the two Lingums are worshipped with equal reverence and adulation. Agnitheertham as it is called is the place where Rama performed the prayer ceremony with fire. Some distance away towards the east is the Ramnathswamy temple that was built in the 17th Century. It has a long corridor with symmetrically layed out colomns of designed pillars on either side. This provides a magnificiet look from the inside. A place called Gandamadana Parvatham is where they believe is the real footprints of Lord Rama preserved for worship. The entire island is dotted with memories of the innumerable incidents that occurred before and after the eventful war between Rama and Ravana. All theres locations have now become places of worship and homage for devotees.

Nearby at Erwadi is another sacred place not related to Lord Rama, the Tomb of Ibrahim Sahid Aulia. Muslims from across the globe visit Erwadi especially during the month of December to participate in the annual festival celebrated as a tribute to the saint Ibrahim Sahid Aulia. Not being able to discover much there about the history of the place I decided to provide for convenience of readers an extract from a published article entitled "A glimpse into the history of Erwadi dharga" by T.S.Sreenivasa Raghavan that appeared in a popular daily The Times of India, Sunday edition dated 8 Aug 2001. "Erwadi Dargah has a history of 400 years. The four dargahs were built here to commemorate Seyyad Ali Sultan Ibrahim Shahid, his mother Fathima, wife Seyyad Ali Fathima and son Abu Thahir who are being held in high esteem since they being the messengers of god who migrated to Erwadi from Saudi Arabia. According to the present imam of Erwadi Dargah, Maulavi Seyyad Ismail Siraji, Seyyad Ali Sultan arrived in India during Hijari 530. When he reached Erwadi, this place was under the rule of Madurai king Sethupathi Maharaja. He pleased the king with his magical powers by performing many an impossible feat. The king who was immensely pleased, gave him 6000 acres of land as a token of appreciation", says the Imam. Though Seyyad Ali lived happily with his family in the land donated by the king for some time, the events in store were not favourable to him. While the king appreciated Seyyad Ali for performing miracles, many non-muslims, especially Hindus, got attracted to him and expressed their desire to embrace Islam religion by accepting his disciplehood. King Vikrama Pandya who succeeded king Sethupathi Maharaja did not like Hindus getting converted to Islam. Hence, a war started between Seyyad Ali and Vikrama Pandya. In this Seyyad Ali attained martyrdom along with his family members. His son Abu Thahir was only 17 then. Since then, the Erwadi Dargah had become a holy place. People bring mental patients here believing that since Seyyad Ali had performed miracles, his magical powers still persist in the Dargah. Ironically, the Dargah is also a symbol of religious harmony. Since the Madurai king Sethupathi Maharaja had patronised Seyyad Ali, his action cemented the bonds between the Hindus and Muslims. Every year, during the month of dulkahath, we celebrate 'chandanakkudam' festival. Hoisting the flag, as is done in many a Hindu temple down south is a celebrated here."

It is believed by devotees here that next to Tirupati, the temple of Lord Muruga at Palani (near Coimbatore) is the major Pilgrim centre in South India. This temple situated atop a 700 step high hill is very ancient. The deity is known as Dandayudhapani Swami. (Danda-yudha-pani would mean the staff in hand) The deity in made of nine minerals called Navabasana. Devotees have a belief that the offering of milk, sandle paste and other auspitious items on coming in contact with the Navabasana attain medicinal properties and gains the power of curing many a desase. When I came here two things fascinated me. First, an electric operated winch—for carring visitors to the hilltop. This contraption I had never seen before. The winch looked like an ordinary dated railway compartment with rows of benches lined one after the other. As each row get filled the doors are locked from outside. About 30 people are stacked inside and the signal is blown.

A cable connected to a pully on top begins to wind and the winch makes its way up rolling over a pair of support rails. Because it is lifted by the cable the elevation of the winch leans beyond the limits of a normal gradiant that we are generally used to, giving a feeling of falling off. The journey takes about ten minutes. I came to know that a more modern cable car has replaced the winch now. Second, this temple establishment has a series of events lined up every year. These events are like festivals that keep the pilgrims merry. Amongst the important ones are: 'Chitra Pournami', a ten-day festival when Lord Muruga rides in the silver car along the streets around the Temple. Festival of 'Agni Nakshatram' is held twice for 7 days when the Lord walks around the hill early in the morning. During the festival of 'Kandhar Shasti' the Lord comes down the Hill, and after fighting a (symbolic) battle with the demons and defeating them ascends the Hill again. This is enacted as a play that is interesting to watch. Several rulers contributed in the making of this 7th Century temple. The first known was a ruler from Kerala known as Cheaman Perumal. Later the Naiks and the Pandyas amongst many other devotees over the course of history contributed in the building of the temple.

The legend on how Lord Murugan arrived here is also an interesting one. Once Narada Muni (a travelling Monk who has access to all Gods at all times) called on Lord Shiva at his abode in Kailash (in the Himalayas in Tibet). When he arrived Lord Shiva was with his family, Parvati by his side and the two sons Lord Ganesha (also called Lord Vinayakar) and Lord Kartik (also called Lord Subrahmanya) around. Narada offered a golden mango to Shiva and said it was a 'Gyanaphalam' (meaning fruit of wisdom) that he had brought especially for Him. Lord Siva gave it to Parvati. Mother Parvati in turn thought of giving it to the children to have. But since there were two of them and both eager to have the fruit they were all left in a fix as the 'fruit devine' cannot be cut. So it was decided that (amongst Ganesha and Kartik) he who could travel around universe and return first would have the fruit. Lord Subrahmanya (Kartik) in a hurry to win the race for the fruit set off on his peacock to take the sprint while Lord Vinayakar (Ganesha) circumambulated around his parents saying that they symbolised the entire universe. Lord Vinayakar thus won the fruit and consumed it. When Lord Subrahmanya returned he was dissapointed and felt let down. He became angry and sad. In his infuriation he left the family and decided to go on exile to settle elsewhere on earth forever. Later when Lord Shiva and Parvati came out in search of their son they found him here (in Palani) on a hilltop. While consoling him the parents told him that He was 'Pazham Nee' which ment that he himself was the fruit ('pazham') of all knowledge and wisdom ('nee' means you. Hence the place was called 'Pazham Nee' that later came to be promounced as Palani.

Another important place in the civilisation of South that signifies a historical heritage is Thanjavur. It was also the seat of authority of the Chola dynasty between the 1st-12th centuries, the Nayakas in the 16th century and the Marathas in the 17th and 18th centuries. It is said that Thanjavur has a hundred temples. But the most important one here is Brihadeeswara Temple that was built during the time of the Cholas (9th to 12th century) and it was also the administrative headquarters. Rajraja Chola I built this temple in 1010 AD. All through this period this town remained the seat of cultural advancement. The monuments and art forms that are found here is evident of their excellecne in this field. Incidentally this region being located in the Kaveri delta is very fertile and is compared to the soil of the Gangeic plains. Evidently the fertility brought with it prosperity and thus came creativity in music, literature, dance, drama, sculpture and the like. Thanjavur has a great history of warfare, empires and their gallantry deeds. Although the Cholas reigned supreme for over a thousand years there were many a struggle with the Muttaraiyar Chieftains, Pandiyan, the Pallava King till they were rendered extinct in the 13th century. The Sultan of Delhi challenged the supremacy of the Pandiyan regime. After invasion by Ala-Ud-Din Khiliji, Muslim rule was established in Thanjavur. Later, Vijayanagar Kings drove out the Muslims by the middle of the 14th century. The Nayak dynasty under patronage of the Vijayanagar Empire ruled for a brief period from the middle of the 16th century. The Vijayanagar Empire ended in the 17th century and after a period of turmoil Thanjavur witnessed the entry of the Marathas in the later half of the 17th century. The turmoil gave way for intervention by the British. Finally in 1799 Thanjavur came under the British occupation. The kingdom remained under the British domain till 1947 when it became an integral part of independent India.

Yet another contribution by the Chola Kings Aditya I and Parantaka I is the temple of Nataraj at Chidambaram. Located about 250 Km south of the capital city of Chennai, this temple houses the idol of Shiva in a dancing posture. Nataraj was the guardian deity of the Cholas. Out of extreme devotion they had covered the shrine roof with gold. This information is deciphered from the inscriptions in the temple as is given to understand. The State of 'Nataraj' signifies 'Ananda Tandava' (the Cosmic Dance of bliss). The name suggests 'Chit'signifies heart or consciosness 'ambaram' would mean openness or open sky or a temple. Thus 'Chitambaram' would mean 'hall of consciousnesses'. In other words, Chidambaram is the heart of the universe where Shiva as Nataraja performed the cosmic dance. This dance of Lord Shiva as per the legend was performed to obliterate the arrogance of the saints and monks (of a place called 'Tharukavanam') who upon learning the books of religion (Vedas & Shastras) had lost all sense of humility. The Lord after getting the news of their egoistic attitude and their ruthlessness towards the subjects decided to arrive there to teach the saints a lesson. He took the form of a beautiful youth and wondered in the forest accompanied by Lord Vishnu masqueraded as Mohini, a charming lady. Their appeal was so alluring that all the young saints would fall for Mohini and the wives of the elderly monks would get attracted towards the handsome lad. When no explanation worked the saints decided to perform the sacrificial ceremony of lighting the fire of annihilation and chant the humns of destruction so that doom would befall on the couple. From the fire emerged an animated tiger that leaped at the Lord and was killed instaneously. Shiva tore its flesh and tied it to its waist. Then appeared a snake that was thrown to the Lord which He tied to his neck similarly several such dangerous beings were hurled at him but all proved futile. Exhausted with all ammunition they then threw the sacrificial fire at him, which he put on his hand but caused no harm. He then began to dance the 'Oorthava thandavam' (an infuriated cosmic dance form) with His hairs flowing in all directions and the earth rumbling to His footsteps. The saints immediately had the revelation that He was non other that Lord Shiva himelf. Realising their offense they immediately fell to His feet in atonement. The pose in which the Lord is depicted here is one of the frozen symbolic postures during the performance of this dance called 'Nataraja'.

Another important abode of Lord Shiva is the Ekambareswara temple at Kancheepuram—considered as earth abode. (Other abodes being Tiru-vanna-malai abode offire, Chidambaram—of Sky, Thiruvanaikoil is of water and Sri Kalahasti—air) This town that is now popular for its immaculate craftsmanship in silk weaving was once the seat of learning. It was the administrative capital of the Pallavas where scholars arrived in persuit of, religious accomplishments. This center of pilgrimage is considered as one amongst the sacred places like Kashi, Mathura and Ayodya.

Situated at the tip of the Indian peninsula is Kanyakumari. This is a lovely little place where the east and the west coast lines of India meet. The shores of Kanyakumari are washed by the Bay of Bengal on the one side and the Arabian Sea on the other. From here both the seas could be seen merging with each other yet the color of the two seas would remain distinctly different on either side forming a visible yet void line of demarcation. The deity with a smiling face inside this temple of Kanyakumari is 'Parasakthi', a virgin Goddess. Kanyakumari as the name suggests (kanya meaning young lady and kumari is unmarried / virgin) is a young goddess yet ill-fated to have remained waiting for a prearranged marriage ceremony that never occured. The legend reminds of the period when Banusura a demon king began over powering the Devas (or Gods) who felt oppressed and pained. 'Devas' then performed 'yagna' (a holy ceremony) when Goddess Parasakthi (a form of 'Parvati the consort of Lord Shiva) came into being. She was sent here in the form of a virgin girl, as it was a surmon for the Devas that only a virgin could kill Banusura. Lord Shiva when he came to know of her fell in love with her and decided to marry. This news reached 'Narada'. He thought that something needed to be done as Shiva was too arrogant to be convinced by argument. Once decided no power could hold him from marrying the young virgin God. Once the marriage is concluded then every chance of anhillating Banusura would be lost. So he decided to play a trick. On the decided day of marriage when Lord Shiva set off from nearby town of Suchindrum for the ceremony Narada engaged him in coversation for quite some time. There after he left and took the form of a rooster to crow and announce the dawning of the day. Thinking that the auspicious time was over Lord Shiva returned calling off the marriage. Parasakthi the bride kanya thus was left a 'kumari'. She too decided never to get married and remaied a vergin all her life. The deity of 'Kanyakumari' dedicated to the goddess Parvathi as a virgin is worshipped very ceremoniously in different forms through the day. In the morning she dresses like a young girl, later in the day she is dressed differently and in the evening she is dressed like a bride.

One of the most wonderful places I have experienced in Tamil Nadu is Kuttralam or Courtallam 135 Km northwest of Kanyakumari along the Western Ghats. It is a place of natural beauty and immaculate landscape. The place is mountaneous with greenery and forests all over. It has a multitude of cascading waterfalls that makes this place unique. The waterfall here serves several purposes apart from just offering a pleasant sight. One can enjoy a shower here freely and experience the feel of a natural spa. The water here has medicinal properties with several curative qualities that make it a popular health resort as well. There are nine such waterfalls that cascade from 150 meters high cliff over the mountains. Pilgrims who come here during their entourage refresh themselves as they take a good shower, have refreshments and rest here for a while before proceeding further ahead.

On the hilltop is a temple dedicated to Lord Shive. It is called 'Thiru-koota-chalan-athar' Temple. Nearby is another Shrine dedicated to Lord 'Nataraja'. Here one can find ancient inscriptions and paintings of various Gods and religious ceremonies. It is believed that this is one of the rare places where the Lord had performed the cosmic dance. A temple dedicated to Lord Muruga is situated in Thirumalai which is about 15-km from Courtallam. Closeby are several ancient shrines that show the religious significance of this place. There is a monolithic image of 'Neminatha' carved in the 12th century (Neminatha, the

22nd Tirthankara or enlightened one of the Jains). This 16 ft idol is also the tallest of all Jain idols in Tamil Nadu. There are three Jain caves that were converted to three shrines sometime in the 19th century. Here one can find another 16th century temple dedicated to Mahavira and 'Parsvanatha' shrine built in the 17th century.

Thus Tamil Nadu the land of one of the oldest human habitance on earth has from time immemorial been in a state of orderliness with skillful rulers who were not only god fearing and sane but also allowed the freedom of religious expression. Irrespective of regime the rulers too professed religious practices and thus built and partronised the construction of temples and monuments with ample liberty to the craftspersons, sculptures and thinkers. These temples today stand as ancient places of worship but also remind us of the immense architectural ability, quest for knowledge and immaculate artistic skills of the bygone era.

PUDUCHERRY, also known as Pondicherry is a small state located within the boundaries of Tamil Nadu and along the coast of Bay of Bengal. The place is richly cosmopolitan perhaps because of the legacy it has been bestowed with. The Pallavas, the Pandiyas, the Muslim rulers invaded and ruled over this place for quite some time. It was once foremost in Vedic teachings that have cast influence on the thought process of people who lived here. British influence from 17th century onwards followed by French and Dutch dominance was also instrumental in shaping the character of the inhabitants. All these have contributed in making Pondicherry truly multi-ethnic in character.

All these are thus reflected in the sacred site in the form of Churches, the Temples and the Mosques in good numbers. Some such significant sites are: English De Notre Dame Das Anges, Sacred Heart of Jesus Church, Church of our Lady Immaculate Conception, The Jamia Mosque, Varadaraja Perumal Temple, Vedapureswarar

Temple and Srimanakula Vinayakar Temple. All these places of worship are beautiful structures with architectural styles that reflect the traditions of their heritage and times. There are innumerable other such places of worship around Pondicherry. During the present times the most prominent place the best-known landmark of Pondicherry is the Ashram of Sri. Aurobindo. Born in Kolkata and educated in Britain Sri. Aurobindo as the world knows was a spiritual thinker. He was a revolutionary from Bengal who later became Yogi (spiritual practitioner) and moved to the then French Pondicherry in 1910. He will always be remembered amongst other things for his contributions to India's freedom struggle and for his spiritual attainments. He has left behind not only his great writings like 'The Life Divine' and 'The Synthesis of Yoga' but also for building the Ashram as a seat of learning and imparting skill for self-sustenance. International Centre for Yoga Education and Research and Sri Aurobindo International Centre of Education are important part of the ashram. The belief here is that "every child is unique in its thinking and the centre of education tries to help them grow and nurture them in their individual way and leave the choice to the children. They don't mingle them together into the frame of one particular syllabus".

Along side the state of Tamil Nadu, sharing the southernmost tip of the peninsula is **KERALA**, the 'God own Land' as they denote to promote touism. Indeed like Tamil Nadu, Kerala too has been a seat of learning and religious attainments from the very ancient times. References dating back to 300 BC confirm the rule of the Keralaputras who ruled over Travancore, Cochin and Malabar. The great philosopher saint and religious reformer of the eighth century Adi Shankaracharya was born here in Cochin. From this southern tip of the country he traveled to all the four corners of India organising and deliberating in public discourses and preaching amongst others the philosophy of advaita (monism). In Hinduism Shankaracharya is revered as a monk of supreme order. The four Matha (missionary) that he had founded during his short span of life (in Puri in Orissa, Sringeri in Karnataka, Dwarka in Gujarat, and Badrinath in Uttarakhand) are still functioning and benefit the cause of worldly welfare and spiritual advancements. Kerala was also one of those rare places on earth where international trade and commerce was conducted way back in the 12th century in quite an organised manner. Trade with the Chinese and Arabs brought revenue for the Zamorins rulers of erstwhile Perumal dynasty. Later with the arrival of Vasco da Gama at Calicut in 1498 trade began with the Portugese. Rising opportunities attracted the Dutch to reach here a hundred years later followed by the British in around 1630s. The Dutch were ambitious and succeeded in their endeavour to grasp political and military power. But this did not last for long. Dharma Raja the ruler of Travencore brought an end to Dutch dominance in 1758. Soon after Haider Ali, the ruler of Mysore and later his son Tipu Sultan invaded and brought the region under their rule. But during the later half of 1700 Tipu's territories in the north began to fall under the British forces and so did Malabar. Then on there was continuous struggle by the inhabitants to oust the British and put an end to their dictatorial dominance. This culminated into merging with the freedom movement that spread all across the country. Finally in 1947 the state along with the country as a whole attained its independence. While Buddhism and Jainism flourished here from the beginning of the Christian era, the history of Kerala got richer with the wide diversity of religious infusions and settlement of the different communities from across the world. West Asian families settling here so did a large population of Jews. Christians migrated here way back in 300 AD much before Chritianity spread to any other part of the world. First Muslim settlement in Kerala the advent of Islam in West Asia happened in the 7th century. Many Syrians migrated to settle here in the 9th century.

As expressed in his book Keralolpathi (The Origin of Kerala) Dr.Herman Gundert, considered the father of Malayalam lexicon, had compiled a version which was published in 1868. There are differences of opinion over his interpretations but according to him "Cheramanperumal, a Chera king of Kodungallure, left for Makkah, embraced Islam, and accepted the name Thajudeen. He married the sister of then King of Jeddah. On his return trip, accompanied by many Islamic religious leaders, led by Malik-ibn-Dinar (RA), he fell sick and passed away. But he had given introductory letters for the team to proceed to 'Musiris' (Kodungallur), the Chera capital. The visitors came to Musiris and handed over the latter to the reigning king, who treated the guests with all respect and extended facilities to establish their faith in the land. The king also organised help for the artisans to build the first Mosque at Kodungallur, by converting Arathali temple into a Juma-Masjid. It was built in 629 A.C., and the area around it had been ear-marked for the team's settlement."

One of the oldest temples in Kerala is Parasurama Temple. Located near the capital city of Thiruvananthapuram at Thiruvallam this temple is dedicated to its mythological creator 'Parasurama' (sixth incarnation of Lord Vishnu). This temple belongs to the late Pandyan period around 12th and 13th century. It is said that ever since the greatly revered saint Sri Adi Sankaracharya performed the religious rituals for his mother after her death, this place has become a holi place for making offering to their ancestors and also offiring holy sacrifices. Here one can find the idols of Parasurama in granite stone along with those of Brahma, and Siva all facing the north. Parashurama is a blessed saint and is one of the rare beings according to Hindu mythology who is immortal. It is said that the idol of Lord Sabarimal Sri Swammi Ayappan located in the mountains at a height of over 4000 feet in the western-ghats was the creation of Parasurama. Later King Rajashekhara of Pandyan dynasty built the temple under the devine guidance of 'Manikandan' (incarnation of the child of Lord Shiva, born out of 'Mohini' an incarnate of Lord Vishnu). Manikandan lived as the son of King Rajashekhar till the King came to know of his real identity. On knowing this, the King was overwhelmed at the gratitude of the Lord. It came to his mind that he should build a temple in honor of Manikandan. He asked Manikandan where he would like the temple to be built. Manikandan said he would spew an arrow from his bow and wherever the arrow would fall would be the site of the temple. So he shot the arrow and it fell on top of a mountain. Manikandan disappeared thereafter. The temple was built there. Then-on people began visiting the temple to worship and honor the God. It has now grown into a pilgrimage center for thousands of devotees irrespective of caste and religion except women between the age of 10 and 50 (entry is restricted for female between puberty and menopause) The journey is an arduous one and the wildlife makes it quite fierce. Thus the local administration keeps vigil all through during the pilgrimage months (coinciding with 'Makarasankranti' according to the Hindu calendar). The trail passes through dense forest and a steep climb to the mountaintop. The route is open only during November and January when the temple remains open. In all other days of the year the passage is closed. The pilgrimage starts with the carrying of the Holy Jewel Casket the home of the royal family to the Temple. On that day it is told that a 'Garuda' (a large fabled bird-like creature of Hindu mythology—similar to the logo of Indonesian Airlines) is said to appear. The 'Garuda' hovering in the sky follows the procession carrying the casket of ornaments for the deity. After reaching the ornaments are put on the Lord. The bird would then circle the temple thrice and would disappear. After this miraculous happening another miracle appears in the evening sky. Makara Jothi (a heavenly flame that looks like a glowing star) would appear on the horizon behind the mounain. This is believed to be a confirmnation of the presence of Lord Swamy Ayyappan and seeing this splendid sight the devotees feel blessed. I have never been on this expedition but I am told by many belivers that it so happens.

Amongst the temples here the biggest one is Padmanabhaswamy temple located in the capital city of Thiruvananthapuram. Tiruvalla Temple at Tiruvalla near Alappuzha is however considered one of the largest Vishnu temples of Kerala. The Padmanabhaswamy temple dedicated to Lord Vishnu is considered one of the holiest abodes of Lord Vishnu. The temple covers a huge area with 100 feet high Gopurum under which rests the idol of reclining Vishnu. The temple in Thiruvananthapuram was built in its present form in 1566 later it is said that Raja Marthanda Varma founded it in 1734.

The deity of Sri Padmanabha Swami, incarnate of Lord Vishnu is seen in reclining posture resting on the holy five-hood anaconda called Anantha Shesh Nag with His left palm resting on a divine Shiva lignum. He is flanked here by Sridevi and Bhudevi who are goddesses of prosperity and the earth respectively. Also seen is Lord Brahma emerging from a lotus that emanates from the navel of the Swami. These are expressions of the sculpture to depict the imaginations of the ruler or who-so-ever may have contemplated to build the temple. Due to the reclining position and its length the Lord has to be viewed separately through the three doors of the temple that exposes the three parts of his body. This idol was originally made out of wood as it is believed. No one created it but was self crated when a large tall tree fell on the ground by virtue of a miracle by an incarnation of Krshna. It is said that this idol got burnt in fire. Thereafter the present one was built out of 1008 'saligrams' (pebbles from the flowing river that take the shape of a 'Shivalingum' or close to it) that were brought on elephant back from River Gandak in Nepal.

Guruvayur is a thriving township in Trichur district and is popular for the temple of Sri Guruvayurappan. This is a very sacred pilgrimage center for all devotees of Lord Krshna. It is believed that Lord Brahma worshipped the idol of Guruvayur (Guru implies Brihaspati name for the planet Jupiter. He is the counsel and guide of the Gods and Vaayu his disciple and the God of Winds). The idol of Guruvayurappan came to Lord Vishnu as a gift from Lord Brahma who worshipped it originally. Lord Vishnu kept it with him at Dwarka during his Krishnavataram. When Dwarka was at the brink of destruction Krishna instructed Uddhava (one of his followers) to seek help of Guru and Vayu's help to find a safe place for the image. Guru and Vayu then came to Parasurama for his help. He advised them to install it near Rudratirtha the holy tank beside which Shiva and Parvati are also present. The idol was installed there and the temple and the town then on came to be known as Guruvayur. There is another sacred 1613 A.D temple dedicated to Lord Krishna located 14 kms from Alappuzha. This temple too has a lovely architecture and liberal in the distribution of sweet milk porridge as prasadum offered to the deity by His devotees

Jewish settlers here have also set up their places of worship in Kerala. One such is the Kochi Jewish Synagogue built in 1568. With very less number of Jews remaining the Synagogue has been reduced to a historical monument more than a humming place of worhip. But churches there are many. St. Mary's Church built in 1579 by Thekkumkoor Maharajah well decorated with murals on the walls. At Mulanthuruthy a beautiful village in the outskirt of Ernakulam city stands the Marthoman Church. This is a Syrian Orthodox Church established between AD 1110 and 1125. Located on a hilltop in Thiruvankulam is the Kyomtha Chapel that was built in 1675.

The oldest Mosque in India and the second oldest in the world is located at Kodungallur near Thrissur. It is the Cheraman Jama Masjid Built in 628 AD, nearly seven years after Prophet migrated to Medina. Strangely this mosque resembles a Hindu temple like the Jamat Mosque in Malappuram built under the act in accordance with the desire of a Hindu family. But the Pazhayangadi Mosque in Malappuram is more Mughal style with white dome and filigree work.

As we traverse the state of Kerala we would have left the eastern coast and begun our climb along the Western Ghats with the Arabian Sea on our left towards the west. Upward of Kerala is the state of **KARNATAKA**. The capital city of Bangalore or Bagaluru as it has been renamed recently. It is a cosmopolital city humming with activity. It is one of the finest locations in the country where the young and enterprising give wings to their imagination. Like its immaculate history the city and the state is a seat of knowledge and also a center for religious fulfillments. The Gavi Gangadhareshwara temple is one of the oldest temples in Bangalore. It is believed that this cave temple dates back to the Tretha Yuga ('Yug' or era /epoch. Tretha Yuga is the second of four yugas of Hinduism. The four yugas are the Satya Yuga, Dwapara Yuga, Tretha Yuga and Kali Yuga that is currently running). This is one of the temples built by the founder of the city 'Kempegowda'. The other temple he built is the Bull temple. While the former is dedicated to Lord Shiva the later is dedicated to his sacred carrier 'Nandi'—a bull.

It is said that Nandi used to devour all the groundnuts/ peanuts grown there. Then the people would pray for him to give reprive. Later this idol was set up and prayers were offered after which the crops were saved from all the menace. In rememberence an exposition was organised after the crops were harvested. This ceremony continues even today and people arrive here to worship and offer prayer to Nandi for safety and security of their earnings and prosperity thereafter. Situated nearby is the Dodda Ganesha Temple at Basavanagudi. This 16 feet wide and 18 feet high statue is carved out of a single boulder and is also known as Satya Ganapathi and Shakthi Ganapathi. The idol is worshipped with lot of love and affection so much so that devolees smear huge amount of butter over the entire body of the idol. Some days they cover it with sandle-wood paste and on some other days with fruits and vegetables. I am sure such shower of love exhausts the God after a while. Sri Banashankari Amma Temple built later in time is worshipped for relief from hardships and poverty. The ISCON temple dedicated to Lord Krshna is situated on Chord road, Rajajinagar on the so-called 'Hare Krshna Hill' dedicated to Lord Krishna and Radha. Located on Airport Road is a large Shiva statue situate behind the Kemp Fort. It is not a temple in a true sense but an interesting creation to attract visitors. Indians as they are they tend to honour the idol of Gods and so did I find people doing here. With all devotion to the gigantic statue they woud offer their prayers and donatons and spend some time in the lovely ambience that has been created there. I was told that the owner of the Kemps chain of shops built this to attract tourists and also to popularize the belief in Shiva, as has been transmited to him in the dreams. In a spirit of true metropolitan character the other places of worship include the Aurobindo Society Ashram, Vivekananda Ashram, Ramakrishna Ashram, Bahai Centre for worship, Osho Nisargam Meditation Centre,

Mahabodi Society, Gurudwara Sri Guru Singh Sabha, Jumma Masjid, Parsi Fire Temple, Parish Priest St. Patrick's Church St. Mark's Church, St. Mary's Basilica, Hudson Memorial Church and many such others.

About a hundred and forty kilometers from Bangaluru is a unique place that is not only the cultural hub of the state but also exhibits the pride heritage of palaces and gardens. The place is called Mysore that draws its name from 'Mahisasura' or the buffalo headed demon. He was the king of Mysore whose atrocious rule was ended by Goddess Chamundeshwari or Durga an incarnation of Parvati (consort of Lord Shiva). Located atop the 3000 ft high Chamundi hill is the huge Chamundeshwari temple built in reverence to the Goddess also called 'Mahisasura Mardini'. The Maharajas of consider the Goddess Chamundeshwari as their tutelary deity under whose blessings the state got reprive and by whose blessings the subjects prospered. The temple is a marvelous structure built in the Dravidian style. The idol of the Goddess made of pure solid gold is worshipped regularly with full ritualistic veneration and reverence. It is said that it was here that Goddess Durga fought a battle with Mahisasura in her quest to bring peace and tranquility on the earth. It is also symbolic of the Hindu faith that the good always prevails over all evils. Goddess Durga or 'Mahamaya' (the Mother of the Universe), is believed to be the creation of the trinity of Brahma, Vishnu and Maheswara (Shiva) who unitedly founded an embodiment of supreme power that found its form in a powerful female entity with ten arms. She is Goddess 'Durga' who then visits the earth to annihilate the evil demon Mahisasura who tormented the Gods for long. As the story goes there was a devil king by the name of 'Rambha' who fell for a beaulifal lady called 'Shyamala' who was cursed to be a water buffalo. Out of this union Shyamala conceived a more ferocious demon called 'Raktabeeja' or 'Mahishasur' ('Mahis' meaning buffalo and 'asur' means a demon). Raktabeeja had satisfied Lord Shiva through his penance and obtained a blessing that if he were wonded in war the each drop of his blood would multiply into another asura and add to the army against the enemy. Thus during his war here in the mountain with Durga the 64 joginis' helped her by slurping every drop of blood and protected proliferation of asura. Durga thus succeeded in anhilating Raktabeeja. This forceful depiction of warior Durga is also called the Chamunda form or 'Chamundeshwari. The temple is in that memory.

My wife and I visited the temple very early in the morning to attend the morning service. Only a fixed number of devotees are allowed to witness this session that too during the auspitious 'Navratri' period. By the time we reached entry was getting closed with a few visitors ahead of us. Luckily for us Mr. Srinivasa who was escorting us made good use of his influence as a government servant and the three of us finally managed to sneak in along with the last ones who were allowed entry. But the experience that we had was worth the mission. The hour-long session that began with the songs of devotion, the fold-over of the curtain with the appearance of the magnificent 'Durga pratima' followed by the offering of the prayer was something extremely satisfying and remained etched in our mind for a long long time. On our way back we halted at the place where the huge black monolithic statue of 'Nandi' (the bull which is the carrier of Lord Shiva) is located. It is a creation one must see. The immaculate form in sitting position built to such precision is quite amazing to watch. From here about 50 Km away is the Keshava temple said to have been built in 1268 AD and is also the last major temple of the Hoysala dynasty. (The Hoysalas who ruled Karnataka region during the 12th century were the most supreme of the all the other dynasties. They were also great builders of temples and monuments).

GOA is an ancient land where since the ancient itmes people of different culture and ethnically varied races had settled from time to time. References are found from the Sumerian Times over 200 years before the Christ era bagan. That time the place was said be called 'Gubio'. In the Mahabharata the place is refered to as a place where Brahmin colonies were set up sometime around 1700 BC. The place is refered to as 'Gomant'. Legends record that Lord Krshan who once traveled the place was so impressed by the cowheards that he named the place 'Go'puri' (Go or Gau in Hindi means cow and puri is place). According to the Mahabharata Parashuram (a mythical sage and the sixth incarnation of Lord Vishnu) who once ruled the place had obliterated the entire community of the 'Kshatriyas' (worriers). This led to anarchy in the state. Seeing this one saint named 'Kashyap' prayed to Parashuram to vacate the place and settle elsehere. Obligingly, Parashuram migrated from the place to find another to settle. Finding no expanse of land he went atop the mountain of the Western Ghats and ordered the Sea 'Varun' to receed to the point where his arrow would drop. He spewed an arrow from there and it fell in the middle of the sea far away. The place came to be known as Bannali. ('Baan' meaning arrow and 'ali is village). Subsequentlty this place came to be known as Benaulim where several settlers from the north of India came to settle. It is said that 'Saraswat Brahmis' who live along the 'Saraswat river in Punjab started to migrate after the river dried up and eventually vanished. Finding no option the Saraswat Brahmis then set-off eastward for Bengal. Midway they changed course and reached what is now known as Goa. Mention is also made of its fertile land and abundant warer resources that made it known as paradise on earth. Later around 200 BC it came under the rule of King Ashoka under the Mauran Empire. The land of Goa also attracted several merchants from overseas particularly the Greek, Roman and the Arabs. All of them had great praises for this blessed land. The Muslim Sultaate of Delhi ruled for a brief period during the 14th century followed by the Vajayanagar kings from Hampi in Karnatak. Later in 1510 Goa was conqured by Dom Afonso de Albuquerque the famous Prtugese naval general officer whose administrative skill and military might helped in establishing authority the in the Indian ocean. As a reward for his deeds Albuquerque was made the duke of Goa. He was the first from outside of the Royal familyto be so positioned. In his persuit to capture the spice trade Afonso de Albuquerque had put an end to free the movement of Muslims and the Turks in this region onland as well as in the sea. Later Goa became the capital of the Portugese Empire in the east and began to enjoy the same status as Lisbon in Portugal. Even after the Indipendence of India in 1947 Goa remained a Prortugese territory and was unwilling to give up to Indian request. The conflict was refered to the Internationa;l court of Justic as well as the United Nations but of no avail. India took control over the territory of Goa after a 36-hour battle in December 1961. The Portugese surrended unconditionally and the land was restored within the Republic of India.

The historical happenings of the place make it quite evident that the place would have several places of religious importance and memorials that have attained religious sanctity. Indeed there are many such in Goa. Perhaps one of the oldest temple here is situated near Valpoi. This is a 5th century temple dedicatefd to 'Brahma' In India one comes across very few "Brahma' temples. One such has been mentioned about in Ajmer in Rajasthan. Other temples dedicated to Lord Shiva includes the Pandavas Caves temple, and Shree Rudreshwar Temple at Aravalem. Another Shree Chandranath Temple at Paroda as the name suggests is dedicated to Lord of the Moon in the form of Lord

Shiva. Shree Nagueshi Temple, Bandode built aroung 1413 is place for worship of the 'Linguam' the symbol of Lord Shiva. The idol of Nandi in black stone adores the foregroung. Here too wood carvings depicting mythological instances could be seen. A temple dedicated to Lord Ganapathi, son of Lord Shiva Shree is located in Farmagudi. This stone image temple is relatively new.

Shree Mahalsa Narayani Temple is dedicated to Lord Vishnu but the deity inside portrays a female form. The wooden images in the temple corridor are a rare form of art that is unique to this place. At Bandode is situated Shree Mahalakshmi Temple dedicated to 'Mahalakshmi' the goddss of wealth and consort of Lord Vishnu.

Among the important Muslim religious sites are the Jama Masjid near Margao and Safa Masjid at Ponda. The Safa Masjid is older, built in 1560 by Ibrahim Adilshan of Bijapur (now in Karnataka). Both these places are prominent shrines where festivals are held with much grandeur.

Of the churches in Goa perhaps the oldest is the Church of Our Lady of Rosary. This is the only place where the conquest of Goa by Afonso de Albuquerque in 1510 is inscribed. The Portuguese however are said to have built the first church in 1521 by converting a prison into a place of worship. The structure later was converted into a museum and a school for teaching philosophy and theology and came to be called as the Rachol Seminary. But the most popular Church in Goa is the 16th Century Basillica of Bom Jesus. This shrine is dedicated to infant Jesus where the mortal remains of St. Francis Xavier are kept preserved in a silver casket. When I visited this place first in 1991, I paid my tribute and offered my gratitude that I owe to Francis Xavier under whose order of mission several institutions of education and enlightenment was built. I did my entire school and college education in two such reputed institutions of the country. I really owe my entire up bringing to these institutions and also believe that all that I have learnt here is what has carried me through in life. Basillica of Bom has now gained the status of a World Herritage Monument. Of all the cathedrals the most splendorous one I noticed was the Se Cathedral. Dedicated to St. Catherine the interior of the chirch is very imposing and opulent. Here one can see the famous Golden bell. In Goa, it is the biggest and said to one of the best in the world.

The cathedral is a tribute to Afonso de Albuquerque's victory over the Muslims in 1510. The victory day coincided with the feast of Saint Catherine and thus was dedicated to her. The structure was later enlarged and completed in 1619 and consecrated in 1640.

The only tower that could be seen today actually had a pair that collapsed in 1776. The Church of St. Francis of Assissi is also one of those few whch has an interior of orthodox setting built by the Portugeses in 1661. Here some wonderful paintings could be seen prettifying the walls. The Church of De Dens dedicated to Mother of God and The Church of St. Ana near Panaji located amidst beautiful surroundings are worth a visit.

Goa is one of the smaller states in terms of size tucked between two larger states Karnataka in the south and **MAHARASHTRA** in the north. Maharashtra as the name suggests is large ('Maha' meaning great). Indeed it is one of the largest and one of the most significant of all the states of modern India. It is the commercial capital and also a major port of transit for travellers and merchandise to and from foreign land. Capital Mumbai (earlier called Bombay) is popular for being the tinsel town and the hub of celluloid world better known as 'Bollywood'.

The name Bombay has recently been changed to Mumbai. Mumbai is said to be the original name and derives from the Goddess Maa Mumbadevi whose temple (now in Bhuleshwar on Marine Lines, Mumbai) once stood on the site of the present Victoria Terminus in the central island. It is said that Koli fishermen built the temple in the 15th century. This deity is an embodiment of strength and power. Maa Mumbadevi is a female deity seen riding on a tiger with 'Maa Annapurna' (the Goddess of food) by her side. The legend attributes the decend of Maa Mubadevi to the prayers of the local inhabitants before Lord Vishnu to protect them from the terrorizing acts of a ferocious demon called 'Mumbaraka'. Seeing their plight Lord Vishnu beckoned a goddess with eight arms who overpowered Mumbaraka and brought him to her feet. Finding himself helpless Mumbaraka beseeched the mother Goddess to adopt his name and in return assured to build a temple in her name. So it happened. The temple was actually built by the demon where the deity of the orange faced Goddess stands. Devotees still believe that the Goddess is the savior of all troubles and an embodiment of strength that could come to their relief to ward off all evils and distress. But the most popular among the religious sites in Mumbai is the 'Siddhi Vinayak Ganapati Temple' at Prabhadevi. Built in 1801, it houses the idol of Lord Ganesha. Lord Ganesh is an auspicious figure in whose name all good things are begun to gain good fortune and success that is desired. He is also the embodiment of 'Siddhi-Riddhi'.

Terms 'Siddhi-Riddhi' is derived from mythological references. 'Riddhi' means prosperity and well being and 'Siddhi' means perfection, accomplishment, attainment and success. These are reffered to spiritual power. The tenets of Hinduism speaks of eight primary 'Siddhi's (called 'Ashtha Siddhi') and ten secondary 'Siddhis'. The Lord has the ability to bestow them. Through another understanding they also refer to 'Lakhsmi' the Goddess of wealth and prosperity (i.e. Riddhi) and 'Saraswati' the Goddess of knowledge (i.e. Siddhi). While it is generally believed that Lord Ganesha is a true 'Brahmachari' (one who follows practiced strict celibacy) but he is visualized as being associated with Buddhi (intellect), Siddhi (spiritual power), and Riddhi (prosperity) as goddesses who are his consorts. 'Vinayaka' on the other hand symbolizes leadership and victoriousness. "Viyate Nayake Iti Vinayaka" that is, "He is a master unto Himself. Many worship Vinayaka In this world but Vinayaka does not worship anyone. He has no master above Him. Even Easwara, the father, worships His son Vinayaka, but it does not happen the other way".

Built at the behest of a rich old lady by the name of Deubai Patil. Deubai was childless. She once conversed with the Lord in her prayers and decided to erect this temple where devotees would come for their wish fulfillment and where childless women in particular would be blessed with a child in fulfillment of their wishes. The deity of Shree 'Siddhivinayak' in this temple is an idol carved out of a single stone. On either side of the idol are the two idols of goddesses Riddhi and Siddhi. For this reason the deity here is also called the Siddhivinayak Ganapati Temple.

The St John's Church is located at Colaba, Mumbai also known as Afghan Memorial Church of St. John the Baptist. Established in 1847 AD it was consecrated 11 years later as a memorial to those who fell in the First Afghan War of 1843 and Sind campaign of 1838.

Elephanta Caves situated 10 Km into the sea from the Gateway of India at Mumbai on Elephanta Island is a major tourist attraction in this region. These caves house the rock cut temples inside dating back to the 5th century BC. Elephanta Island was so named by Portuguese after they found a statue of an elephant on landing on the island. These temples rich in sculptural content are dedicated to Lord Shiva Mahadeva.

The mausoleum of Haji Ali situated on the sea half a mile of the beach at Mumbai can be reached by a walkway. Here lies the mosque and tomb of Haji Ali.

Haji Ali was an affluent merchant who denounced his wealth and riches in devotion to the almighty. It is for this reason and the deeds of wisdom that all honors him. It is believed that he died while on pilgrimage to to Macca. But drawn by his love for home and his people the chest of his coffin floated back here. This miracle mesmerized everyone and the casket was respectfully laid to rest here. The monument apart from being a place of pilgimage also serves as a place of shelter for all those who set out for pilgrimage to the holi city of Mecca.

A hundred kilometers away from Mumbai is Pune. This city is the bithplace of one of the most accomplished warrior and legendary hero of Indian history named 'Chhatrapati Shivaji Raje Bhosle' popularly known as Shivaji. This great military leader of India was born on 19th February 1630 to King Shahaji in Shivneri Fort, Junnar, 60 kilometres north of Pune. He was so named by his mother Jijabai after Goddess Shivai, to whom his mother prayed for having a son. Shivaji had an excellent upbringing under the guidance of his father. Several experts in warfare and educationists were put together to mentor his career. Most notable amongst them was well-ordered personnel Dadoji Konddev Gochivde whom Shahaji appointed as the guardian for Shivaji. Shivaji was taught swordsmanship horse-riding, Hindu ethos and languages like Persian and Sanskrit. All this groomed the young prince into a courageous warier and a conscientious governor. Shivaji took over the charge of Pune in 1647. Shivajis pursuit to expand his Maratha kingdom by eradicating the Mughals out of his homeland and establishing self-rule in Maharashtra, he fought many a battle and proved his mettle. The Marathas under Shivaji soon became a major threat for the Mughal Emperor Aurangzeb. Amongst several successes and setbacks Shivaji and his empire emerged as a formidable force to take on the Mughal who ruled most of Hindustan. On his coronation on June 6, 1674 at the Raigad fort Shivaji was formally crowned 'Chatrapati' ('Chatra' meaning umbrella or protection shield, and 'pati' is guardian. i.e., representing the protection he bestowed on his people. It is also interpreted as 'head or King of Kshatriyas'). Shivaji died on 3rd April, in 1680 at Raigad, after running a fever for weeks as a result of infected digestive system that severely damaged the intestinal lining.

Shivaji will always be remembered as a representation of the 'fight for freedom' a stimulus for resurgence of post Islamic India and for his contrbution towards strengthening of Hindu assertiveness. Chhatrapati Shivaji was a committed Hindu but he had utmost respect for all religions in his domain. Though he fought against the Muslim dominance he had high respect for the Sufi tradition of Islam. His ideology was one of inclusivity and tolerance of other religions. His subjects too enjoyed the freedom to practice the religions of their respective choice. While he fought to protect the rights of Hindus he was opposed to forced conversion.

The inspiration he infused and the regimentation he had implanted in his militia, the Marathas sustained the twenty-seven years war that was started in 1681 by Aurangazeb. Over the years the crusade compelled the mighty Mughal Empire to weaken and eventually withdraw. There on the Mughals never resurfaced to contest. It was only after three major Anglo-Maratha wars between 1775 and 1818 that the Marathas succumbed to the British and became a part of the British rule that by then had conqured most of India. The state of Maharashrta was later formed in 1961 when the Marathi and Gujarati speaking areas of former Bombay state were separated and Bombay city became the capital of the new state.

The plurality of religions and the spirit of tolerance amongst people and rulers of this region witnessed thriving of innumerable religious places in the form of temples, mosques, gurudwaras, ashrams and the like. Around pune one can find so many of them. One important temple is the Shree Ballaleshwar Vinayak temple in Raigard near Pune. Here Lord Ganapati is also known as Lord Ballaleshwar. The uniquness in this form of Ganesha is that this is perhaps the only idol that is named after the name of its devotee. Ballal was a young kid who developed a great attraction towards Ganapati. He became a staunch devotee and would often get into trans while concentrating on the Lord. Once put in distress by his father who was infuriated by the complaints of neighbours he prayed before the Lord. Ganapati is said to have appeared before him in human form. It did not take much time for Ballal to recognize him. Pleasesd by his devotion the Lord in disguise asked him to express his wish. To this he asked the Lord to stay here always to remove the miseries of the people. So it happened and he vanished into a stone nearby. God desired that henceforth 'your name would appear before my name and the stone would be known as 'Ballal Vinayak'. One Nana Phadnis a well-known intellectual in Maratha Darbar later built a temple around it 1770 during Peshwa rule. Another important Ganapati Temple is situated at Sangli on the banks of river Krishna. Sangli is some 450 KM south of Mumbai is a place of natural beauty. There are mountains, forests, several rivulets, waterfalls wildlife sanctuaries and forts. The idol here was installed and sanctified in 1843 by the Patwardhans.

On way to Pune sixty kilometers away from Mumbai is a small village town called Ambarnath where the famous Ambarnath Temple is situate. 'Ambernath' as the name suggests is dedicated to Lord Shiva. This temple is pretty old. The temple was built in Saka 982 or 1060 AD as inscribed on the north-facing door of the temple. That was the time of the Silhara dynasty that ruled North Konkan, comprising the modern Thana, Bombay and

Colaba districts, from 800 AD to 1240 AD. The elegance of the temple lies in its richly carved stone blocks that form the external walls. Seeing this one is reminded of the Dilwara temple of Rajasthan.

In Pune one can come across yet another important Siva temple known as the Nageshwar Temple or Nagnath Temple ('Nag' means serpant that adorns the tresses of Shiva). Nageshwar temple is considered as one of the oldest temples of Pune that are associated with the work and times of Saint Gyaneshwar (1271 AD) a spiritual leader, poet and a master of yoga and Tukaram (1600 AD) a well regarded poet saints of the country). Close by is a beautiful place called Bhimashankar. It's a natural paradise and also the origin of river Bhima. This river is said to have sprung out of the heat and intensity that generated during a fierce war between Lord Shiva (also called 'Shankar) and Tripurasura rakshas (demon). Here one can find a temple dedicated to Lord Shiva that is considered as one of the 12 Jyotirlingas in India. Another temple dedicated to Lord Shiva is at Parnakuti on a hilltop.

This temple is also one of the oldest known temples in Pune. Closeby is a small town known as Karla or Karli that is famous for the Karli Caves—a 1st century BC Buddhist temple or chaitya cut out from stone. Driving twards Aurangabad one comes across Meharabad a pilgrimage center dedicated to Meher Baba. Persian by origin Meher Baba became a devine preacher "explaining creation, evolution of consciousness through infinite variety of forms, re-incarnation and involution of consciousness in a language intelligible to an average man's understanding and at the same time scientific and logical in convincing the rationalist".

Ganesh Peth Gurdwara, Gurdwara Shri Gurusingh Sabha and Ramgodia Shivajinagar Gurdwara are important Sikh temples where people gather in large number to offer their prayer. Chand Tara Masjid, Inaam

Masjid, Janwadi Mosque and Aundh Masque are places of Islamic worship. Shree Mahaveer Digamber Jain Temple, Shree Mahavir Jain Temple and Shree Chandraprabhu Jain Temple are places of worship for the Jains. Similarly one can find Jewish Synagogues, Buddhist shrines and several Ashrams set up by popular preachers.

One such located in Pune is the Osho Ashram or Osho International Meditation Resort founded by Bhagwan Rajneesh. Osho was born on 11th December 1931 and his original name was Rajneesh Chandra Mohan Jain. Later he gained enlightenment of some sort and preached the course of peace and happiness in his own unique way. He soon became popular and also controversial because he spoke against the institutionalized religions, and made a mockery of Gods, religious practices and prominent saints. His approach towards sexuality also made him known as the 'sex-guru'. But the Bhagwan had tremendous knowledge of Yoga, Tantra, Taoism, Zen, Christianity, Buddhism and scriptures such as the Upanishads and the Guru Granth Sahib. His power to articulate and captivate the mind of his listeners drew a large following particularly the rich and the famous. His charisma led him to USA where he went with the purpose of medical treatment in 1981 and ended up establishing an Internatinal Community in Oregon with the active participation of his innumerable followers. But for certain alleged involvement in wrongful acts of his followers he got implicated and prosecuted against. His subsequent imprisonment and widespread misapprehension brought much disrepute to him and his institution. After a long drawn legal battle he left America and retured to India to his old Ashram in Pune in 1987. A year later he denounced his title and preferred to be called as 'Osho' alone (meaning religious master). Osho died On January 19, 1990 at the age of 58 at the Pune Ashram. The inscription where his mortal remains are burried reads

"OSHO Never Born, Never Died. Only Visited this Planet Earth between Dec 11 1931-Jan 19 1990." Though his career got maligned during the last stages he is still remembered by many eminent people and those who have come across him that he was as a free and independent thinker who tried to enlighten the people and teach them to liberate themselves from the shackes of convention. His reflections on the various facets of human existence are still postmodern and indeed thought provoking. Even today, so many years after his death more that 200,000 visitors still pay visit to his ashram each year at Pune.

Amongst the other places of religious interest are the 8th century Panchaleshwar Temple, an ancient rock cut Pataleshwar Temple, which is also of the same time, Parvati Hill and Temples dedicated to Lord Shiva, Goddess Parvati, Lord Ganesha and Lord Kartikeya, the family of Lord Siva, which were built by Balaji Baji Rao and the Trishundya Ganapati Temple. Pune also has one rare Zoroastrian Fire temple built by Sir Jeejeebhoy in 1844, which has the Holy Fire and Sacred Holy Book in it.

A five-hour road journey from Pune is Shirdi. This is where the Temple of 'Sai Baba' is located. This temple is a beautiful shrine that was built over the Samadhi of Shri Sai Baba. Nothing is known about the birth, parentage or early life of this spiritual Saint except that he occasionally appeared as a quiet and unpretentious person who lived in an old and dilapidated mosque in Shirdi. Gradually people came to recognize him through his miraculous deeds and kind words that he uttered. He was identified as an ordinary fakir. Gradually as time passed by his teachings began to draw visitors from different parts of the country. People came to realize the enormity of his spiritual powers. The miracles he performed were not to mesmerize but to cure the incurably sick, help those in need and in reading the minds of others. He drew unto himself countless souls caught up in ignorance and opened their eyes to the true meaning of life. It is said that as long as he lived Sai Baba attempted to awaken every man from the darkness of ignorance and set in motion a wave of spirituality, which still continues to spread all over the world. His glorious life came to an end on October 15, 1918 but his teachings and the devotion towards him still continues to spread at an even faster pace amongst Hindus, Muslims and all religions alike. As seen in most of his pictures he is found seated on a black stone block. That stone is still there preserved with reverence. When I visited the temple it was just passed midnight. The main temple door was closed by then. As I had to reach Pune the next morning I could not see the main statue of the Saint that is worshiped there. I had to remain content with the black stone. This stone afterall is a real object of continuity that was in physical contact with Sai. The idol is only a manufactured one intalled at a later date.

Amongst other important Ashrams is 'Sewagram'. Mahatma Gandhi set up this Ashram in Wardha in the year 1934 under patronage from a rich businessan named Jamnalalji Bajaj. May not be a religious place in that sense but certainly a place of pilgimage for many as here lived the Mahatma. Gandhiji carried out his freedom movement from this Ashram. Sewagram ('Sewa' means service and 'gram is village) is the epitome of Gandhiji's teachings of simplicity and truth. Opposite to the ashram there is a guesthouse complex spread over a large expanse of land and equipped with all facilities for boading and lodging. In February 2007 I too had the opportunity to stay here for a couple of days to attend a Servas conference. During that time I also visited Vinoba Bhave Ashram at Paunar, near Wardha. Vinoba Bhave the most trusted lieutenant of Mahatma Gandhi at Sabarmati Ashram was sent to Wardha to start a similar Ashram. Vinoba Bhave started his own Ashram at Paunar, where he continued to stay till his death on

15th November 1962. Vinoba lived in accordance with the eleven vows, included in Gandhian daily prayer, viz. non-violence, manual work, truthfulness, absolute honesty, chastity, poverty, fearlessness, temperance, respect for all religions, independence in the matter of money and non-recognition of cast distinctions.

Other religious spots near here are Vishwa Shanti Stupa or the prayer place for of Budha Community in India, Varad Vinayak (Lord Ganesh) temple at Kelzer and the 1905 Laxmi Narayan Temple of Lord Vishnu and Laxmi.

On way to Wardha I passed through Nagpur. I have fond memories of Nagpur where I had spent the earliest days of my childhood. We left this city in 1964 and thereafter this was my first visit after 43 years. I found that the little town I lived in had grown into a beautiful city but had not become nasty as most others have. The greenery and the clenliness still exist. I was put-up in a hotel which I realised was standing in a place that used to be a barren land then beside our school premises. I visited my school the famous Bishop Cotton School on Church Road. That was my first school. The bulidings and the playing fields still are the same except for a few encroachments at the rear near the baby field (that was meant for us then). The assembly couriyard, the notice board and the office building where I first came for an interview with my father existed as it was then. Mr. Newman was the Head Master at that time. I do not remember the names of my teachers but I only remember they were beautiful Anglo-Indian ladies and wonderful gentlemen who had the perfect knack of teaching the young. Memories about them may have faded but I do owe them a lot for their contribution to my up bringing in the very formative stage of my life. I liked my school very much and most of all I liked going to school. As narrated in 'Nation Master'—Encyclopedia "The Bishop Cotton

School, Nagpur is an old co-educational school which had been established in 1862, by Bishop George Edward Lynch Cotton, son of an Army Captain, who died leading his Regiment in a battle. A scholar of Westminster, and a graduate of Cambridge was appointed Assistant Master at Rugby by Doctor Thomas Arnold, one of the founders of the British Public School system. Bishop George Cotton drowned in an accident on 6th October 1866 while touring Assam in the Governor's yacht on the river Gorai. To perpetuate the memory this school in Nagpur was established."

Founded on the banks of the River Nag, Nagpur city today is India's "zero mile" being situated right at the centre of the country. Nagpur is also famous for its large mandarin Nagpur oranges. This is why the city is also known as the 'Orange city'. There are no pilgrimage centers in or around Nagpur. Perhaps this is a reason why the serenity of the place has not got spoilt. The only place connected to mythology is perhaps 'Ramtek' located about 50 Km away. Here it is said that Lord Ram, Sita and Laxman, had visited here on way to south, hence the name Ramtek ('tekri' in Marathi means hill). Also the place is cherished for being the place where one of India's greatest Sanskrit poet and dramatist 'Kalidas' (of 6th century AD) wrote the epic poem, 'Meghdoot' (meaning Cloud Messenger). To commorate this there is a Ram Temple and a Kalidas Memorial. This place is also famous for producing a high quality 'beetel-leaf'.

Nagpur falls within the Vidharva region of Maharashtra. Inspite of the better possibilities there, I feel terribly bad because this region is more in the news for the large number of farmer commiting suicide here. People here are devoted to Goddess 'Ambadevi'. A temple dedicated to Amba Devi is situated at the heart of the city of Amaravati, which is 155 km from Nagpur. Goddess Amba Devi is the personification of power and vigor, the prevalence of good over evil and bestower of strength to overcome hurdles. It is said that 'Rukmini' (the first and most prominent of Lord Krishna's 16,108 queens) is also considered as the reincarnation of the Goddess of wealth and fortune Lakshmi) had come to pray at the Amba Devi temple when Shri Krishna abducted and married her. There is also an interesting anecdote connected to this historical temple.

Once upon a time there lived a king named 'Bhishmaka' who ruled in the region now known as Vidarbha. Bhishmaka had a daughter named 'Rukmini' who was most beautiful, virtuous and adored amongst the most eligible princess on earth then. Krshna who lived in Dwarka was also the most charming and sought after by the women folks. Though they lived miles apart the two had fallen in love with each other. On coming to know of their likings, Rukmini's parents decided to carry the proposal of marriage to Dwarka. But Rukmini's brother 'Rukmi' was strongly opposed to the idea and persuaded Bhishmaka to hold the nuptials. The reason for Rukmi's dissent was that he was under the partronage and alliance of another ruler by the name of 'Jarasandh'. Jarasandh had once decided to give his daughters in marriage to king 'Kansa'. But Krshna had killed Kansa. So Jarasandh became a natural foe of Krshna. Instead, Rukmi proposed that she be married to his friend 'Shishupala', the crown prince of 'Chedi' and also a confederate of Jarasandha and hence an ally of Rukmi. Bhishmaka yielded to the argument but Rukmini, who had overheard the exchange, was perturbed and felt terribly led down. In defiance she called her friend and secretly arranged to deliver a letter to Krshna through a trusted messenger. In that letter Rukmini narrated the unforunate happenings and the dangerous situation that was likely to arise if the marriage was formally organised. She thus suggested to Krshna to come to Vidarbha and abduct her and claim to marry her. This in her view was the only way to avoid war and bloodshed. She also suggested the day when she would be going to the Amba Devi temple alone. She also added that if Krishna refused to comply she would end her life in the depths of despair.

On getting this message at Dwarka, Krishna set off for Vidharba with his brother 'Balaram'. Meantime while Shishupal was unworried and rejoicing about soon getting married to one of the most attractive woman on earth, the shrewd Jarasandha was suspicious of a possible reprisal. So he deployed his spies to keep him informed. Bhishmaka by now had come to know of the plans of his daughter and readily sided with her. Draped in her marriage attire Rukmini proceeded for this very Amba Devi temple on the D-day to offer her prayers. After her prayers were over she looked around. There was no one. She was too disappointed that Krshna had not come. But when she stepped out of the temple she became jubilant. The sight of Krshna waiting with his chariot to carry her away was like a dream come true. She waited for this moment all her life and the time had finally arrived when she would become one with her beloved. Sparing no time Krshna grasped her and fuung into the chariot and sped away. From far a happy Bhishmaka bid them goodbye and showered his blessing to the two. But the real face-off was far from over. Shishupala noticed them eloping in a charriot. Soon Rukmi and Shishupala started their chase while Jarasandha's forces began to follow. The indomitable Balaram engaged Jarasandh's army but Rukmi soon cought up and intercepted Krshna's chariot. The duel that followed resulted in Krshna's triumph. Krshna was about to kill him but Rukmini fell at Krshna's feet and begged for her brother's life. Merciful Krshna spared his life and freed him but not before shaving his head in punishment. Krishna and Rukmini got a rousing welcome on their arrival at Dwaraka. Soon after they were ceremonially married with great pomp and grandeur.

Shishupal's meeting his doom in the hand of Krshna was pre-destined by the voice of heaven at the time of his birth. Shishupal was born to a lady who was sister of 'Vasudev'. Thus in a way he was related to Krshna. After his birth Shishupal was born ugly with two extra limbs and three eyes. He was thus abandoned after birth. When his disgusted father decided to kill him there was the voice from the heaven asking him not to kill. 'Once the child is taken in the lap he would immediately get rid of his ugly features and become a nornal human'. But he 'who will pick him up will also become the cause of his death at a later stage in life'. So no one dared to pick the baby and he was left on his own. Unaware of all this, compassionate Krshna came to see the newborn. Finding him unattended Krshna picked up the infant and placed him on his lap. Shishupal soon became a normal baby and all his appendages fell off . . . His mother rushed to the place and told Krisna about the surmon from the sky and prayed to Krshna to think a hundred times before he killed her son. Later in a Rajasuya function organised by Yudhishthira for honouring Lord Sri Krishna, Sisupala appeared and began to insult Lord Krshna and commit blasphemy. He hurled slanderous abuses at the Lord and began to threaten him as well. This annoyed everyone. Having done with a hundred insults Shishupal exhausted all his options of survival. His appearance before Krshna was actually his death that brought him there. Lord Krshna left with no option summoned His Divine discus. As Sisupala rushed at Sri Krishna with his raised sword, the sharp blade of the discus landed on Sisupala's neck severing his head from the body.

The Amba Devi temple at Amaravati is said to be the same very temple where Rukmini prayed before she met Krshna and fled away. Amba Devi is also regarded as 'Maha Lakshmi' and Rukmini the beloved consort of Krshna is also considered as an incarnation of Goddess Mahalaxmi.

Another famous Mahalaxmi Temple dedicated to the worship of Amba Bai is located at Kolhapur near Mumbai. This place has grown into a center for spiritual enlightenment. This is a 7th century temple constructed by Chalukya rulers. Faith and architecture of this exquisitely carved monument attracts thousands of devotees from all over the country and abroad. A visit to 'Chakreshwar Temple' is located near Kolhapur, is regarded as a part of pilgrimage while visiting the Mahalakshmi temple at Kolhapur.

Kolhapur is also a place of pilgrimage for the Jains. Nana Hill close by is the abode of sage Bahubali (Digambar Acharya Samantabhadraji Maharaj Saheb) who meditated here during the mid-seventeenth century. Installed here is the nine-meter tall white marble statue of Bhagvan Bahubali Khadgasana (standing) posture and temples of the 24 Jain 'Tirthankaras' or Saints. A temple of goddess Durga adores the hilltop and draws devotees from far and near. This place has thus become a sacred place for both Hindus and Jains.

But Kolhapur in recent times has gained a celebraty status for its unique brand of slippers called the 'Kolhapuri Chappals' ('chappals' meaning casual slippers). It is an age-old trade here of making the footwear by hand. This makes each product unique and inimitable. Wearing a 'Kolhapuri chappal was once very fashionable. Unfortunately this trade like many other handicrafts is fast slipping into obscurity and may soon become extinct.

An overnight journey from Nagpur and about 400 Km from Mumbai is Aurangabad a town named after the great Mogul emperor Aurangazeb. Aurangabad was developed as a trading hub some four hundred ago. This town was a major trade route that used to connect north and western India's sea and land ports to the Deccan region. Today it is famous for the well-known world heritage caves of Ajanta & Ellora. These caves were carved during 350 A.D. to 700 A.D. They depict the stories of Buddhism and represent the three faiths of Hinduism, Buddhism and Jainism. These are some of the finest examples of cave temple architecture that remained in obscurity till were discovered in the 19th century by some British Officers during a tiger hunt. One can find an ancient Shiva Temple in the village of Ellora, 30 km from Aurangabad. It is reported to be the largest of the 34 excavations at Ellora. It took about a century to complete this task that involved reassembling of 200,000 pieces of excavated stones. Apart from the 30 meters by nearly 55 meters idol there are several stone engravings along the pricincts of the temple that depict scenes from the Hindu mythology including the Ramayana and Mahabharata. Shiva is worshiped in this temple. A festval of dance and music is also held periodically here. The 'Anwa Temple' is located close to Aurangabad is dedicated to Lord Shiva. The temple dates back to 12th century. 'Bibi Ka Maqbara' built in 1678 by Prince Azam Shah; son of Aurangazeb is situated 5 km away from Aurangabad. This is a monument that resembles the famous Taj Mahal was built in the memory of his mother Begum Rabia Durani.

A little over 500 km from Mumbai, beyond Sholapur is a small town of Ganganapur. Here one can see the shrine of Dattatreya, who was an incarnate of Lord Vishnu. Temple dedicated to Dattatrya is seldom seen in any other part of the country. I have never come across one. Dattatreya was the son of a sage named 'Atri' and his wife 'Anasuya'. Atri's 'tapasya' (penance) was so severe that all the three Lords of the universe Brahma, Vishnu and Mahesh appeared before him. They asked him as to what he desired. He said he wanted a son who would be blessed with such divine powers that he will have the qualities of all the three of them. The Gods said 'so will it be'. Of the several sons born to him namely 'Soma', 'Dutta' and 'Durvasa' were the 'avatar' of Brahma, Vishnu and Mahesh respectively. Out of the three 'Dutta' following the footsteps of his father gained profound knowledge through extreme meditation and devine learning. His astuteness and wisdom attained such high order that in him is believed to vest the features of the three. Thus Dutta came to be called 'Dutta-treya'. In the temple here the 'padukas' (pair of footware) of Dattatrya is worshipped. Sixty-five kilometers away from Sholapur on the banks of river Bhimarathi is another place of Vishnu worship called Pandharpur. Here there is a temple of Lord Vithoba. He is considered and revered as Vishnu. It is a large temple and even larger is the admiration it draws from the people across the country. Devotees of Lord Krishna too pay visit to this temple where Lord Vithoba is shown standing along with consort Rukmini. It is said that great Vaishnava saints like Tukaram, Namdev, Jnaneshwar and Eknath have enhanced the glory of the place during their visit to the shrine between 13th to 17th Century AD. Going by the inscriptions in the temple as deciphered and the references drawn by local experts' the image in this temple dates back to the 5th century.

Travelling northwards along the coast of the Arabian Sea one crosses the picturesque territories of **DAMAN, DIU AND DADAR & NAGAR HAVELI**. These were Portuguese colony (along with Goa) till about fifty years ago, now Union Territories of India. Situated within the Saurashtra Peninsula of Gujarat, Diu attains mythological significance from the understanding that during the 'Mahabharata' period the place was under the kingdom of the 'Yadavas' under Lord Krishna and that the 'Pandavas' stayed here for a while during their period of exile. Historical monuments, like the 1610 St. Paul's Church and St. Thomas Church are reminders of the Portugese past. The 17th-century-old Se Cathedral and the Church of Our Lady of Rosary are a major attraction of tourism in Daman.

Treading over these stunningly wonderful coasts one gets to get the feel of **GUJARAT** the home state of Mahatma Gandhi. Along the banks of river Sabarmati in the capital city of Ahmedabad Mahatma Gandhi founded an ashram in 1915. He called this the Satyagraha Ashram. It was from here, that the Mahatma began his famous 'Dandi March' in 1930 to protest against the Salt Tax imposed by the British. Today it is called the Sabarmati Ashram and is one of the most important pilgrimage centers of modern India and the world. The state of Gujrat is indeed a blessed one. It has not only given birth to the Mahatma but several stalwarts and above all the people who are blessed with the supreme skill of enterprenureship that makes Gujrat the most industrialized states of India today. It is also blessed because here resided 'Dwararkadhis the Almighty Lord Shri Krishna after his migration from Mathura. He settled and established his terrestrial kingdom at Dwarka, in Jamnagar. The original Dwarka where Krshna actually lived is said to have been submerged in the Arbian Sea. The 16th century Dwarkadhish Temple was built to commemorate the kingdom of the Lord. Lord Krishna is also called Dwarkadish, which means Lord of Dwarka. The original temple built over 'Hari-Graha' (Lord's residence) is said to have been built by Krishna's grandson, Vajranabha. The Jagat Mandir has a recorded history of 2500 years. The temple diety is represented by Lord Vishnu with four-arms. The other temples are of Lord Krshna's brother Balarame, Krshna's son Pradyumna and another of grandson Aniruddha. Other shrines are of Lord Shiva, mother Devaki (Krishna's mother). Another temple here dedicated to Lord Vishnu is called Beni-madhava temple (Beni & Madhava both are synonymous to Lord

Krshna). Shrine of Purusottama, Kuseswara Mahadeva shrine, shrines of Radhikaji, Lakshmi-Narayan and Saraswati are other monuments that adorn the location.

Moving southward along the coast is a small town called Porbandar that is known for being the birthplace of Mahatma Gandhi. Mythology also reflects that one of Lord Krishna's childhood friends 'Sudama' was also born here. Lord Krishna and Sudama studied together at sage Sandipani's Gurukul. After their academic learning was over Shri Krishna and Sudama entered their respective field of work. Krishna served as a ruler while Sudama returned to his native place and started his married life. In due course of time Sudama's economic condition went from bad to worse. With a wife and several children he was unable to make the ends meet. His wife Sushila then suggested to Sudama to meet Lord Krshna his childhood friend hoping that He could ameliorate them from the miseries. Sudama was reluctant but was also helpless considering the miserable condition of his family. He decided to take a chance. It came to his mind that he should not go empty handed to his friend's palce. At best he could afford some parched rice for his friend. Tied a handful in a cloth pouch he set off for his friends place in Dwarka. As it was long since they had parted after the gurukul days and had never met in between he wondered whether Krshna would be able to recognize him at all. On reaching the gates of the Lord's palace he sent the message of his arrival. Hearing this Lord Krishna rushed to the gate for his friend and adoringly ushered him inside. He took Sudama to his personal room in the palace and made him seated on a chair. Overwhelmed by the visit of his long-lost childhood friend Krshna began to wash his feet. Seeing the pitiful condition of his friend He held Sudama's feet and tears rolled down Krishna's cheeks. Then food was offered to him and comforting him in every possible way he chatted with him holding his hands and recalled the time when they were together in the Gurukul. They recalled that once they had gone to the forests to collect fuel wood for their Guru when a trrible storm had set-in. They were caught in a heavy storm and rain. The weather went so bad that they had to spend the night in the forest without food. But Sudama had some morselful tucked in his clothes. Unable to bear the hunger he had silently devoured it alone without letting Krshna know about it. At sunrise, when Guru Sandipani came to know about this, he had himself arrived in the forest. Seeing their dedication to duty and responsibility for the Guru he blessed them that all of their ambitions be fulfilled. Krshna then said it is the teacher whose grace gets peace and all the luxuries of life. To this Sudama added that he was privileged to receive Krshna's company at the Gurukul. Krshna in the meanwhile could understand from his conversation that Sudama was living in a precarious condition. But during the course of his stay Sudama never uttered a word about his distress or asked for favor. Rather he only expressed his love and happiness of meeting his long lost friend. Krishna on his part had decided by then that he will now give him such wealth to his dear friend that would be rare even for the Gods to possess. He wittily asked Sudama what he had brought for him for this visit. Sudama having seen affluence of Krshna life style was too embarrassed to open the rag pack of rice. But Krshna on seeing the bundle forced him to show what he has brought. When he opened the bundle Krshna was overjoyed. He exclaimed: "O friend, you have brought me a wonderful gift". Saying this, He took a morsel of the favourite childhood foodstuff and ate a handful. The satisfaction that appeared in his expression and the affection that showed in his eyes delighted Rukmani. She said to Lord Krshna "O soul of the universe, please give this man prosperity in this world and in another. Eating one handful of parched rice is enough to bestow the desire that you have in your mind". It is said that the pain of hunger that He had experienced in the forest at childhood had lingered since. It was quenched on taking this handful now. On reaching home the next morning Sudama was perplexed to find that his dwelling hut was not there and in its palce stood a splenderous palace that he had never seen before. People in the neighbourhood who looked at him with sympathy now welcomed him. On hearing the arrival of her husband Susheela was full of joy. She at once came out of the palace and greeted him touching his feet. She was adorned with different types of ornaments and surrounded by maids. Sudama realised that it was the deed of his friend to bestow this relief on him and made him so wealthy in every respect. Sudama said to himself that Krshna could read the minds of his devotees but would remain silent. Such is the generosity of Shri Krishna that a gift so meager for him but given with love and truthfulness according to ones means fills him with such esctacy and he in return pours his choicest blessings to the giver that keeps him fulfilled everafter. Elated Sudama prayed that he in his many births gets the love and friendship of Krshna and only long for love for his feet. Unaffected by all the allurements, Sudama lived along with his wife Susheela in the palace that they had received as a bounty from Krishna. Day by day, their love for Shri Krishna grew. After their death, they joined the Lord in His heavenly abode.

This place is thus made holi and the other temples that have been erected from time to time there are the Sudama Mandir, Bharat Mandir, Gayatri Mandir, Gita Mandir, Hanuman Mandir and the Kirti Mandir.

Further down on the coast is Someshwar Mahadev temple at Somnath in Junagadh district. It is said that Soma, the moon God was married to the 27 daughters of King Daksha Prajapati. (Daksha Prajapati is considered as the son of Lord Brahma. He is said to be presiding over procreation and protector of life—thus 'Prajapati'). But Soma was obsessed with Rohini (one of the 27 sisters) only. The other daughters were left utterly neglected. This infuriated Daksh and when he lost his patience he cursed him with an incurable illness. Soma was dipressed but was not crestfallen. He decided to go to seek Lord Shiva's blessings. So he prayed to the Lord with dedication and devotion. In due course his illness got cured by the blessings of the Lord. Soma constructed this temple as a gesture of gratitude to Shiva. According to legend, Soma had built the temple in gold.

On way to Amba temple in Junagarh is the Jain shrine of Neminath (the 22th Tirthankar). This rectangular temple is said to have been built between 1128 AD and 1159 AD. Vastupal and Tejpal, two brothers who were ministers of a clan king and devotees of Jainism and who had built several Jain Temples also built Mallinath temple dedicated to the 19th Tirthankar in 1231 AD. The Rishabhadev temple and Parshwanath temple of the 15th century are also found here. Here one also comes across a temple dedicated to Surya or the Sun God constructed in 1026-27 AD.

Junagurh is the seat of Ambe Mata, the mother goddess. Situated on the hill in the Aravali Range of mountains the 12th century Ambaji temple stands in testimony to this. She is a form of Parvati, the consort of Lord Shiva. Ambe Mata is the Adya Shakti (original source of all strength, the fundamental female power). It is believed that Goddess Amba's blessing ensures eternal conjugal bliss for all married couple. Ambaji is one of the 52 main Shakti Piths. According to tradition Sati's heart fell here at Ambaji making it one of the most auspicious and sacrosanct of the religious places. It is said that the goddess revealed herself on the Gabbar Hill nearby and left her footprints. The Maha Kali temple enshrines an image of Kalika Mata nearby. Here Goddess

Kali is worshipped as Dakshina Kali, and is worshipped according to tantric rites as enshrined in the Vedias.

Navsari a nearby town 30 kms south of Surat is the place of first settlement of the Parsis—a Fire temple 'atas Beharam' stands here in testimony to the same. The sacred fire here was brought from Persia and conveyed in to this temple. As the history goes—the Arab invasion of Persia in the 7th century brought an end to the dominance of the Zoroastrians' in the kingdom. The Muslim rulers inflicted atrocities on the Zoroastrians. They were treated brutaly. Persecutions were rampant and were unreasonably discriminated against. Soon life became miserable and unbearable for the Zoroastrians. A few of them decided to quit their land and move to Hindustan. Persians used to denote the land beyond the Indus River as Hindus. The name Hindustan thus was coined (the suffix 'stan' in Iranian connotes place). They first landed in the island of Diu (in Saurashtra, South Gujarat). A decade later about 18-20 thousand of them migrated to the mainland of Gujarat and sought refuge from the the Hindu King named Jadi Rana. The king was generous but rational. He laid down certain conditions for their stay, like disowning weapons, adopting the local language, adopting the local attire for their women and conducting marriages only in the evening like the Hindus. They agreed to all the conditions and began to live in peace. Seeing their conduct, their devotion to faith, and the tranquility in their oration the king acceded to their request to set up a fire temple and kindle the Atash-Beharam, the highest grade of sacred fire known to Zorastrians, for which the religious requisites had to be brought especially from Khurasan. As these new inhabitants began to be known as the Parsis (The term Parsi is derived from 'Pars' the place where they once dwelled), this place came to be known as Sarjan—a place in Khorasan province of Iran where from they hailed.

Zoroastrianism is a faith founded on the teachings of the Prophet Zarathustra, who lived sometime between 1500 and 600 BC in Persia. Zarathustra preached three virtues—Humata, Hukhta, Huvarashta,—meaning Good Thoughts, Good Words, and Good Deeds. The Persians are tought to hold Good Deeds the highest in the order. They believe in 'The Wise Lord' or 'Ahura-Mazda' as they call with whom ones soul must spiritually unite through good deeds on earth. 'Ahura-Mazda' is a belief that gives its followers the free will to obey the divine natural universal laws or to disobey them. They believe in the cycles of rebirths on this earth and based on their deeds it is believed that a soul will progress on the path of 'Asha'. (Asha is an essential part of the Wise Lord is also the tool with which in His Wisdom, Mazda promotes the Living World).

Historically, the first settlement of the Parsis took place in Navsari in 1142 A.D. Navsari is also recognized as the birthplace of the great business tycoons such as Dadabhoy Naoroji, Jamshetji Tata and Sir Jamshetji Jeejeebhoy. Historically this place also draws importance because it here that Mahatma Gandhi along with his followers, walked upto from Sabarmati Ashram (Ahmadabad to Dandi, Navsari) to make salt in protest against the British salt tax in colonial India.

The Parsi community in Inda has made immense contribution to the Indian economy. They are one such migrant community that has tended to blend compassion to business interest and have seldom resorted to ruthless commercial interest. They have only worked to contribute and never plundered or took special favour. Inspite of their small and dwindling population they never sought any special privileges from the state. They are a dynamic Indian community that has honestly excelled in business, arts, law, politics, military, sports and so many other fields. They have been institution builders, employment providers and income generators for the nation. Because of their integrity and compassionate frame of mind they are also one of the truly philanthrophic kind. Some names that deserve mention amongst many more are the Wadias, the Godrejs, Tatas, Air Marshal Engineer, Admiral Jal Cursetji, Field Marshal Sam Maneckshaw, Dr. Homi Bhabha, Zubin Mehta and Feroz Gandhi et al. Parsi Vad and the various other edifices of this place that are built in the authentic Parsi style are the reminiscence of the byegone era. Navsari, the first dwelling place of the Parsis is now an important tourist attraction. Not only the Parsis but also tourists from the different places of the country come here to have a look at Navsari.

Jamnagar in Saurashtra interestingly has a Bala Hanuman Temple that has earned a place in the Guinness Book of Records. Dedicated to Lord Hanuman who was an ardent disciple of Lord Rama this temple has witnessed the 24 hours chanting of 'Sri Ram, Jai Ram, Jai Jai Ram' continuously since August 1964 and thus entered the record books.

We had reached Gujrat after crossing Maharashtra. Both these states have a common neighbor with which Maharashtra shares the longet border and Gujar the shortest. This is the state of Madhya Pradesh. The splendour of **MADHYA PRADESH** lies in its being a truly multi-religious state with diverse topographical features. For that reason place has several important historical monuments, temples, mosques, shrines and monasteries. The famous tenth century ruler of the 'Parmar' dynasty called Raja Bhoj founded capital city of Bhopal. Raja Bhoj was a versatile character and was bestowed with expertise in diverse fields. He was a competent commander of the armed forces who had won several accolades at war with other kings and Muslim intruders. Apart from his skill in civil archtecture, medicine, veterinary science oceanic knowledge and spiritual understanding he was a great literarian, a philosopher and a poet in Sanskrit. During his rule he laid great emphasis in educating the people and imparting of knowledge in diverse fields. He named the city as 'Bhojpal' (after his name) that later became 'Bhopal'. Later the city of Bhopal came under the governance of the Afgan and Mughul rulers for over a century from the mid 17 th century. One can thus find large and immaculately architectured Masjids like Moti Masjid built in 1860 by Sikandar Jahan, the daughter of Kudsia Begum, The Taj-ul Masjid, Shaukat Mahal designed by a Frenchman built in Gothic architectural patterns and Sadar Manzil that is situated near Shaukat Mahal. This building was to be converted into the office of the Bhopal Municipality. Bhopal also has one of the Birla Temples dedicated do the famous Lakshmi and Narain deities.

Although its capital Bhopal has a significantly old history but the concentration of the important religious sites are mainly in the neighbouring districts particularly Ujjain and Indore. Both these cities have Temples dedicated to Lord Ganpati or Ganesha (the son of Shiva). Ganpati Temple of Indore was built in the year 1875 and the idol is perhaps the largest in the whole world and measure 8 m in height. This is also thus called the Bade Ganeshji Ka Mandir ('Bade' meaning big). A temple by the similar name is also there at Ujjain. In the center of the temple one can see a rare 'Panch mukhi Hanuman' (Panch meaning five, mukh means face). The significance of Ujjain however is because of the Mahakaleshwar temple that is one of the twelve sacred 'Jyotirlinga' shrines of India. Shiva Linga is Shiva personified and symbolises his eternal power on earth. The architectural beauty of the temple and its ornamentation of the marble porticos with symmetrical row of pillars are worth a visit. There is a unique reflection of a blend of Rajput as well as Mogul architecture. The river 'Shipra' that flows along the town is sacred too. It is made secret by the drops of 'Amrit' (holi necter) that spilled in its water when the pitcher that emerged during the course of 'Amrita Manthan' was being jostled around by the Gods and the Demons. [Amrita Manthan or the Churning of the Cosmic Ocean is refered to in the Ramayana and also Mahabharata and other epics which is an event undertaken at the behest of Lord Vishnu. This churning would help in extracting the ultimate nector of immortality called 'Amrita'. Though this manthan was ment for the Devtas (Gods) but the Asuras too ganged in (Demons) to participate in the process to gain access to the Amrit—devouring which they would become immortal. But as the Manthan (churning) progressed what initially emerged was a ghastly dreadful poison that could obliterate the entire universe. Terrified, they rushed to Lord Shiva for respite. Shiva in his quest to save the universe devoured the poison himself. Parvati (his consort) on seeing this rushed to Shiva and stangulated his thoat to hold the poison to tricle down further. In a short while the poison clotted and remained in the throat for ever. This is why the throad of Shive is seen blue in color—and he is also called 'Neel-kanth' (blue-throated). The Manthan rersumed with greater enthusiasm now as the poison was gotten rid of. Finally, the Amrit energed from the ocean in a bundle shaped as a pitcher. The Asura were smart and got hold of the pitcher and began to escape as the Devtas chased. On seeing this Vishnu intervened. He took the form of 'Mohini' a very seductive woman who enticed the Asuras to hand over the pitcher to her. She succeeded and gave the pitcher to the Devas to drink. One Asura named Rahu guised himself as Deva joined the queue. Surya the Sun-god and Chandra the Moon-god detected this trickery and informed Lord Vishnu. In his fury the Lord reached just in time as Rahu had just taken a sip. Finding no option Lord Visnu beheaded Rahu to stop the nector get further down the throat. This way while his torsoe perished with time his head remained immortal.

Other places of religious significance at Ujjain are the Harisddha Temple where idol of Goddess Annapurna (the Goddess of nourishment and consort of Lord Vishnu) is seated between the idols of Mahalaxmi and Mahasaraswati. Also a sacred 'Sri Yantra' that symbolises power of fortune is kept in the temple. The Gopala Mandir and Navagraha Mandir (Nine-planet Temple) are other sacred places of visit in Ujjain.

It is here in Ujjain that Ashoka (304 B.C.-232 B.C.) the Great came to know about Buddhism. Ashoka was the son of Emperor Bindusara who ruled over Patliputra. Brainwashed by the step brothers of Ashoka, Emperor Bindusara had sent him on exile. During a violent encounter in a battle in Ujjain (then known as Ujjayini) Ashoka was severely injured. He had to be treated in hiding to protect him from the mercineries of the Susima (one of Ashoka's step brothers) who looked for opportunity to exterminate him. During this time the Buddhist monks and nuns treated him. It was then that Ashoka learned about the teachings of Buddha. Young Ashoka was drawn towards 'Devi' the daughter of a merchant who was his personal nurse during the curative period. Both fell in love. Later Ashoka married her after he recovered. On coming to know that his son had married a Buddhist, Emperor Bindusara got infuriated and disallowed his entry to Patliputra. He was asked to stay in Ujjain and act as the provincial governor. Ashoka originally built the famous Sanchi Stupa located near Ujjain when he was the governor of Ujjayini. Sanchi forms a cluster of monasteries and temples dating back to the 3rd century B.C.

Amarkantak a serene mountain course between the Vindhya and the Satpura mountain ranges springs the rivers 'Narmada' and 'Sone'. The two take divergent course Narmada flows west while Sone takes an eastward course towards Bihar to merge with the Ganga. While Mother

Nature has blessed Amarkantak, Lord Shiva has blessed Narmada. It is thus that the Narmada is considered as having unique purifying powers that is superior even to the powers of Ganga. The flow of Narmada has taken such a course that it has formed an island in the shape of the holiest of all Hindu symbols, 'Oum'. (I could not make out this shape). The island is also known as 'Oumkareshwara' where at the Oumkar Mandhata temple the Jyotirlinga (one of the twelve throughout India) is worshipped. As the river flows westwards into Gujarat it touches quite a few places of religious importance. Amarkantak is one where several temples of Shiva, Radha-Krshna, Durga and other depictions of the Gods are located and worshipped with great honour. Passing through the majestic marble and lime-stone rock mountains in Bhimghat, Jabalpur it reaches Omkareshwar where the medivial Brahminic architectured Omkareshwar Temple and Siddhanath Temple are located. Further down the stream reaches the holy town of Maheshwar. Temples of pilgrimage located here are Ahileshwara temple, Kaleshwara temple, Rajaraheshwara and Vithaleshwara temple.

Geographically Amarkantak is located in the middle of the two mountain ranges namely Vindhya and the Satpura to the south of it. Indeed an amazing creation of nature and a fascinating place to be in. Amidst the valley of Satpura is a lovely place called Panchmarhi. After its discovery in 1857 by a British Army officer named James Forsyth it was developed as a sanatorium and later became a popular hill station.

In the north of Madhya Pradesh is Gwalior a historical place that preserves several architectural specimens like forts and edifices. The city was also a center for art and culture. Ruled and flourished during the period of Tomar Kings of the Rajput clan, Gwalior experienced the Golden Period of thirty years from 1486 during the rule of Raja

Man Singh Tomar. The Tomar clan arrived at Gwalior to establish their kingdom after they lost control over Delhi. This king Man Singh Tomar was one of the greatest of Tomar kings who also was a great admirer of art and music. He brought together musicians from different places. Research in music that was cultivated during his time gave rise to a different school of learning in music called 'Gharana'. He is said to be the father of 'Dhrupad' a unique form of Indian classical music. One of his nine jewels who adorned his court was Tansen who exhibited extra—terrestrial power through his music. Raja Man Singh Tomar was an equally great warrior who could never be conquered by the Lodhi Kings of Delhi. It was only after his death that Ibrahim Lodhi could subjugate the kingdom. Incidentally, the Tomars are considered as the descendents of Pandavas and follow the lineage of the warrior kin Arjun. It may be of interest to mention that Akbar recognised and respected the exceptionally skillful military competency of this Rajput clan. Understanding that it would be extremely arduous to overcome them in his persuit to expand his kingdom he resorted to diplomacy through marriage to assure alliance with the brave Rajputs. The magnificient fort built by Raja Man Singh Tomar in the 15th century is one of the most well equipped and most impregnable citadels constructed by any Indian ruler anywhere else. So much so that even Akbar's grandfather and once the undisputed ruler of Hindustan the Great king Babur was spell bound when he saw this immaculate architecture on the step slopes of the mountains sprawling like the Great Wall of China. Within the fort are several places of interest and religious significance that were all walled up within the fort or were built later. One such is a 9th century AD Vishnu temple called the 'Teli Ka Mandir'. The temple structure exhibits north Indian architectural styles with that of southern (perhaps of the Telangana region that draws similarity to its name). Another dedicated to Lord Vishnu is the twin temple called 'Saas-Bahu' built in the 11th century. ('Saas & Bahu' in Hindi literally means 'mother-in-law and daughter-in-law). But I'm told it has got nothing to do with that. The name has mysteriously got coined that way for reasons unknown). Inside the fort are several artificial tanks and water bodies with streams and tributaries that were purposefully created. On such well inside the Man-Mandir Palace is the Jauhar Kund ('jauhar'—is suicide. 'Kund' means a well). This place gained historical importance when in 1232 the kingdom once fell in the hands of Delhi sultan Iltutmish. All the surviving Rajput wives and ladies of the harem jumped into the well or self immolated on its banks to honor the esteem of the Rajput who could never allow the enemies to even touch them alive. The Gujari Mahal seen here was built by Raja Mansingh Tomar in memory of his courageous and beloved wife Queen Gujari Devi Mrignayani who mostly accompanied him at war. The Tomar dynasty also founded the city of Delhi during the time Tomar king Anangpal Tomar-I in 736CE. This brought back the revival of the city that was once created by their ancestors the Pandavas.

A few hours journey from Gwalior is **NEW DELHI**. Situated about 200 Km south of the Himalayas located near the western bank of river Yamuna, this city is now the National Capital of India. Some 4000 years ago this barren expanse of land was gifted disdainfully by the 'Kauravas' to their cousins the 'Pandavas'. The Pandavas under advice of Lord Krshna engaged architect 'Moy' to develop the place. In due course this deserted terrain got converted into an incredible wonderland that even the Kauravas began to envy. Thereafter the city was rebuilt over the ages as several dynasties came and went. In 800 BC a king by the name of Dhilu founded ancient Delhi. Later came the Tomar Rajputs the descendants of Pandavas ruled Delhi till 1182 A.D. Turkish dynasty also known as the Slave Dynasty led by (Turkish Slave) Qutb-ud-din Aybak conquered Delhi in 1193. Delhi Sultanate made Delhi their capital from 1206. This followed by Khilji dynasty, the Tughluq dynasty, the Sayyid dynasty and the Lodhi.

The 14th century Turco-Mongol conqueror and founder of the Timurid Empire and distant descendent of Chengis Khan 'Timur' layed the seed of the Mogul rule in India after he entered Delhi in 1398. He plundered the city and returned the following year to central Asia to fight battles in Egypt, Syria, Georgia and the great Ottoman Empire in Turkey. In 1404 he died of plague while preparing to wage a war against the Ming Dynasty in China who had originally driven them out in 1368. Though succeeded by his son Shah Rukh the first leader to set foot in India at Delhi was Zahir-ud-Din Mohammad more commonly known as Babur and the then king of Usbekistan. King Babur layed the foundation of the Moghul Empire in 1526 after defeating the Afghan ruler Ibrahim Lodi at the battle of Panipat.[27] There after except for a brief period of fifteen years from 1540 during the time of Humayun, Delhi was under the reign of a visionary ruler Sher Shah Suri who had driven the Moghuls beyond Multan (now in Pakistan). Moghuls ruled for over 300 years. Islam was the official religion of the Mughal Empire and the official language Persian. Later a Sanskritic Hindi version of language called Urdu emerged that also had a Persio-Arabic formation. Though the Moghuls were uncompromisingly Islam but Akbar's disposition was quite liberal. He was considerate towards other religions too. He abolished toll tax on non-Muslims that was in vogue at that

---

27 The Mughal Empire By John F. Richards Published by Cambridge University Press, 1987 ISBN 0521566037, 9780521566032 320 pages

time. He also introduced the tropical solar calendar in place of the Islamic lunar one. In order to neutralise the obvious dissent of Muslim clerics, Akbar decided to introduce a new religion that he called 'Din-i-Ilahi' (which meant faith of God). Perhaps he felt that merging other faith into one religion would bring communities together as this diversity of belief was the cause of animosity and turmoil. His son Jahangir, son of a Hindu mother continued religious liberalism during his rule and later under the rule of Emperor Shah Jahan. But the practice of political tolerance for non-Muslims and allowing non-Muslims to practice theirs without too much interference faced a challenge under Aurangazeb's rule. Aurangazeb the valiant son of Shah Jahan was a fundamentalist Muslim and quite an unforgiving ruler. He even did not spare his father and had him imprisoned during the entire phase of his last life. His onslaught against the Hinuds, the Sikhs and others in his persuit to expand his kingdom and more particularly the damages he caused to the places of worship and persons of high order bred hatred and enough animosity amongst religions. Unlike his forefathers he was myopic and could not envisage that the hatred against Muslims could one day turn revengeful. He professed conversion of non-Muslims to Islam and significantly favoured Muslims over non-Muslims particularly the Hindus. This caused the resurgence of Hinduism and saw the consolidation the Hindu rulers to stand up to such offensive. Also the events of Sikh Gurus martyred by the ruling Mughals militarised the Sikhs to take on the Islamists. Thus apart from the several good things particularly art and architechture, cultural ettiquetts, norms of nobility, skillful craftsmanship, the spirit of chivalry and exquisite culinary the Mughual rule also left behind several scars that still trigger bitterness and revulsion. The rebelliousness amongst discontented subjects and other communities' finally led to the weakening of the Moghul rule. The Europeans, who by then had established themselves, were yearning to surmount and plunder the wealth in this foreign land did not spare a chance. Sequence of events that followed destabilized the Mughal throne and finally in 1858 Delhi came under the rule of the British Empire. In 1911 George V, the then Emperor of India shifted the capital of the Raj from Calcutta to Delhi. The Britsh rule lasted until August 1947 when India gained independence to lay the foundation of a democraic republic with Delhi as its capital.

New Delhi today with its multi-ethnic and multi-cultural composition has become a truly cosmopolitan city. Being adjoined to Punjab Delhi has a large Punjabi population that practice Sikhism. The religion founded by Guru Nanak that preaches a code of practice for humans based on service to mankind and free from all kinds of discrimination as prevalent in Hinduism. Sikhism till today is practiced and preached the way the different Gurus have deliberated upon from time to time and the places of worship are referred to as the Gurudwara ('Guru' refers to the wayfinder and 'dwara means the doorway). Five important Gurudwaras that adorn Delhi actually commemorate the visits of five of the Gurus. These sacred places of Sikh pilgrimage are: Gurudwara Majnu ka Tila Sahib that commemorates the visit of Guru Nanak the first Guru and founder of the Sikh religion in the 15th century. The name 'Majnu' is of a Sufi saint who lived here in a cottage during the reign of Emperor Sikander Lodhi. Gurudwara Nanak Piao also commemorates the visit of Guru Nanak who stayed here in 1505. The term 'Piao' which means serving water has been attached to remind that the Guru himself used to serve water to the people visiting him. Gurdwara Bangla Sahib is dedicated to the eighth Sikh Guru of the Sikhs Guru Harkrishen who stayed during in 1664. It was actually Bangla (garden house) of Raja Jai Singh to he was a guest during the visit. This Bangla was later converted into a Gurudwara. Gurdwara Sis Ganj built in honor of Guru Tegh Bahadur the ninth guru of the Sikhs who was beheaded here in 1675 by orders of Mughal Emperor Aurangzeb for disobeying his command of converting to Islam. After this one of his devotees Lakhi Singh escaped with the body of his Guruji to his house where he carried out the performed the last rites and cremation respectfully. After that in order to remove all evidence he also torched the house reducing everything to ashes and buried the ashes under the ground. On this place in 1732 Lakhi Singh Banjara raised a majestic white temple that came to be called the Gurdwara Rakab Ganj.

Muslim rule in Delhi over long period of time has left several admirable places of worship that constitute the precious heritage of the country. Qila-I-Kuhna Masjid is an imposing mosque constructed by Sher Shah in 1541 AD even before the Mughuls. But the largest and the most brilliantly architectured one is the Jama Masjid built by Shahjahan in 1656. The three domes and two monuments of this structure is a unque feature that makes it stand out amongst the several mosques that Shah Jahan built across the country. Another three dome structure is the Moth-ki-Masjid built in the 16th Century by Miyan Bhuwa a minister of Sultan Sikander Lodi. It is said that while on a walk the Sikander picked up a seed of lentil (moth dal as called in India) and in a light mood handed it over to Bhuwa saying it to be a gift. Least was it realised then that Miyan Bhuwa would plant it in the field and the yield that would come of it would in a span of few years lead to abundunce in the cultivation of the crop. As a result it generated enormous revenue and Miyan Bhuwa decided to build a place of worship in admiration of the one who made it happen. This mosque still stands to remind that even the smallest of gift if accrepted with reverence and love can blossom into a marvel to cherish.

Hazrat Nizamuddin Dargah dedicated to the much-revered Saint Sultan-Ul-Mashaikh Hazrat Khwaja Syed Nizamuddin Aulia, also known as 'Mehboob-i Elahi' or Beloved of God is a place of pilgrimage for all Muslims across the world. Born in 1236 and having arrived in Delhi with his mother he became a disciple and successor of the Saint Shaikh Farid Shakarganj. His attainments, his love for people regardless of their professed faith drew several devotees to him from distant places. Amongst them were the rulers Ala-ud-Din Khalji and Muhammad Tughluq. Though Hazrat Nizamu'd-Din died in 1325 a nobleman named Faridu'n Khan built this tomb two hundred years later sometime in 1562. There are other tombs too in the precincts of the Dargah. Notable amongst them are of Khizr Khan, son of 'Ala-ud-Din Khalji, of Shah Jahan's elder daughter Jahanara, Amir Khusraw, a celebrated poet and also the chief disciple of Shaikh Nizamu'd-Din Auliya, grave of the famous poet Mirza Ghalib and a few others.

Moti Masjid (pearl mosque) is located inside the majestic Red Fort. The fort was built by Shah Jahan between 1639 and 1647 after he shifted his capital from Agra to Delhi. His son Emperor Aurangzeb built this beautiful private mosque inside the fort in 1662. Moti Masjid is built with highly polished marble. This mosque displays Mughal design and well crafted marble wok. The carved cornices and bulbous domes make it a unique spot of beauty inside the crude environs of the relentless citadel.

There are two important colonial Churches at Delhi one the Church of the Sacred Heart built in the 1930s and Cathedral Church of the Redemption built a decade earlier. Henry Alexander Nesbitt Medd who served as the Chief Architect to the Government of India for twelve years till India's indipendence in 1947 designed both these churches. Here one can find a golden cross and a picture that were donated by Lord Irwin in gratitude to God for saving his life when his train was blown up in 1929. Lord Irwin was a deeply religious person by nature dignified, aristocratic and a much respected politician of his generation.' The English statesman Edward Frederick Lindley Wood, 1st Earl of Halifax was Viceroy of India from 1926 to 1931. He later served as foreign secretary and as ambassador to the United States during World War II'.[28]

World Buddhist Centre is one of the most famous Buddhist temples located in Delhi. Established by Rev. Gyomyo Nakamura and Rev. Eigaku Kouchi in 1996, it undertakes the noble mission of propagating Lord Buddha's teachings. Other places of Buddhist worship located in Delhi are Buddha Vihara, Ladakh Bodha Vihara and Tushita Mayahana Meditation Centre all of which are locatd in South Delhi.

Like the Christains and Buddhists the Jews too are a minority community whose population is very little and the Judah Hyam Jewish Synagogue built in 1956 is the only synagogue that caters to the handful of Jews residing here.

A Parsi fire temple called Kaikhushru Pallonji Katrak Dar-e-Meher is a place of worship for 1000 odd Parsis of Delhi. Established in 1960 the Delhi Parsi Anjuman premises is a highly revered place for the community where ritualistic prayers are offered to the fire five times a day remembering the great saints and kings of Iran. 'Delhi Parsi Anjuman, which was formed 75 years ago, and the Parsi graveyard here, which is almost 116 years old, the fire temple was consecrated quite late but it has

---

28 Roberts, Andrew, *The Holy Fox: a biography of Lord Halifax*, London: Weidenfeld and Nicolson, 1991.

nevertheless helped strengthen and preserve the already strong rituals'.[29]

Moving around Dehi one comes across large writing on wall saying way to 'Praachin Mandir' meaning ancient temple. I do not know how ancient these temples are. I have also not been able to find any inscription either in the temple pricincts or any reference book so I am not certain about the period to which these temples originally belonged. But going by the belief and the perception of the people it could have some reference to the past. The oldest of the Hindu temples is a Jain temple built during the times of Emperor Shah Jahan in 1656. Constructed in red sand stone and located opposite the Red Fort in the old Delhi region this temple is called the Sri Digambar Jain Lal Mandir. Later one chief of the Agarwal community Harsukh Rai, appointed an imperial treasurer of the Moghuls built another majestic temple called the 'Naya Mandir' or the new temple in 1807. It is said that during the Moghul rule affluent Jains were invited to finance the regime for different purposes. These invitees were given land where they could settle and also construct their place of worship. It was thus that this temple got installed. There after other temples were also constructed. It is said that there are a hundred and sixty-five Jain temples in Delhi.

Situated in the Old Delhi is the temple of 'Gauri Shankar' (Lord Shiva and his consort Gauri) where the Lingum is believed to be of 1100 A.D. Other two temples that are quirte old include the the Hanuman Mandir situated near Connaught Place built in 1724 by Maharaja Jai Singh and the Kalkaji Temple situated in the heart of South Delhi that dates back to 1764-1771. The fomer is

---

29 'Parsi fire temple to celebrate anniversary' Article appeared in the Hindustan Times Delhi edition 20 Dec 2007

dedicated to Lord Hanuman the primate chieftain and an ardent loyalist of Lord Rama who played a pioneering role in rescuing Sita from captivity while the later is dedicated to Goddess Kalka Devi. The Lingam is a Hindu temple. Chattarpur Mandir dedicated to goddess Durga and the Sheetla Devi temple situated at Gurgaon in the National Capital region of Delhi dedicated to Mata Sheetla Devi are very popular places of Hindu worship. Sheetla Devi temple is considered a sacred 'Shakti Peeth' and hence is a place of pilgrimage for all Hindus.

In recent times majestic temples have been built that are better equipped, with good architechture and well managed. Some such that deserve mention are the Lakshmi Narayan Mandir or Birla Mandir dedicated to Lord Vishnu and his consort Goddess Laksmi, the ISCON temple dedicated to Lord Krshna (reincarnation of Lord Vishnu) and his consort 'Radha' who are reincarnations of Lord Vishnu and Goddess Laksmi, the Bahai temple—shaped like a lotus, and the newly built Akshardham Temple that is dedicated to a Saint 'Bhagwan Swami Narayan'. Bhagwan Swami Narayan lived between 1781 and 1837. He renounced the world and spent several years meditating in the Himalayas and travelling across the country. He finally settled in Gujrat and professed the principles of peace, non-violence and love. His followers built temples in his memory the world over. The two important ones in India are at Ahmedabad and Delhi. The 109 meters wide and 43 meters high temple in Delhi, completed in November is an entrant in the Guinness Book of World Records for being the world's largest Hindu temple complex.

Delhi is also famous for housing several Ashrams Hindu hermitages where persons of spiritual attainment have lived and preached. Some such are Ramakrishna Mission Ashram established in 1927, the Aurobindo Ashram, Maa Anandmayi Ashram, Osho Ashram and

Osho Rajyoga Dhyana Kendra, Shivananda Yoga Vedanta Nataraja Centre the Bengali Kali Bari or the House of Goddess Kali, Tushita Mahayana Center, India Islamic Cultural Centre, World Buddhist Centre and others all of whom provide the platform to promote to preach and profess in their own respective way the universal principles of love and peace irrespective of faith, caste, creed and color.

The oldest of the relics discovered in Delhi region are those that belonged to the forth century B.C. Nothing much is decipherable from the few articles that have so far been discovered from the place where the old fort now stands. From this we can perhaps conclude that Delhi region proper has not been an ancient religious location compared to its neighbouhood. It only goes to re-establish the fact that the place, as enumerated in the Mahabhatara was indeed barren prior to the time the 'Pandavas' came here to settle. But then this is only a point of view considering that there is no convincing evidence to prove anything to the contrary. Talking of ancient claims I cannot ignore to mention of the temple of Baba Bhairon Nath (descent of Lord Shiva) located behing the old fort. Flanked by the idol of Kali in ferocious form the idol of Baba Bhairon Nath is seated inside. History of the temple is not known but said to have been here since the Pandava era (3000 BC?—sounds absurd). Its uniqueness lies in the fact that while every Indian place of worship prohibits alcohol, here it is considered a divine offering. We conceive Lord Shiva as a God with simple life-style, humble attires and generally a cool headed wish fulfiller. Aids in the domain of Shiva are known to have dry hallucinatory stuffs and not expensive liquor that ostentatious Gods would have if they were to have. But as a matter of faith people here offer bottle of rum, whisky whatever from which the priest pours a portion on a salver and returns the rest as 'Prasad'. Devotees believe that the offering works and the Lord and Maa Kali have been blessing them with wish fulfillment.

Delhi the seat of power today houses one of the the most magnificient circular edifice in the world. Designed by Herbert Baker in 1921 and inaugurated by Lady and Lord Irwin in 1927 this is a monument that every Indian fells proud of. It is called the Indian Parliament House. Being the fountain head of the largest democracy in the world it is today the greatest place of pilgrimage of the modern India that transcends all religious beliefs but represents every such in this secular country called India. It indeed epitomizes a modern Temple of Democracy in which is imbibed our faith.

Annexures

Fifty-two-Pithasthanas of Hindu Worship

Fifty-two-Pithasthanas of Hindu Worship

Sl.	Place	Organ or Ornament	Shakti
	Sri Lanka		
1	Nainativu, Jaffna	Anklets	Nagapooshani
	Pakistan		
2	Naina, Karachi	Three Eyes	Mahishmardini
3	Hingula Baluchistan	Head part , Brain	Kottari
	Nepal		
4	Muktinath Pokhara,	Temple	Gandaki Chandi
5	Pashupatinath, Kathmandu	Both Knees	Mahashira
6	Mithila,, Janakpur	Left Shoulder	Uma
	Tibet		
7	Manas, Mansarovar	Right Hand	Dakshayani
	India		
8	Amarnath, **Kashmir**	Throat	Mahamaya
9	Shri Parvat, **Ladak**,	Right Anklet '	Shrisundari
10	Kangra, **Himanchal Pradesh**	Tongue	Ambika
11	Jalandhar, **Punjab**	Left Breast	Tripurmalini
12	Kurukshetra, **Haryana**	Ankle Bone	Savitri
13	Birat, Bharatpur, **Rajasthan**	Left Feet Fingers	Ambika
14	Gayatri hills, Pushkar,	Two Bracelets	Manibandh, Gayatri
15	Prabhas, Junagadh, **Gujarat**,	Stomach	Chandrabhaga
16	Anart, Ambaji, Gujarat,	Heart	Ambaji
17	Haridwar, **Uttarakhand**	Teeth	Panchsagar Varahi
18	Chitrakuta **Uttar Pradesh**	Right Breast	Ramgir, iShivani
19	Vrindavan, Uttar Pradesh	Ringlets of Hair	Uma
20	Allahabad, Uttar Pradesh,	Finger (Hand)	Prayag Lalita
21	Varanasi Uttar Pradesh,	Earring	Vishalakshi & Manikarni
22	Shondesh, **Madhya Pradesh**	Buttock (Right)	Amarkantak, Narmada
23	Kalmadhav Amarkantak	Buttock (Left)	Kali
24	Bhairav Parvat, Ujjaini	Upper Lips	Avanti
25	Nasik, **Maharashtra**,	Chin (Two Parts)	JansthanBhramari
26	Kalighat, **Kolkata**	Right Toes	Kalika
27	Hooghly, **West Bengal**	Right Shoulder	RatnavaliKumari
28	Vibhash, Medinipur (E)	Left Ankle	Kapalini (Bhimarupa)
29	Burdwan, West Bengal	Left Arm	Katwa, Bahula
30	Burdwan, West Bengal	Lips	Attahas, Phullara
31	Burdwan, West Bengal,	Right Wrist	Ujaani Mangal Chandika
32	Khirgram Burdwan	Great Toe (Right)	Jugaadya
33	Murshidabad, West Bengal,	Crown	Kireet Vimla
34	Kankaleshwari, Birbhum,	Bone	Devgarbha
35	Nalhati, Birbhum	Bones of the Feet	Nalateshwari Kalika Temple
36	Sainthia, Birbhum	Necklace	Nandini
37	Bakreshwar, Birbhum	Eyebrows Portion	Mahishmardini
38	Salbari, Boda, Jalpaiguri	Left Leg	Trisrota, Bhraamari
39	Dantewada, **Chattisgrah**	Daant (Teeth)	Danteshwari
40	Biraja, Utkal, **Orissa**,	Navel	Vimla
41	Radhakishorepur, **Tripura**,	Right Leg	Tripura Sundari
42	Kamakhya, Guwahati, **Assam**	Genital Organ	Kamakhya
43	Rajamundry, **Andra Pradesh**	Cheeks	Rakini or Vishweshwari
44	Kanyakumari **Tamil Nadu**	Teeth (Upper Jaw)	Shuchitirtham Narayani
45	Kanyakumari Tamil Nadu,	Back	Sarvani
46	Karnat place not known	Both Ears	Jayadurga
	Bangladesh		
47	Shikarpur, Barisal	Nose	Sunanda
48	Sitakunda Chittagong	Right Arm	Bhawani
49	Falizur Sylhet.	Left Thigh	Jayanti
50	Shri Shail, Sylhet	Neck	Mahalaxmi
51	Bhabanipur, Bogra,	Left Anklet '	Karatoyatat, Arpana
52	Ishwaripur, Satkhira,	Palms & Feet	Jashoreshwari

Twelve -Jyotirlinums: Holi Places of Shive worship

Sl.	Place	India
1	Amarnath, Kashmir	Naturally formed ice-Linga
2	Benares	Lord Shiva's own cilty. He stayed here for a while.
3	Chidambaram	Lord Shiva as Nataraja theLord of the Dance.
4	Deoghar	Lord Shiva as Vaidyanath (Lord of Physicians),
5	Girnar	Shrine of sage Dattatreya, incarnation of Vishnu.
6	Kankhal, Haridwar	Shiva destroyed his father in law Daksha's sacrifice.
7	Kailas, Tibet	Dwelling place of Lord Shiva
8	Kanchipuram	Shiva as the Lord of Mt. Kailas and Ekambareshvar
9	Kedarnath	Shiva revealed himself to the Pandava brothers
10	Rameshvaram	Lord of Lord Rama, Shiva's Home
11	Somnath	Shiva as Somnath the Lord of the Moon.
12	Ujjain	Shiva as Mahakaleshvar the Lord of Death.

Twelve-Vishnu Temples: Holi Places for Vishnu Worship

Sl.	Place	India
1	Badrinath, Uttarakhand	Image found and installed by Adi Shankaracharya
2	Mathura, Uttar Pradesh	Birthplace of Lord Krshna
3	Brindavan, Uttar Pradesh	Lord Krishna grew up in this village
4	Dwarka, Uttar Pradesh	Kingdom of Lord Krishna
5	Girnar	Temple of Dattatreya, an incarnation of Vishnu.
6	Kanchipuram, Tamil Nadu	Lord Vishnu remembered as Lord of Vaikuntha
7	Nasik, Maharashtra	Forest home of Rama and Sita, kidnapping of Sita.
8	Nathdvara,	Lord Krishna as Shrinathji.
9	Pandharpur,	Temple of Vithoba deity worshipped as Lord Vishnu
10	Puri	Temple of Jagannath ,worshipped as Lord Krishna);
11	Rameshvaram, Tamil Nadu	Lord Rama worshipped Lord Shiva and set off to war
12	Tirupati, Andhra Pradesh	Temple of Venkateshvara, a form of Lord Vishnu

One-Brahma Temple: Holi Places for Brahma Worship

Sl.	Place	India
1	Pushkara, Rajasthan	Sole temple in all of India dedicated to Lord Brahma

Four Places of Kumbh Snan (Bath of Purity)

Occurance	Place	Holi River	Periodicity
Held every third year at one of the four places by rotation	Haridwar	Ganga	Ardha Kumbh is held hereevery sixth year
	Allahabad	Confulernce	
	Nasik	Godawari	Each of these places every twelve years
	Ujjain	Sipra	

Nine-Avatar (incarnations) of Lord Vishnu

Avatar	Evolution stage	Assumed similarity with the Theory of Evolution
Matsya - fish	Acquatic form	Starting with a single celled organism, over ttime the first creature to evolve were aquatic creatures.The came amphibions followed by land animals and airborne birds. After that half-man-half-lion (Narasimha) in the fourth incarnation. Finally came the evolution of humans
Koorma - tortoise	Amphibian	
Varaha - boar	Land animals	
Narasimha - half man- lion	Transition to human	
Vaman - dwarf man	Homo sapiens	
Parashuram - man with axe	Savages	
Rama - moral man	Family and social life	
Krishna - philosophical man	Philosophy & teaching	
Buddha - teacher	Spiritual life	

Adi Shankaracharya Institutions

Four Dhams(*Cardinal monasteries*)		Four Maths(*Monastries*)	
Title	Places	Title	Places
Uttar•mn•ya Math (to the north)	Badrinath	Jyotir Math	Badrinath
Pkrv•mn•ya Math (to the east)	Puri	Govardhan Math	Puri
Dakshin•mn•ya Math (to the south)	Rameshwaram	Sringeri Math	Sringeri
Pa[chim•mn•ya Math (to the west)	Dwarka	Sharada Math coast	Dwaraka

Holi Scripture of Hunduism

Hindu scriptures	
Sruti scriptures That which is heard. Heard by Vedic seers, during meditations and realized through intuitive perception. These include the following four Vedas said to of 10-7000 BCE	**Smriti scriptures** That which is remembered. Written elaborations of the Vedas for common people. All Holi scriptures beside the Vedas and are said to be of 6,000 BCE era
Rid - Song of Gods, the cosmic powers	Dharma Shastras
Yajur - 3988 verses, assemblage of mantras	Puranas / Vedangas
Sam - 1,540 verses, chanting during rituals.	Nibhandas / Itihasa
Atharva - 5,977 verses, people daily needs	Tantras / Darshanas

Vedantas (end of Vedas) or **Upanishads**						
13 principle Upanishads of the 1180 are:						
Aitareya	Brhadaranyaka	Chandogya	Isa	Kaivalya	Katha	Kena
Mundaka	Maitri	Mandhukya	Prasna	Svetasvatara	Taittiriya	

Dharma Shastras		
Ac•ra: Daily rituals, Life-cycle rites and Duties of four defined castes	Vyavah•ra: Procedures for resolving doubts about dharma and rules of law	Pr•ya[citta: Punishment and penances for violations of the rules of dharma.

Puranas			
Vaishnava Puranas		**Brahma Purana,**	**Shaiva Purana**
Vishnu Purana	Bhagavata Purana	Brahma Purana,	Shiva Purana,
N•radeya Purana	Garuda Purana	Brahm•nda Purana,	Linga Purana,
Padma Purana	Varaha Purana	Vaivarta Purana,	Skanda Purana,
V•mana Purana	Kkrma Purana	M•rkandeya Purana,	Agni Purana,
Matsya Purana	Kalki Purana	Bhavishya Purana,	V•yu Purana

Vedanga (parts of Vedas)
Shiksha: Phonetics, phonology and morphophonology- the scientific study of speech sounds, how they are produced, used in a particular language and union of words.
Kalpa: Ritual- an established and prescribed pattern of observance, e.g. in a religion.
Vyakarana: Grammar -system of rules by which words are formed and put together.
Nirukta: Etymology study of the origins of words or parts of words.
Chandas: Meter Pattern of rhythm in verse, of beats that combines to form musical rhythm
Jyotisha: Astrology- the study of the positions of planets and their motions affect human s

Itihasa narrated events of bygone days		
Mahabharata legends of the lunar dynasty	**Ramayana** legends of the solar dynasty	**Itihasa-Purana**{ These narrate the saga of eternal past and includes cosmogony, myth, legend and history of events that are also partly myths
Bhagvat Gita	The national gospel contained in Mah•bh•rata	

Tantras (*94-Scriptures*)		
Bhairava Tantras (64)	Rudra Tantras (18)	Ziva Tantras (10)

Darshanas or *Darshan Shastras portrayssix schools of philosophy*
Poorva Mimansa: rituals for material prosperity .**Nyaya:** discerning the difference between maya, matter, and God. **Vaisheshika:** happiness through renouncing worldly desires. **Sankhya:** releases the soul from material attachment binds the soul in the cycle of birth and death. Yoga Darshana eliminated mental anguish associated with ignorance, ego, attachment, hatred, and the fear of death. **Uttar Mimansa Brahm Sutra** true liberation is only attained through surrender to God.

Sacred Rivers of India

Ganga	Saraswati	Godavari	Brahmaputra	
Narmada	Sindhu	Krishna	Kaveri	Yamuna

Nine Planets in Vedic Astrology

Roman	Hindu				
Planets		Gods	Element	Body Part	Influences
Sun	Surya	Agni	Fire	Bone	Soul
Moon	Chandra	Varuna	Water	Blood	Emotion
Mars	Mangala	Subramanya	Fire	Marrow	Career
Mercury	Buddha	Vishnu	Earth	Skin	Intelligence
Jupiter	Brihaspati	Indra	Ether	Brain	Knowledge
Venus	Sukra	Indrani	Water	Sex organ	Vices
Saturn	Shani	Kali	Air	Muscles	Labour
North & South Node	Rahu	Durga	Air	Head	Dissence
	Ketu	Ganesh	Earth	Skni	Spirituality

Notable Buddhist Sites in the sub-continent

	Monastries	Place	Importance
1	Lumbini	Nepal	Birth place of Buddha.
2	Bodh Gaya	Bihar	Buddha attained enlightenment
3	Sarnath	Uttar Prdesh	Buddha first taught the Dharma
4	Boudhnath Stupa	Nepal	Holy site of Buddhist followwers.
5	Bumthang Valley	Bhutan	spiritual heart of Bhutan
6	Ajanta-Ellora	Maharashtra	Rock-cut cave monasteries
7	Kushinagar	Uttar Prdesh	Buddha reached Mahaparinirvana
8	Rewalsar,	India	sacred lake associated with the Buddhist
9	Taktshang	Bhutan	Sacred places for Buddhissts across the world
10	Tooth Temple	Sri Lanka	A tooth of Lord Buddha is placed here.
11	Taxila	Pakistan	Teeth and bone fragments of Buddha here.
12	Sitagarha Hill	Hazaribagh	Mauryan Period stone carved Buddhist shrine
13	Alchi Gompa	Ladakh	rich collection of ancient Buddhist literature,.
14	Tabo Monastery	Himachal	HQ of Tibetan Govt one of the most ancient
15	Tawang	Arunachal	largest and the oldest Buddhist monasteries
16	Rumtek	Sikkim	preserves some of the ancient manuscripts

Admired Jain Shrine in India

Shrine	Place	Importance
Udaigiri, Khandagiri	Orissa	1BC rock temples carved by Jain monk
Palitana Temples	Gujrat	Most sacred of all Jain Temples
Dilwara Temples	Mount Abu	Lord Mahavira-the founder of Jainism
Mudabidri	Mangalore	An ancient center of Jain learning built 1430
Taranga Temples	Gujarat	A 1121 Statue of Adinatha is the central idol
Ranakpur	Rajasthan	Of Lord Adinath, the first Tirthankara.
Jain Golden Temple	Rajasthan	90 kg. of gold adors temple dome and idol.
Sravanabelagola	Karnataka	The 57-feet tall statue of Gommateshvara
Kalugumalai	TamilNadu	Of Neminath Mahaveera Parvanatha.
Lal Mandir	Delhi	of Lord Mahavira, the 24th Tirthankara
Sittannavasal	Tamil Nadu	A Rock-Cut Temple Of The 7th Century AD
Chitral	Tamil Nadu	Rock-Cut Sculptures Of Tirthankaras
Hati-gumph	Orissa	Rock-cut inscription and architecture
Tirupparut-Tikunram	Tamil Nadu	Of Vardhaman Mahavira and Chandra Prabha
Girnar	Gujrat	Of Neminath, the 22nd Jain Tirthankar
Ajitnath	Gujrat	Of Ajitnath, the 22nd Tirthankara of Jains
Vallimalai	Tamil Nadu	10 AD temple of Mahavira and Yakshi

Few Important Places of Islamic Worship in India

Title	Places	
Cheraman Masjid (0628)	Thrissur	First mosque of India and oldest in the world
Moinuddin Chishti Darga	Ajmer	Kwaja Moinuddin Chishti's final resting place
Jama Masjid (1650)	Delhi	Founded by Shahjahan the then Emperor of India.
Haji Ali Dargah (1431)	Mumbai	Dovout Haji Ali's coffin was laid to rest here.
Fatehpur Sikri (1585)	Agra	Built by Emperor Akbar when blessed by an heir
Moti Masjid (1860)	Bhopal	Built by Sikander Begum in the year
Nakhoda Mosque (1926)	Kolkata	Built by Kutchi Memon Jamat from Kutch
Wallajah Mosque (1795)	Chennai	Built by the Nawab of Arcot

The Five Pillars of Islam

	Surmon	Performance
1	Shahadah	Reciting sincerely the Muslim profession of faith
2	Salat	Performing ritual prayers five times each day in the proper way
3	Zakat	Extending charity) payment or tax to benefit the needy poor
4	Sawm	Undertaking fast during the month of Ramadan
5	Hajj	Participating in pilgrimage to Mecca

The Five Takhts (Thrones) of Sikhism

Takhts	Place	Significance
Akal Takht	Amritsar	Seat for dispersal of Justice and temporal activity.
Patna Sahib	Patna City	Guru Gobind Singh was born here in 1666
Keshgarh Sahib	Anandpur	Guru Gobind Singh propounded Khalsa order
Damdama Sahib	Bhatinda	Guru Gobind Singh scipted the Guru Granth
Hazur Sahib	Maharashtra	Guru Gobind Singh left for his heavenly abode

Some Famous Churches In India

Churches and Year	Place	Influence
Malayattoor church 0052 AD	Ernakulam Kerala	Indian
Marthamariam Cathedral, 0920	Kottayam, Kerala	Indian
St.Francis Church 1503	Kochi, Kerala	European
Santa Cruz Basilica 1505	Kochi, Kerala	Portuguese
Vallarpadam Church 1524	Kochi Kerala	Portuguese
The Basilica of Bom1605	Old Goa	Portuguese
Se Cathedral 1510	Goa	Portuguese
All Saints Cathedral, 1887	Allahabad, U Pradesh	British
St. Paul's Cathedral, 1847	Kolkata	British
St. Mary's Church 1550	Kottayam, Kerala	Portuguese
Sacred Heart Cathedral , 1931	New Delhi	British
St. Philomena's church, 1939	Mysore	Indian

Some Important Parsi Temples in India

Atash E Behram Highest grade of sacred fire	Navsari, Gujrat 1765	Bhagarsath Anjumana
	Mumbai, Maharashtra 1783	Seth Nosherwanji Dadiseth
	Mumbai, Maharashtra 1797	Zarthosti Anjumanna
Atash E Adaran Next higher grade of the fire	Surat , Gujrat 1827	Jamsetji Jejeebhoy Adaran
	Kolkata, W Bengal 1912	Zoroastrian Anjuman Adarian
	Jamshedpur, Bihar 1969	Cursetji Maneckji Shroff Adarian
Atash E Dadgah Lower grade of sacred fire	Boisar, Maharashtra 1820	Jamshedji Nasserwanji Petit
	Surat, Gujrat 1908	Kekobad Rao Daremeher,
	Bangalore, Karnataka 1926	Cawasji Dhunbai Daremeher

Some Jewish Synagogues in India

Pardesi Synagogue , 1567	Kochi, Kerala
Beth El , Synagogue 1856	Kolkata, West Bengal
Magen David, Synagogue 1884	Kolkata, West Bengal
Keneseth Eliyahoo, Synagogue 1885	Mumbai, Maharashtra
Magen Abraham Synagogue, 1934	Ahmedabad, Uttar Pradesh
Gate of Mercy Synagogue, 1796	Mumbai, Maharashtra
Ohel David Synagogue, 1867	Pune, Maharashtra

Lexicons

Term	Description
Agni	Literally means 'fire' and signifies the necessary element for sustainance of life. Hidu mythology believes Agni to be the son on Bramha and his wife is called 'Swaha', he is the most important Vedic God.with more than 200 hymns in the Rig Veda devoted to Lord Agni. Its ability to purify makes it indispensible in all solemn ceremonies, sacrificial offerings, prayrs, festivals, worships and the supremely sacred witness to any oath.
Ahimsā	The first letter 'A' here connotes 'un' or negation while 'hingsa' or 'himsa' means to physical attack or violence. This principkle not only applies to warfare or enimity but also includes cruelty to all forms of life. one of the greatest proponents of ahimsa was Lord Mahavir the founder of 'Jainism' a sister religion of Hinduism founded in the beginning of the Christ era. The application of these principles is a careful decision based on relevance. While in recent times the world has witnessed how Mahatma Gandhi used it as the mightiest weapon against all odds on the other hand while 'Arjun' desired to adopt 'ahimsa' when faced with his adverseries in the battle field Lord Krshna himself dissuade Arjun and sways to to take recourse of war that he designates as 'Dharma Yuddh'
Astra-Shastra	'Astra' are weapons / ammunitions that are shot or thrown at enemies, while 'Shastras' are held in the hand.like a sword.
Asur	(The first letter 'A' here connotes 'un' or negation,'sur' means godly). They are generally the demons, legendary evils mischievously opposed to the Gods. As war mongers Asur keep the heaven and earth terrorized but are inevitably defeated by the Gods. Some goblins are superior and spiritually accomplished like Ravana while there are others who are called 'pisach' who haunt battlefields and places of violent deaths, 'Vetala' or vampires who take their abode in corpses. In addition, Bhuta and Preta are ghosts known to wandering souls who have either died in obscurity or who have not been ceremoniously seen off by performing rituals by his/her kin.
Avatar	Liyerraly means incarnation or descent and ofeten refered to Avtar of Vishu.
Bhoot	In Hindu mythology bhoots are mischievous spirit of those who have died and whose dreams have remained unfulfilled. They are also believed to have either died a violent death or whose funeral rites have not been performed fully. It is said that they haunt the newly married, women and children. Unlike prêt who could be unknown to the persons they haunt bhoots are spirits of a diseased persons known in the family. Bhoots however have a limited active operation span.
Char Dham	are the four cardinal points of the subcontinent as grouped together by the great 8th century reformer and philosopher Shankaracharya (Adi Sankara), they are the representative pilgrimage circuit of four important temples----Puri, Rameshwaram, Dwarka, and Badrinath. Visiting these four points are said to be virtuous and thus essential in the life time of a true Hindu.
Dharma	Often wrongly refered to religious beliefs, it is indeed meant to suggest moral principle of universal law based on the Hindu tenets 'truth'.
Graha	Graha are planets. In Hinduism this 'grahas' have a great influence as the mathematician sages have deciphered volumes of tangible and proven knowledge studying the constellation of palnets and their inescapable impact on living particularly human as well as inert beings. The cluster of nine-planets is denoted as 'Nava-Grava' ('Nava' means nine).
Gurvaani	These are the virtuous words of enlightenment that emanated fron the mounts the ten (Sikh) Gurus and as are inscribed in the Guru Granth Sahib. Guruvani speaks of of enlightenment and salvation. The fourth Guru, Duru Ram Das wrote "the word is the embodiment of the Guru and the Guru is the embodiment of the word within which are contained the immortalizing elixir" -

	of life's fulfilment.
Halal	in Arabic refers to permitted or acts allowed under Islamic law. These mainly refer to food but other aspects of life too covered under it. In other words what is non-'Halal' would fall under the category of 'Haram'.
Haram	in Islam refers to forbidden acts or actions that are sinful in nature. Some acts are 'Haram' ab-initio like murder, robbery or illicit sexual act or relation. Other forms of haram are cheating, swindling, charging interest, consuming alcohol, lying and so on. In other words the Holy Scripture has laid down the do and don'ts of life so than man remains disciplined and there in harmony in the society.
Kama	Indicates lust, a longing for sensuous pleasure and aesthetic enjoyment.to elaborate further it is one of the thirteen virtues but of 'tamas' (abhorrent) category of desired human qualities, [Raag (rage), Dvesha (animosity), Kama (lust), Krodha (anger), Lobha (greed), Moha (acquisitiveness), Mada (intoxication), Matsarya (displeasure), Iirsha (jelousy), Dambha (arrogance), Darpa (haughtiness) and Ahamkar (egoistic) are the thirteen Sanskrit names of the types of tamasic gunas].
Karma	Denotes action or deed. Based on the Vedic principle of 'reap what you sow' the principle of 'Karma professes to abide by 'goodness' of deeds. The influence of 'Karma' impinge on the present as well as subsequent lives. Bad deeds culminate into accumulation of blemish known as 'paap' (as opposed to 'punya'). Religion preaches purification of deeds through benevolence in . words we speak, thoughts we behold, actions we perform and directions we render.
Mantra	A simple 'prayer' and 'mantra' addresses the same issue of praising the God, paying him respect and seeking His divine blessings. But the word 'mantra' has an enhanced connotration that delves into the discipline associated with rhythm, pronouciation and vibes. Mantras have been skillfully composed by extremely learned Hindu saints of ancient times. They kept in mind the choice of words, phonetics, and chanting style that would not only help devotees to converge his mind and prayers with the almighty but also help emiting the right energy needed to succeed in the effort and time dedicated in doing the prayers.
Masjid	In simple words it is a place of worship for the followers of Islam. The word masjid means to prostrate, the time and place of prostration. The Masjid serves as a place where Muslims can come together for prayer (salah) lead by the Imam, exchange information, impart education and settle disputes ment.
Mazar	It refers to a (Sufi) Shrines. It is a site erected in memory of a respected Islamic saint whose deeds during his lifetime have been admired by people. After the holiness departs this world this shrine remains a as a mausoleum for visit for paying homage. In Persian it is perhaps refered to as 'Dargah' and in Arabic called 'Maqbara' (both terms also prevalent in India). While Islamic practices vary from country to country, in India a structure is built on the grave. A soul of higher order may see a mosque or a madrasah built closeby for higher respect.
Moksha	Means liberty. It is the supreme liberty and the ultimate emancipation that can be attained from the continual cycle of death and rebirth. He who attains 'moksha' finds place in the abode of the almighty in heaven.
Murti	Common phraseology it would define it as a stone, metal or wood idol. Generally refered to idols of Gods or Godly deities in a place of worship. Establishment of such idols is followed by certain ceremonies notably 'sthapna' and 'pran-pratisthan', which instills in the idol the sybolic life and awakening the minds of devotees.
Nirvana	Nirvana means extinguishing, whereby the worldy desires and

	attachments are extinguished. This state when attained the spirit is liberated from the cycles of death and rebirth. This reference in Buddhism is synonymous to 'Moksha' in Hinduism.
Puja	refers to idolization or worshipof the diety by performing the rituals and offerings using the designated accompaniments like fire, water, bell, chonc shell, chanting of mantra and such auspicious and appropriate items with which a devotee invites the diety andestablishes contact with its cosmic energy. This practice is said to have the magic of instilling composure in the performer and enhancing his ability to ward off the evil.
Qurbani	Qurbani is a ritual in Islam. It entails sacrifice of an animal cows, goat, or sheep by butchring it in a prescribed manner setting its spirit off to its godly journey soon after its throat is slit. But Qurbani also entails within the philosophy of sacrifice which means refrainment, abstainance or renouncement for the cause of higher virtues in life.
Sadhana	Suggests concentration. In spiritual parlance it would mean meditating with deep concentration focused on one single object of attainment.
Samadhi	It is a state of attainment in the process of meditation. While through mmeditation one focuses ones mind on one and eliminates all else the stage of Samadhi is attained when the mind is silenced and spiritual grace is achieved. It is here that one is able to switch off the natural workings of the mind and becomes a detached being qualifying himself to vie for highest level of spiritual awareness but hereon he is faced with terrible impediments and allurement that deter him from reaching the highest form of awareness.
Sansara	is the bodage of human relationship in the world that we live in and entails the cycle of action and reaction culminating into birth, death and rebirth.
Shaastra	Ancient scriptures of knowledge that explains sacred methods of following rituals, understanding of astrological influence, of physics (bnautic shastra), economics (arth shastra), architecture (vastu shastra) and so on.
Shakti	Literal meaning is power. Here we see it as the supreme power of womanhood to combact evil the power of creation and agent for change. It is a non-dependent power and suppliments the feminine energy of Shiva. Shakti is personified through Mother Goddess in diferse forms viz., Durga, Kali, Amma, Maha LAxmi and others as are worshipped in the 51 'Shakti Piths'.
Stotra	These are scripted hymn addressed to Almighty For all or most devine dieties there are stotras written that are chanted by devotees in praise of the God - more particularly on days stipulated by the ephemeris assigned to respective God. .
Sufi	Sufi Truthful (person) Sufis are proponents of the pure form of Islam. Sufism is a science of purifying ones soul therby diverting away from materialistic wants and moving towards God. According to spiritual thiker Idries Shah " Sufism not as an ideology that molds people to the right way of belief or action, but as an art or science that can exert a beneficial influence on individuals and societies, in accordance with the needs of those individuals and societies ... Sufi study and development gives one capacities one did not have before."
Tandava	Tandava is the celestial dance of destruction, This is an extreme yogic dance that it rouses dormant energies which has the power to reshape world order. Its cosmogonic energy instills in the dancer new and higher traits of power and vigor. The arch yogi of all Gods, the consort of Shakti is also 'Natraj' who is said to be the originator performed the Tandav for a purpose. There are seven forms of this dance Anandtandav, Sandhya Tandav, Kalika Ttandav, . Tripura Tandav, Gouri Tandav, Sanhar Tandav and Uma Tandav. All these dance forms have principles and depict imparting divine knowledge to fearsome demonstration of destructive force.
Tantra	Often conceived as black magic and witchcraft and performance of a mysterious formula that causes miracle that are at times

	harm causing, It is actually a metord of gaining spiritual ascendancy through the.application of cosmic sciences and nessesarily includes the worship of 'Shaki' in yhe form of Kali and Shiva. Literally Tantra combines two words Tattva (Truth or Brahman) and Mantra (mystic syllables). '
Tapas	Drawn from the word 'tap' which in Sanskrit denotes heat the Vedas refer to it as inner heat. This inner heat is spawned and regulated by deep meditation and practicing severe austerities.It is believed that through this practice •Praj•pati', the creator God brought the world into being. The saints and yogis believe that this practice with chastity and poverty is the only path to enlightenment and purificationof the body to prepare it for the more exacting curriculum of spiritual performances leading to Moksha.
Taqt	Taqt is throne, often refered to the 'Ahaal' Taqt which means the throne unbound by time.
Tirtha	Pilgrimage. Tirth-Yatra means traveling for that purpose, tirtha Sthal means place of pilgrimage. In Hinduism as also in other religion vsit to certain 'tirth-sthal' are supposed to be obligatory for all at least once in a life time. Though it is also believed that it is the Gods call alone that one gets fortunate enough to visit places of pilgrimage. Going on pilgrimage does not necessarily mean visit to a holy place but it entails a cycle of events and a sequence of ritualistic performances over a certain period to truly qualify for a "tirtha"
Wriddhi Siddhi	Riddhi epitomises wealth and prosperity while Siddhi depicts intellectual and spiritual powers. They are two characters who have often been associare with Lord Ganesha. Even said to be the consorts of Ganesha who were created by Lord Brahma. Out of their marriage Lord Ganesha had two sons-- 'Shubha' meaning auspiciousness and 'Labha' representing profit and a daughter 'Santoshi'- contentment. But Lord Ganesha is also refed to as a 'brhamachary' (maintaining celibacy for life).the perception thus is that the spouses of Gaṇe[a are the personifications of his powers, manifesting his functional features.
Yantra	The word means contraption that in Hindu mythology denotes an efficient meditating tool designed with geometric precision in harmony with spiritual insinuations. These geometric visdialisations can lead the practitionaer to attain union with God. Yantras could also be cosmic drawings in papera and used used to derive astronomical position of planets over a given date and time. Yantra accompanied with Mantra and Tantra forms the trio While 'Mantra' symbolizes 'Gyana marg' or knowledge, 'Tantra' denotes Bhakti or devotion while 'Yantra' embodies 'Karma-Sanyasa Marg' or the path of detachment. Application of all these in the prescribes form of practice can pave the way to invoke universal forces needed for spiritual advancement.
Yoga	it is a disciplined endeavor of reaching the supreme goal of spiritual accomplishment in life. Hindu saints have documented the methodologies that find reflection in the Yoga Sutras, the Gita, upanilshads and other scriptures. There are various stages of attainments that finally culminate into achieving the supreme goal of 'moksha' or 'nirvana'.' Karma Yoga' (the path of right action), Jñāna Yoga' (the path of wisdom), 'Bhakti Yoga' (the path of love and devotion) 'Rāja Yoga' (the path of meditation) are the various course of the discipline that enables one to move towads the said goal. Modern Yoga code flows from the teachings of Maharishi Patanjali the ancient Indian Yoga philosopher, who is believed to have compiled his Yoga Sutra around the 3rd or 4th century BC.
Yuga	It is unit of age in time. Broadly in hindu mythology there is said to be four 'Yugas' or phases in the life span of this universe. They are 'Satya Yuga', 'Treta Yuga', 'Dwapar Yuga' and 'Kali Yuga'. While Satya Yug is the Age of Truth the ones following keep degrading in quality of human existence. Thus 'Kali Yuga' is the age when the human qualities get to the lowest ebb' We

	now live in 'Kali Yuga' and it in this phase thathe world is destined to see impurities and vices swamp all virtues that humans are required to be possessing with. With the passage of time human being will even be devoid of knowledge and will be left with the physical body and a mind fallen prey to deformity. All except those very few who do good unto others and lead a life devoid of sinful acts will bear a lesser burden of pain and sufferings. As situation would worsen it is believed that "Lord Shiva shall destroy the universe and all the physical body would undergo a great transformation. After such dissolution, Lord Brahma would recreate the universe and mankind will become the 'Beings of Truth' once again".

May faith imbibed not be blinding,
May religion be devoid not of blending.